UNBELIEVABLE!

MICHAEL WINNER

UNBELIEVABLE!

WITH CARTOONS BY THE AUTHOR

First published in Great Britain in 2010 by
JR Books, 10 Greenland Street, London NW1 0ND
www.jrbooks.com

A catalogue record for this book is available from the British Library.

ISBN 978-1-907532-26-9

1 3 5 7 9 10 8 6 4 2

Printed and bound in Great Britain
by Clays Ltd, St Ives plc

Contents

INTRODUCTON

Eating with Michael Winner

I have been eating in superb restaurants from the age of five, which means I've had a 70-year-long binge. We all remember the food we first ate with great clarity. The food at my co-educational Quaker school is emblazoned on my mind. It was vegetarian. It was during World War II. In order to help the war effort the headmaster was so dumb that he instructed us to eat grass from the cricket pitch. This was served with the salads. Needless to say, it was completely indigestible and we all became ill. But we produced the best milk in Hertfordshire. As the school was vegetarian and meat was rationed, I used to go down to what was called the Corner Post Office, a lovely little Edwardian building selling everything. We'd get meat paste in little jars which was meant to be put on bread or toast and scoop it out with our fingers. I also used to go to a lovely café with the music teacher (who was extremely gay but I stayed out of his clutches) and have sausage, gravy and chips. I decided that was the greatest food ever and I would never eat anything else. A promise which I later broke.

In spite of rationing I remember the food during the war as being very good. When the war was over the food in the 1950s was far better than the food today. First of all it was not chemicalised, mass-produced and deep-frozen. It was fresh. Every vegetable had an individual taste. As did the meat and fish. It was simply presented, without plates being full of ridiculous red and yellow squiggles. It was generally described as meat and two veg. That means you got some meat, two green vegetables and potatoes. Of course, there were variants of that. Since the plate decorators and poncified chefs took over, food has not improved at all. It has become pretentious. It has become mini-portions where the description on the menu takes longer to read than the food takes to eat.

My first trip abroad was to Switzerland in 1946. I stood on a balcony of the Palace Hotel, Lucerne and reeled back at the sheer beauty of the lakeside view that faced me. It was one of those great old grand hotels. I went back recently with John Cleese on his divorceymoon tour. It had become dreadful beyond belief. The room was full of pornographic channels, the furniture was absolutely terrible. It was for conventions rather than individuals. That has happened, sadly, to a great many of the large hotels which used to feed and house the gentry. They can't find enough gentry so they let in business conferences and groups. I don't blame them. But it hasn't exactly 'classed up' the general atmosphere.

Contrary to popular belief, which has me, in the minds of some people, as a screaming, petulant, pompous twit terrorising waiters, chefs and anyone connected with restaurants – I go in very quietly, eat quietly, thank everybody and leave. This often disappoints people at the next table. They go home and people say, 'Oh, you sat next to Michael Winner! What happened?' The true answer is,

'Nothing really happened.' Eventually people get tired of saying that and realise it would be better if they had a story to tell. So they invent one. This happens again, again and again. One example is that I was sitting at the bar of The Ivy, having had my lunch, waiting for my girlfriend, who was in the loo. A man came in, looked at me and I sensed that he was going to be trouble. He went on into the restaurant. The next day one of the newspaper diaries rang me and said, 'We hear you were barred from The Ivy yesterday. They wouldn't let you in to have your lunch.' Obviously this man had phoned them and said that. I pointed out that I'd already eaten my lunch, I was sitting in the bar waiting for my girlfriend. The story was, as so many are about me, complete rubbish.

I admit that I have somewhat encouraged the view of me as a lunatic eccentric rampaging round hotels and restaurants. I choose the letters printed in the *Sunday Times*. Rather than choose the majority, which say how much they love what I write and how it's the first thing they turn to in the paper, I pick the funny ones which are insulting me. I set myself up as an Aunt Sally. Those letters are far more amusing than letters saying how wonderful everything is. Occasionally I get a genuinely vicious letter of attack. I remember one in particular, which was not that different from most of them, where this person went on and on and on about how awful I was (not knowing me at all) but finished up saying, 'Best wishes, carry on the good work.' The column has become a bit of a game. It's there to entertain. I don't profess to be the most knowledgeable person in the world about food. I don't believe the readers want an analytical breakdown of the sauce or the gravy or anything else on the plate. They want a fun report on my life in restaurants and they want to know whether I think what I ate was good or bad. One thing I know for sure: if I say it's good the place is full for weeks to come. If I say it's bad, unfortunately it doesn't always close a restaurant. Although some restaurants have accused me of being the reason they closed. Of course, the reason they shut down was because they were no good and people weren't coming. I don't believe for one minute that the place was full until I murdered it and then it was suddenly empty. People are not that easily misled.

My transformation from film director, producer and writer to food critic, returning occasionally to films and frequently to commercials, was quite by accident. The editor of the *Sunday Times Magazine* asked me if I'd write an article. At the time I'd had the most awful dinner at Terence Conran's La Pont de la Tour where everything was wrong – the fish seemed off, we got the wrong food, people got the wrong courses and I was finally driven to distraction by seeing two waiters looking at a large tray of coffee for a table of 14 people. They had no idea who had ordered which sort of coffee. At this point it was one of my rare moments of, shall we say, exuberance. I went into the main restaurant and shouted for the restaurant manager. Seeing me, he walked away. So I shouted again. He walked further. This time I shouted so loudly I could be heard in South Africa. I then told him what I thought of the service in the restaurant. The next day I wrote to Terence Conran and said most of his restaurants were excellent but this had been a horrific evening. Terence Conran wrote back, 'I've received your film script. I will investigate.' From that moment on the investigation continued forever. Terry and I slagged each other off in the press for six years. Then I was in Venice at the Cipriani hotel by the swimming pool and I saw Terence Conran with his wife Vicky and a couple of friends. I thought, 'I'll go over and say hello.' After all, a public slanging match is one thing but it doesn't have to go into private life. I will never forget Terry's face as I walked over. It was fear. You could see him thinking, 'Oh, my God,

Winner's going to create a scene! This will be too awful!' Instead I greeted him warmly and he greeted me warmly. Later that evening his wife rang me and said, 'We're booked into Harry's Bar tonight for dinner. The only place to be is to sit downstairs in the bar, but we're upstairs. Could you help get us downstairs?' So I rang my friend Arrigo Cipriani, the owner of Harry's Bar, and got Terry in the right place. Since then we have been very friendly. I welcomed him to my engagement party a couple of years ago.

From rather shaky beginnings my restaurant column has run for 16 years. I've had over 900 columns printed, never missing a single week, including when I was in intensive care in hospital and drugged up to the gills. Nobody seemed to notice the difference. So perhaps I'm a bit round the bend anyway. I do hope so, normality is not a plus.

I hope you will enjoy this book and the various stories therein. If you don't read my *Sunday Times* column already I hope you will in future. Either way I wish you a wonderful life.

Michael Winner eats with his friends

an unbridled Report

Eating with Warren Beatty

I became good friends with Warren Beatty having been introduced to him in 1968 by Michael J. Pollard, who'd starred with him in *Bonnie and Clyde* and who had been in my film *Hannibal Brooks*. I gave a dinner for Michael J. Pollard in my apartment in Kensington and Pollard asked if Warren Beatty could come. Of course I said, 'Yes. Delighted.'

Warren came to dinner, which was done by a couple of old lady caterers. At the time Geraldine was with me. We had a number of, shall I say, liaisons over the years. I had a beautiful spiral staircase going from the bedroom area above down to the living room below. As she came down the stairs Warren Beatty went absolutely bananas. He said, 'My God, who's that?' I said, 'Warren, it's my girlfriend. Keep your hands off her.' Warren had just been to the airport to see Julie Christie off. He was with Julie at the time and indeed stayed with her for quite a long time. One of the girls at my dinner party was a beautiful English actress called Carol White, who was blonde and looked a bit like Julie Christie. To nobody's surprise Warren left with Carol White and doubtless they greatly enjoyed each other's company thereafter.

I used to see Warren quite a bit when he was in London.

Some years later he was in town when he was 'with' the Mamas and Papas singer Michelle Phillips. He came to dinner at my house. After dinner we went to my private cinema where I would get films prior to West End release. This evening it was John Schlesinger's movie *The Day of the Locust*. A film about old Hollywood. I had then a proper celluloid projector and a projectionist who was always drunk. I shared him with Stanley Kubrick. In those days, before DVD, I had to run celluloid films and I was always given by the distributors the copy of the film that was to play in the West End of London. That meant that it was a copy where the director had personally worked on the grading. It was what they called an original negative print rather than a copy negative which goes out on mass release. So these prints were very valuable. I was terrified that my drunken projectionist would drop them on the floor or damage them and thus destroy the West End opening.

The Day of the Locust was a terrible film. I like and admire John Schlesinger, but this was not one of his great efforts. So I'm watching it sitting in the front row with my then girlfriend. Warren Beatty is on a sofa at the back with Michelle Phillips. Occasionally I would sneak round to look and they were doing something which I will not describe because I'm of a delicate disposition. It would normally be done in the privacy of the bedroom. I don't blame them really because the film was a bore.

A few days later I was telephoned by Alf Jarrett, the head of UIP, one of Britain's biggest distribution companies, and he said to me, 'Michael, I'm afraid I can't give you any films any more.' I said, 'What are you talking about, Alfie? What have I done wrong?' Jarrett replied, 'I gave you a print of *The Day of the Locust* and Warren Beatty has been going around ever since saying it was one of the most awful films he's ever seen.' This got back to John Schlesinger, who asked, 'How on earth could Warren Beatty have seen the film? It isn't out yet.' Somebody told him he saw it in my house. Schlesinger went absolutely ballistic. I'm not surprised. I would have done too. But showing films in advance of screening is common in Hollywood. Prints go out all over Beverly Hills. I think only Kubrick and I ran them here in England. I begged Alf to keep supplying me with movies, otherwise my extremely expensive cinema would be hardly worth having, as UIP was the distributor for about five of the American major companies. I promised that from then on, I would not have anyone in the cinema apart from myself and my girlfriend. And I didn't. Shows how careful you have to be when you ask stars to dinner!

Eating with Marlon Brando

To say that Marlon Brando enjoyed his food is to put it mildly. I had endless meals with him, each one an enormous pleasure. He was the most witty and marvellous companion. In no way the mixed-up, sour, bitter person that some people thought he was.

My first meal with him was a salad lunch at his house in Coldwater Canyon, Beverly Hills. Everyone used to say to me, 'Marlon lives in Tahiti ,doesn't he?' to which I'd reply, 'No, he doesn't. He lives in Beverly Hills like everyone else.' As we ate and discussed my movie *The Nightcomers*, which he was later to star in, a small group of men were playing a board game further down the hill. 'That's Jack Nicholson,' explained Marlon, 'he's my neighbour.' When Marlon died, Jack bought Marlon's house (quite a modest one really) so there would not be anybody looking down on him who he didn't want there.

On my movie sets I always have a special place for the stars to eat rather than serving them in their caravans. When I made *The Nightcomers* with Marlon Brando I had a special room in the stately home near Cambridge where we were filming. The first day my assistant director came to me on the set at quarter to one after Marlon had been dismissed for lunch and said, 'Mr Brando refuses to eat in the special room. He's going to the marquee where the crew eat.' So I went to the tent, where Marlon was sitting at a trestle table with his entourage of make-up man, stand-in from America, assistant and others and I said, 'Marlon, it may amuse you to eat with the crew but the fact of the matter is they don't want you. They don't want me here and they don't want you here. They'd much rather have their lunch out of the sight of the bosses.' Marlon muttered, 'Yes, but I would rather eat here than in the room you kindly provided.' So I said, 'Marlon, that's inconvenient of you. I now have to go to the room and get all the special plates and cutlery and bring them here.' I went to the room with my assistant and we brought the special plates and knives and forks from the posh room and put them on the trestle table. As the actors and actresses came in Marlon, waved his arm as if beckoning them to sit down. He did this to Stephanie Beacham and a girl called Verna Harvey. Of course they all walked straight past. I said, 'Marlon they're terrified of you. No one's going to sit with you. I don't know why you're bothering. We could all be sitting in a nice room with a log fire eating properly.'

The next day we were filming in a graveyard next to a church and I had a lunch room ready in the church. I went in there with the producer Jay Kanter. Marlon came in a tiny bit later, bringing with him, having sought them out, Thora Hird and Stephanie Beacham. They sat in absolute terror, not saying a word. Until Marlon made the great mistake of saying to Thora Hird, 'Well, what work have you done?' Now for Thora Hird to stay quiet at all was a miracle and Marlon's question opened the floodgates. She started a soliloquy, 'Well, you know, Marlon, I'm very famous in this country. I've done three TV series and I'm know as Mrs Whatever and my daughter Janet married an American singer called Mel Tormé who was very ugly and do you know I got up this morning, Marlon, I had on one red sock and one green sock . . .' She went on and on. Marlon, who could not understand her accent, sat there looking totally glazed. Luckily a man came with all the cheques to sign and I just ignored the whole thing and signed the cheques. Later, as we were walking round the graveyard filming, I said to Marlon, 'Well, that's wonderful, Marlon. Don't worry about eating alone. I'll see Thora Hird joins you every day for lunch.' Marlon said, 'I didn't understand a word she said. You were no help anyway, you sat there signing cheques.' After that Marlon ate in his dressing room, I ate in the special room and life continued in a quiet and orderly fashion.

On Marlon's last day of the film I walked into the special room for my lunch with Jay Kanter the producer. Marlon and all his entourage were sitting there. I thought, 'That's nice of them, at least they're turning up for the last day as a gesture for me.' How wrong I was. As soon as I entered the room Marlon, all his entourage and Jay Kanter got up and walked out and went into the tent with the crew. They of course had fixed this as a gag. I then made a farewell speech for Marlon in the tent with the crew and Marlon made a wonderful speech in reply. I wish I'd recorded it. I may have done but if I did I've lost the recording. I remember he said, 'We are ships that pass in the night but I will remember with great pleasure working here even with Michael Winner shouting from time to time.' It was a typically gracious speech. The next day Marlon, who was meant to be so difficult and egotistical, came back even though he was not on call to work, and went round every member of the crew chatting to them and shaking their hand and thanking them for their work on the movie. This I've never seen before or after with any artist I've employed. This is what I call a true man.

I had a cook who made very good chocolate cake. Marlon absolutely adored her cake. I gave a party for him on board a boat in the Thames with an orchestra and a very glitterati guest list. I bought a chocolate cake especially for Marlon. It was the only time in the 30 years I knew him he was a pain in the arse. He was the last one on the boat, not late but the last one to arrive; I could see he was in a terrible mood. I bounced cheerfully towards him and said, 'Good evening, sir.' Marlon said, 'I've just been assaulted, Michael.' I said, 'Goodness me, so what do you mean assaulted?' Marlon replied, 'As I came along the quayside two photographers took my photograph.' I said, 'Yes, Marlon, they were here before. I don't know how they got here.' Marlon said, 'Did you ask them to come?' I said, 'Of course I didn't. Maybe the caterer did. Maybe one of the agents who I rang to get guests who you'd never met. Who cares?' Marlon sat and sulked for the entire trip, looking out into the river and refusing to talk to any of the people who had come to the party who included Eric Clapton, Ringo Starr, Christopher Walken, Faye Dunaway and many more. I said to the producer of our movie Elliott Kastner, 'I'm going to throw this bloody chocolate cake over his head.' Instead, I carried the cake over to Marlon's table saying, 'I've got a chocolate cake especially for you.' Marlon said, 'Don't disturb me, I'm looking at this marvellous view.' Bloody pig, he was then. The only time he wasn't a lovely person.

I was due to take him around Cambridge the following Saturday, five days later, but I was so pissed off that I dropped him a note to his hotel saying, 'Marlon, in view of your behaviour I really can't be bothered to take you around Cambridge. Another time perhaps.' People didn't write that to Marlon. They all sort of worshipped him. In fact, the nicest thing anyone's ever said about me was said by Brando, who told everybody, 'Michael Winner is the only person I know who doesn't talk to me in the manner in which he thinks I wish to be spoken to.' As a result of my note, I got an abject letter of apology from Marlon saying, 'I cast a pallor on your boat party. I'm extremely sorry. I don't know why I behave like this.' He sent me two crates of very good wine and gave my girlfriend a wonderful necklace. So friendship was fully resumed.

On another occasion I was dining with Marlon in one of the many canyons around his house. With us was Philip Rhodes, his make-up man, a long-time friend who had worked with him as an actor in the 50s in New York. We all ordered ice-cream for dessert. When I started eating my ice-cream Marlon looked at his and then looked at our ice-creams. Eventually he said to Philip, 'Your ice-cream is bigger than mine.' Philip Rhodes said, 'Well would you like to have my ice-cream Marlon?' Marlon said, 'No.' Then he called the waiter over and said, 'Waiter, I'll have a second ice-cream.' And he wondered why he was fat! When he was in serious trouble towards the end of his life from overeating he would phone me night after night and say, 'Michael, I lost 30 pounds.' I would then speak to friends of his and say, 'Isn't that wonderful, Marlon's lost 30 pounds.' They would say, 'He hasn't lost anything at all, he's getting fatter than ever.'

Another time I took Marlon to the restaurant Bibendum in the Fulham Road. The corner table of restaurants is invariably the best. And the best seat is in the corner looking out at the room. Naturally I offered this to Marlon. Marlon declined and sat with his back to the room, looking into the corner. He didn't want to be recognised or troubled.

Another memorable meal with Marlon was tea at the village of Shere in Surrey. I was taking him on a trip around the English countryside in an open car. He liked it so much he later rented a house in Surrey and stayed there for the summer. There was a very good tea shop in Shere on the corner and Marlon liked his tea and cake. I went inside. It was absolutely packed. Outside there was a queue. I said to a rather fey young man who seemed to be running the show, 'I've got Marlon Brando outside. I can't put him in a queue because he'll be mobbed, is there anything you can do to help? There's four of us.' Four ladies were about to leave a table. The man immediately put the chairs against the table and said, 'Get him in here quick.' So I went out and said, 'Marlon, I've just done one of the great achievements of my life. I've got you ahead of the queue for the tea shop in Shere. Get a move on or they'll give the bloody table away.'

On another occasion I was dining with Marlon in Beverly Hills. He was again accompanied by his make-up man Philip Rhodes. At the end of the meal I grabbed the bill. Marlon said, 'You are not to pay. I'm paying tonight.' I said, 'No you're not, Marlon, just shut up and let me get on with it.' At that point Marlon stood up and took the pitcher of water that was on the table and held it over me and let a few drops fall on to the top of my head. He said, 'Unless you give me that bill immediately I will throw the rest of this water over you.' I had not the slightest doubt he would have done. So I gave him the bill.

I could go on with dozens of stories about eating with Marlon, but there is not the space. They are memories that I treasure because he was the most wonderful person. Whenever I go into the restaurants I went into with him I re-live the times we spent together there.

Eating with Charles Bronson

Charles Bronson ate very little when he was young. He was brought up in a hut in a mining camp in Pennsylvania owned by one of the big coal mining companies. He would describe to me in horrific detail how the family of 14 lived in a two-room hut. With his mother dying of cancer in one of the rooms. He used to wear women's clothes because the child above him was his sister and so her clothes were simply handed down to him.

It was only because Charlie was drafted into the army that he became an actor. Because when he came out of the army they offered you training and he chose to train as an actor.

I first met him in 1971 when he starred in my film *Chato's Land*. When I arrived on location in Almeria, Spain, his wife Jill Ireland (who had been a girlfriend of mine) said, 'It's nice to have you here, Michael because I'll need my old friends when Charlie goes.' I said, 'Where's he going?' She said, 'Well, he's very old, you know.' I said, 'His autobiography shows he's only 52.' Jill said, 'You don't believe that do you?' She later told me he was eight years older. This was only revealed by me when he died.

Charles and I would eat every night in a hotel in Aquadulce – that is me, Charlie and Jill. He didn't like his co-star Jack Palance, because Jack's background was rather similar to his. Charlie refused to have dinner with Jack Palance. So Jack had to eat alone a few tables away reading *Country Life* magazine. This is very unfair because Jack was a very nice person. Charlie would have a Campari soda regularly before lunch and only ate a very small dinner because he kept very fit and thin.

When I was unable to be there for some reason or other toward the end of the film, Charlie ate with Jack Palance and said to me, 'You know, Jack Palance is really a very nice man.' I said, 'I've been telling you that for weeks, Charlie.'

Charlie always had an American instant coffee called Yuban. He was suspicious of anybody and everything, although we later became great friends. One day he said to me, 'You're watering down my Yuban coffee!' I said, 'Why should we do that, Charlie? I don't understand.' I guess Charlie was so suspicious he thought if we watered down his coffee it meant we spent less giving him this coffee which we had brought in from America. My assistant Stephen who made his coffee assured him he wasn't watering it down and of course he wasn't.

When we made *Death Wish* and other movies where Charlie was a great sharpshooter we would go to lunch every day. We'd share a dessert and often share a main course. We'd have two plates and scoop half of it on to my plate from his or vice versa. I lost a lot of weight with Charlie. Charlie would also keep forgetting his reading glasses so he'd say to me, 'Would you read me the menu.' This was rather sweet as there he was on set shooting people off buildings a hundred miles away as a great sharpshooter and he couldn't even read the menu.

Charlie kept the most immaculate and beautiful house in Bel Air run by Jill Ireland, who was a fantastic wife to him. The cutlery, the crockery, everything was exquisitely done. Charlie always insisted on eating at 6:30pm so he could see the news at 7pm. If you kept him longer on the set he would become extremely irritated. Later on he simply refused to work after 6pm. When I begged him to do so to complete something for the day, he'd say, 'Michael, it took me 40 years to become a star and those are the terms in my contract and I'm afraid I'm going to stick to them.' I really don't blame him for that at all.

There was an unfortunate incident in Naples. Jill, who was the love of Charlie's life beyond belief, decided to play a little game. When we came back from a long day's shooting she said, 'I've ordered a special dinner for you.' We sat down and this spaghetti came up which was absolutely horrific. It was all gooey and sweet. Charlie didn't say anything because it came from Jill. He was so in love with her he just kept quiet and ate it, but I could see he was hating it. I said, 'What is this rubbish, Jill? It's absolutely ghastly. What are you trying to do, kill us?' She said, 'No, it's a special thing I've done, it's spaghetti with chocolate sauce.' I said, 'Charlie, stop eating it at once, your wife is fucking mad. Let's get a decent meal – we've been working all day.' Although funnily enough I read quite recently that there is some sort of spaghetti they're now doing with chocolate sauce, which shows how appalling taste has become since 1971.

Another classic meal I remember with Charlie was in Ravello. We were filming on the mountainside and I'd been to a firm called G Appa who did wonderful cameos carved by a man called Professor Notto. I told them I wanted Charles Bronson and his wife to come but they couldn't make it. 'So if you want to come down to Ravello we're having lunch in the hotel and if you come down with a trestle table, it's well out of season, and if you've got nothing else to do, I think you'll do very well,' I advised. So we came into lunch at Ravello and there was this long trestle table with all these Italians in very formal clothing with the carved jade and coral laid out in front of them. I mentioned to Charlie that I'd been to G Appa and got some stuff that I liked. After the first course Charlie went over to the table and picked up a piece of coral. He looked at it, he looked at the men in the posh suits and said, 'This is absolute rubbish.' Then he threw it back on the table and returned to where we were dining.

I could see the men were insulted and were starting to pack up. So I went over and I said, 'Excuse me, go if you wish. But I can assure you've just made an enormous sale.' The men looked absolutely stupefied. But they decided to stay. After the main course Charlie went again to the table, picked something else up, and said, 'Dis one is not bad.' Then he looked at a few other things and then he walked back to continue his meal. By the end of the meal Charlie had spent, in those days in 1971, $200,000 on various items for Jill including the most beautiful pink coral necklace which I can still see to this day. He bought something for me. He bought something for my then girlfriend. He bought something for my assistant Stephen. The people from G Appa went away very happy and totally bemused.

Eating with Michael Caine

I first met Michael Caine in 1963 when he was one of the leading players in the theatre in a show called *Next Time I'll Sing to You*. Whereas all other theatre actors at that time were talking in posh accents, Michael spoke cockney. He also spoke directly to the audience. It was a mesmerising performance. After the show at the Criterion Theatre I went to a pub with the cast because the actor I was with knew Michael Caine. Michael was totally unknown. He was 31 years old and the gist of his dialogue at the pub was that he was a jobbing actor who would never be any more than a jobbing actor. His friends Terence Stamp and Peter O'Toole and other people had become stars but he (per Michael) would never become a star. I said, 'I think you're completely wrong. You will become a star. There's no question of it.' Later that year he got his first big break in the film *Zulu* and became a star.

I've had more meals with Michael Caine than with any other film star I know. We go back so long. I've had them in London, Barbados and in particular at his home. Currently this is a fantastic house in Surrey where Michael personally cooks Sunday lunch. He has a bit of help but he does cook. You come there and he's stirring pans and putting things in the oven and getting burnt and generally chipping in at the coalface. There is no doubt at all that Michael Caine's lunches offer the finest food I have ever eaten or ever will eat. Most of it is fresh from his garden, that is vegetables and fruit. The rest is carefully chosen and beautifully prepared. There is an enormous selection put out on a large table top in the kitchen. Michael carves the meat at a second table top. It's self-service and the guests go and sit in a delightful atrium or in his dining room next to the kitchen.

Michael is also the wittiest and most gracious and charming and caring of hosts. When I do my one-man show or lecture or whatever you want to call it, I'm often asked, having told funny stories about movie stars, 'Tell us a story about Michael Caine.' Amazingly I find this very difficult. If not impossible. This is not out of a sense of modesty or discretion. It's quite simply that I can't give any outrageous incident that makes a very funny story that has ever happened with Michael Caine. The nearest I can get is when we were making a film called *Bullseye*. Michael, Roger Moore and I used to eat every day in a restaurant near the location, being careful to get back precisely within the hour allowed for the unit lunch. These meals were so good that Michael and Roger were putting on weight. To make matters worse the stills photographer, who was very famous and very good, was extremely short. It was Orson Welles who taught me years ago that if the camera is held at eye level or a bit above, the person being photographed looks slimmer. In this case we had two movie stars getting fatter by the second being photographed from well below by a very short stills photographer. Eventually I had to say to this person, 'You're going to have to stand on a little platform.' This he found deeply insulting and quit the picture. Whereupon I got a taller stills photographer.

Michael, as well as being as a great actor, was for quite a while a famous restaurateur. He had Langan's (not a place

I ever cared for much) with Peter Langan, who was always drunk on the floor, and a third partner. Then he had the Canteen, where he bought Marco Pierre White (whom he introduced me to) from the wilds of some ghastly area in South London to be his partner in this restaurant in Chelsea. There was then a major falling out. Marco Pierre White is definitely the easiest person in the world to fall out with. He's absolutely ridiculous. And the restaurant closed. Not before Michael Caine had put Marco Pierre White into the Hyde Park hotel and been very helpful in getting him his third Michelin star. For which, of course, Marco Pierre White never showed any gratitude. Marco was unquestionably the most marvellous chef and worked very hard in the kitchen from early morning until nightfall and beyond. Since he stopped working in the kitchen he's become a bore.

Michael on the other hand is the most marvellous raconteur, has written two autobiographies, one of which will be out at the same time as this book and which I strongly recommend you to buy, called *Elephant to Hollywood*. There are more stories about his career, which blossomed again after he played an American for the first time successfully in *Cider House Rules*. This opened up a whole new career for him which is most well deserved.

Can I tell you any secrets about Michael Caine's eating habits? Not really. Except he invariably ends the meal with a Fernet Branca to aid his digestive system. I always have some in the house when he comes round. That may not be the most scandalous revelation you've ever heard. But then Michael leads an absolutely exemplary life.

I remember years ago reading in the *London Evening Standard* an article which lumped a number of actors and stars together, including Sean Connery and Michael Caine. It said they all had things in common. They were unfaithful to their wives, they did not write their own autobiographies and they were friends with Michael Winner. That was a serious libel. Michael Caine has never had a whisper of impropriety about double dealing in his private life. He has the most marvellous wife ever, Shakira. The wisest thing he ever did in his life was to get married to her. He's always been totally faithful. Furthermore, he not only wrote his autobiography, he wrote it by hand. So I was immediately on the phone to Michael to get on to them through the lawyer (I recommended him a lawyer) and go for enormous damages. Michael never likes to get involved in these disputes to a large degree. So he settled for an apology and hardly any damages. I love getting libel damages from newspapers.

When I started my police charity, the Police Memorial Trust, it was practically financed by libel damages from newspapers. I've never taken a penny for myself. A recent 'donation' came from the *Daily Express* for a pathetic libel carelessly and inaccurately printed, written by the most boring man in the world, the writer Frederick Forsyth. I wish he'd insult me again inaccurately, then I could get some more money for the Police Memorial Trust.

As for Michael Caine, he continues to be a best friend and as fine a human being as I've ever met in my life. On top of that he can cook! If that isn't rare, I don't know what is.

Eating with John Cleese

One of my greatest friends in the world is John Cleese. We met in Barbados many years ago. One of our first meals was on New Year's Eve. John was staying at a small hotel and I went there to dinner. Amazingly the hotel wasn't doing a proper New Year's Eve event. The only people in the dining room were John, his daughter Cynthia, a TV producer and his gay friend and me and my girlfriend. It was an absolutely marvellous evening and I spent many other New Year's Eves with John, including one at the Sandy Lane hotel, where we had the meal and then walked away from the terrible noise and din and sat on a wall for an hour and a half waiting for midnight just chatting away together.

It's always a pleasure to see John eat because he finishes his plate. There's nothing left on the plate at all. It looks absolutely clean. He's not averse to taking things from other people's plates. He's also given me three of the greatest moments of humour in my life. Once we were sitting in the rotunda tea room of Sandy Lane, Barbados. John is a very serious person. He's been through a lot of psychiatry. He considers life in a very measured intellectual way. Suddenly he got up and did about 40 seconds of funny walks. I don't know why, it's most unlike him. But it was absolutely brilliant. Then he sat down. Another time we were walking along the coast in Barbados with our feet in the water going from my hotel to his. The sun was glistening on the sea, the flowering bushes were out. It was absolutely idyllic. John turned to me and said, 'You know, Michael, there must be more to life than this.' Another great remark which I hesitate to put in this book, but I'm going to anyway, is when we were travelling in Switzerland together on a divorceymoon trip, not to celebrate, but to try and get over the horrific divorce he went through where his ghastly wife Alyce took him for $13m cash (leaving him with considerably less) plus another $1m a year for seven years. We were in a hotel in Lucerne being taken up in the elevator to our rooms. There's always a strange silence in elevators. People feel uncomfortable. They don't know quite what to say or what to do. The manager was there with me and John. John, who's very tall, said in a snooty voice to no one in particular, 'Personally I think all Jews should be treated abominably.' The manager's face was an absolute picture. He didn't know what to do or where to look. He couldn't believe what he'd heard! I thought it was extremely funny because John and I mock each other about subjects which are extremely politically incorrect. So it meant nothing to me because he's not anti-Semitic, he's a marvellous fellow.

Even though he takes pride in telling people that, at our first ever dinner, he had a moustache which he shaved off leaving just a Hitler moustache so he looked like the Führer. Also, when I was telling John that I had quite a large part in a Danny Boyle (the man who directed *Slumdog Millionaire*) television film, John looked down at me very sneerily and said, 'What are you playing? Shylock?' After that, when we went on holiday I had stickers made saying 'Shylock Tours' and I had a little flag made with Shylock Tours on it and I wrote to John on notepaper headed Shylock Tours. This may not be everyone's idea of a joke, but if you can't laugh at yourself and your race, what's the point of it all?

Eating with Simon Cowell

I met Simon Cowell in December 2000 at the Jalousie hotel in St Lucia. This has the best beach in the world. Although the hotel doesn't quite match up to the beach. I had no idea who Simon Cowell was and nor did anyone else. Even his mother had difficulty recognising him. A group of people turned up at breakfast one day on the terrace. There was Simon, a blonde Page 3 girl who was with Simon, Simon's mother, Julie, who is the most wonderful person ever and the only human being who Simon loves more than himself, his brother Nicholas and a blonde girl, Mandy Perriment, an actress who I'd had playing a small part in one of my movies. I went over to greet Mandy and was introduced to Simon and the rest of the group. Simon had not at the time been on television at all. He was a record company executive who's company had occasionally gone bust. I found him immensely pleasant, likeable and witty. So was the party with him.

The reason Simon was on the balcony of the Jalousie hotel is that he'd been at another hotel managed by a total idiot and when he came down to breakfast in his bathrobe they refused to let him into the open-air area to eat breakfast. They also declined to let Mandy Perriment into the breakfast room because she was wearing a sarong.

Which was extremely elegant. So Simon left in high dudgeon for the Jalousie. I was staying at the Jalousie because the Sandy Lane hotel had been closed three years for rebuilding. It was in fact now open for a trial run that Christmas and New Year and the super boss of the hotel, a marvellous man called Dermot Desmond, rang me and said, 'Michael, you're the first person I'm asking to come and stay with us without charge for the accommodation on a trial run at Sandy Lane this Christmas and New Year.' I said, 'I'm not the first person, Dermot, I've spoken to four other people all of whom have been asked!' I then read a very nasty article in the *Evening Standard* about how dreadful the hotel design was (untrue, it's great) and that it was still being built and builder's dust and clanging and banging were going on. So I decided not to go.

I booked after Christmas to the next best hotel on the island, The Royal Pavilion, where I had a house with three bedrooms and two sitting rooms. To cover myself I also booked two suites at the Lone Star hotel just down the road from The Royal Pavilion. Thus I had a choice of where I wanted to stay. If I didn't like one piece of accommodation I'd go to the other. Or possibly I'd go between the two, which was only a very short walk along the beach. I was due to go there before New Year. My friend, the musician Chris Rea, was not initially asked to be one of the guests trying out the Sandy Lane hotel over Christmas and New Year but racing driver manager Eddie Jordan was asked. He was unwell so he suggested they ask Chris Rea in his place. I rang Chris Rea at the Sandy Lane hotel and said, 'Is it full of dust and noise and horrible?' He replied, 'It's absolutely unbelievable. There's about 40 people here and 300 staff. The sun loungers are miles apart on the beach and it's fantastic.' At this point I decided I should go. I rang Dermot and said, 'I'd like to come if I still can, please.' He said, 'Yes.'

I was now in the amusing position of having two rooms at the Sandy Lane hotel, three bedrooms and two sitting rooms at The Royal Pavilion hotel and two suites at the Lone Star hotel. I told Simon I was going to Barbados immediately after Christmas. He said, 'I've always wanted to go to Barbados. We tried to get in but we couldn't.' I said, 'Simon this is your lucky day. I can get you in to Barbados in The Royal Pavilion hotel, let me do that for you.' Simon, was delighted and I was let off the hook for paying for the rooms. The Lone Star hotel managed to let the rooms so it didn't cost me anything very serious.

The Sandy Lane hotel was definitely the best it has ever been. For New Year's Eve I gave a dinner party at the hotel in the terraced dining room which was occupied by very few people because all Dermot's guests were going to the John Magnier party, to which I was asked but I preferred to be at Sandy Lane with my own people. So for New Year's Eve dinner about the only other person in the restaurant was the famous cricketer Sir Garry Sobers. One other table was occupied. We had a large table for me and my guests, including Chris Rea and family, Des O'Connor and his girlfriend (whom he later married), Simon Cowell's party of five, a friend of mine in the theatrical game called Adam Kenwright with one of his friends who was with him. It was a very nice group indeed. Except for Des O'Connor, who is a monster.

I never criticise people of the profession in public but I'm quite prepared to criticise Des O'Connor. He is the meanest sod in the world. He had previously been to one of my New Year's Eve parties a couple of years earlier. These cost, even in those days, at least £350 per person. Des never even wrote and thanked me, never sent a bottle of wine or flowers to my girlfriend. Nothing. Now I'm asking him again and he suddenly said not only did he want to bring his girlfriend, he wanted to bring his daughter. So there were now three people there, which cost me around £1,500. Once again I got no letter of thanks, no flowers for the girlfriend. Nothing. Des O'Connor during the meal, where everyone else was speaking as a human being, spoke like he was on television doing an interview. While he was at the dinner he asked Simon Cowell to lunch with him the next day. Simon turned up to lunch with Des, who only wanted Simon in order to try and promote a record deal for his girlfriend. Not surprisingly, Simon ended up paying the bill.

To return to my dinner party: when the time came for the bill I suddenly saw Simon was paying it with his credit card, he was not even that successful in those days. I became extremely agitated. I said, 'Simon, you are my guest. I've asked everybody here. You cannot possibly pay this bill.' I've often demanded to pay bills, even when I was invited in as a guest. Very few times, other than a token objection, has anyone stopped me from paying the bill. Simon was absolutely adamant that he paid for half of the party. This involved paying for more people than his group of five. I could not stop him. I thought to myself, 'That is a real decent human being.' Simon is in fact a fantastic person. Very together, very focused. His success does not surprise me. I couldn't be happier for him. We had a number of meals thereafter all over the place – one being at my engagement party at the Ritz hotel, London, where I made a sort of 'roast' speech about many of the guests. Toward the end of my after-dinner speech I said, 'If I may end on a serious note. Each night I kneel down and I pray to God.' I could see the audience thinking, 'Oh, he's had all these illnesses and nearly died, he's now going to be very serious indeed.' I continued, 'I get on my knees in my bedroom and I say, "God, please, do one thing for me. Please let it be that I wake up tomorrow and don't have to see Simon Cowell's fucking face in the newspapers again." But of course I did. There he is every day beaming at me with those fake teeth and that made-over face. It really is beyond belief.' That got a good laugh from everybody. Afterwards Simon said to me, 'I didn't realise you could be so funny.' I think it's absolutely essential that people are able to laugh at themselves, which many performers are not able to. Simon can laugh at himself and that's what contributes to making him a rounded human being.

Eating with Salvador Dalí

It is somewhat untrue to say that I dined with Salvador Dalí. Nevertheless it was one of the most memorable moments of my life. I was sitting in the Tour d'Argent restaurant in Paris in the window seat which has an incredible view over the River Seine and the Notre-Dame cathedral. I looked around the room, and there at a centre table was Salvador Dalí. At the time I used a Polaroid camera and I had it with me. I really regret not taking a picture of Salvador Dalí because he was so fantastic. He was very old and his hands were shaking. I'll never forget the sight of Salvador Dalí when the dessert trolley was wheeled over to him. He leant over and looked at every item very carefully holding his hand out which was shaking madly. Eventually he chose his desserts and ate them. We never spoke. I never photographed him. I still remember it.

Eating with Chris de Burgh

One of my most memorable meals was at the Sandy Lane hotel, Barbados. At that time they had a pianist playing during breakfast. I was sitting with Chris de Burgh and his wife and I said to Chris, 'Get up there and play the piano and sing a song, Chris.' He said, 'No, of course I won't do that. I'm on holiday.' I like stirring it up. So I said, 'Come on, Chris, don't ponce about, we'd like a song. It would be very nice to go with the bacon and eggs. Get up there and sing.' Chris was now getting a bit shirty and said, 'No I won't.' About five minutes later the local Barbadian pianist who was at the piano started to play and sing Chris de Burgh's famous hit song 'Lady in Red.' Chris listened for about 20 seconds and got so furious (although I thought it was quite good) at the way it was being played and sung that he shot up, rushed over to the piano, more or less pushed the pianist aside and sat down to play. I went over to the piano with him. So there was Chris playing and singing 'Lady in Red' absolutely brilliantly. I'm listening. The guests are listening. The pianist has no idea who Chris de Burgh is, so he turns to me and he says, 'He's pretty good, isn't he, man?' I couldn't be bothered to say, 'Yes, this is the fellow who wrote it and made it a hit and performs it all over the world.' I just said, 'Yes, he's quite good for a guest.'

Eating with Alain Delon

The French star Alain Delon was with me when I directed a film called *Scorpio*. We were the same age. His birthday was two days before mine. That is why we called the film *Scorpio*, because he was a Scorpio, co-star Burt Lancaster was a Scorpio and I was a Scorpio. We inherited a very dodgy title, *Dangerfield*. So I changed it to *Scorpio* and wrote a line in the film about it.

Part of the film was made in Washington DC. I was having dinner with Alain Delon in the Watergate hotel. We were both staying there on the day the Nixon people robbed it. They might have robbed it but they wouldn't have stayed to dinner. The food was terrible.

The next day we were sitting on the film set in Washington DC, I sat with Delon and Burt Lancaster was a few yards away in his chair. Around Burt Lancaster were hundreds of people queuing for his autograph, taking photographs and treating him as a major star. There was nobody near Delon and me. Alain Delon turned to me and said, very nicely because he was a terrific human being and very modest, 'You know, Michael, here in Washington they all know Burt Lancaster and they're all around Burt Lancaster. Next week we are in Vienna and it will be quite different because I'm very famous in Vienna. I'm famous as an actor and I also took out for years Romy Schneider, who is the Queen of Vienna. You wait and see.' A week later we were sitting in Vienna in a lovely old square, Alain and I are together and Burt a little distance away. Thousands of Viennese are clambering round Burt Lancaster. They're taking his photograph. The few who can get close to him are asking for autographs. It's exactly the same as it was in Washington. It is equally the same because no one is taking a blind bit of notice of Alain Delon. I turned to Alain and I said, 'Alain, you told me in Washington it would be quite different here. That you would get all the attention in Vienna because you were so famous.' Alain said, 'Not in this quarter of Vienna.' Very witty fellow he was.

I managed to wean him from Evian water to Malvern water, which he greatly liked. Then I tried to get him to have my coffee, which he absolutely hated.

I was rather fat in those days and every morning Alain would come on to the set and say, 'Is it twins, dear, or is it triplets?' We were filming one day in the real Central Intelligence Agency – I'm the only person to have shot in the Central Intelligence Agency. I was sitting with Alain, who at the time was the subject of rumours about being involved in the death of his chauffeur, who was found in the boot either of his car or of someone else's, I can't remember. He was definitely dead. He was definitely Alain's chauffeur. He was definitely in the boot of a car. I heard massive police sirens going by. I said, 'Alain, dear, they've come to get you. If you need bail I'll do my best to get you out.'

Eating with Faye Dunaway

When I employed Faye Dunaway for *The Wicked Lady* people said to me, 'You've charmed a lot of the most difficult people in Hollywood – Marlon Brando, Charles Bronson, Robert Mitchum, Burt Lancaster – but you ain't seen nothing until you work with Faye Dunaway.'

Not only was Faye present on the dot, as she was throughout the film, she was one of the greatest professionals I've ever met – she wouldn't even leave her horse to go and sit in her chair. I have a photograph of her in the rain, on her horse, with a plastic bag over her head, resplendent in full late-17th-century costume.

We were having lunch on set and from time to time Faye would say, 'Do I have a day off anywhere on the schedule?' I said, 'We never know, Faye. What may be a day off could be wiped out if the schedule changes because of weather or other problems.' Eventually I said, 'Faye, why do you need a day off?' She replied, 'I want to nip over to Barnet [which was near our location] to get married to Terry.' She'd been with photographer Terry O'Neill for some time. I said, 'Faye, I'll fix a day off. Why didn't you tell me it was that important?' So Faye and Terry got married very secretly. I was sworn to tell no one. As the film premiere loomed, I said to Faye, 'I'd like to tell the press of your marriage shortly before the premiere. Give us a bit of publicity.' Faye agreed, then she went and threw the information away in an interview with the *Daily Express*, who gave it no prominence at all!

Faye was immensely careful about what she ate, and still is. Hence she has never put on weight. I went to Wilton's restaurant with her once, and witnessed the same routine. Wherever you went with Faye, she took small round scales from her bag and placed them under her plate. The food on the plate was on the scales. Faye would then scoop the food off until the scales showed a certain weight measurement. When I asked her once, 'Are you still using the scales, Faye?' she said, 'Yes, people laugh at me but I don't care, it keeps me slender.' I think it's a brilliant idea because I've always said, as I do in my diet book, you can lose weight simply by eating less. It doesn't matter what you eat. Just eat less.

Faye, being a Capricorn, has the wonderful habit of pursuing anything she wants not only relentlessly but super historically relentlessly. I remember when she was planning to be in a film for Menahem Golan with Mickey Rourke she needed advice. She phoned me at the Sandy Lane hotel endlessly. I said, 'Faye, you've now interrupted breakfast, lunch, tea and dinner.' She said, 'I know, darling, but I desperately need your advice . . .' They kept cutting her salary and offering her a percentage of the film. I said, 'Faye, if you think the film is going to be a success as you tell me take the salary cut, it's an important film for you. Just do it. There's no point in sitting at home looking out the window when you could be doing this movie.' In fact, the movie, *Barfly*, was superb and did Faye a lot of good in her career.

The most memorable meal I had with Faye was at a restaurant called Ceccone's, which at the time was run by a dreadful man called Enzo Ceccone. It was quite the 'in' restaurant. Ceccone exploited that and when I last went the tables on one side of the room were very close together and crowded and Ceccone said, dismissively of his customers, 'That side is the East End, this side is Beverly Hills.' Meaning the side he was sitting me at was for the stars and people he thought were important.

Enzo Ceccone now lives next to the Cipriani hotel in Venice, where he used to be the manager. He haunts the place like some dreadful spectre. When I went for my 70th birthday there and I had a group including Michael Caine, Andrew Lloyd Webber, Roger Moore etc., we were sitting outside the Cip's restaurant one evening waiting to get on the boat to go to Harry's Bar. Ceccone was eating in the Cip's restaurant. He came out and went up to Michael Caine and spoke endlessly, totally uninvited. Like he was Michael Caine's best friend. When he left, Michael said to me, 'Who was that?' I was also told by Arrigo Cipriani that at the Cipriani restaurant in London (now called C London) Ceccone wandered in and sat down with Elton John. As he left, Arrigo said, 'You really can't do that, Ceccone.' Ceccone said, 'But Elton John's a very good friend of mine.' The next time Elton John rang he said, 'I want to make a reservation but not if Ceccone's there.' The last time I saw him I was having lunch in the Cipriani by the lagoon and Ceccone was haunting the place going around talking to people non-stop.

But I am wandering. The meal at Ceccone's with Faye Dunaway was particularly memorable because her then husband, the most marvellous human being and someone I absolutely adore, Terry O'Neill, one of the greatest photographers ever, was, shall we say, slightly disturbed by the use of substances. His marriage to Faye was not going well. She could, in privacy, be very difficult indeed. Although I only saw a wonderful side to her. There we were in Ceccone's. Terry O'Neill had been with me that afternoon to a costume fitting with Faye. Unbeknown to me he had walked away from the Faye session and got the costumiers to lend him an outfit that made him look like Mussolini. He was thus dressed in this Italian restaurant Ceccone's. He started a memorable performance, telling the waiters the Italians were cowards and they hadn't fought properly in the war and doing various Nazi salutes. The staff took it very well. If he'd been a customer on his own they probably would have taken him around the back and beaten the shit out of him. But as he was with me and Faye Dunaway they put up with it.

The final scene I'll always remember was Faye Dunaway and Terry going off in a chauffeur-driven Mercedes that the film company was paying for with Terry standing on the seat, his head and upper body sticking out of the open top of the car giving the Italian fascist salute and screaming, 'Fight on! We shall soon be in Abyssinia.'

When I got home Faye rang me and said, 'What did you think of Terry's behaviour tonight?' I said, 'It was very spirited, darling. He's a wonderful person. I wouldn't worry about it.' That was a very brief period in Terry's life. Before then and for the many decades since, I speak to him and meet him regularly and he's absolutely perfectly behaved. Not, shall we say, under the influence.

Another memorable dinner with Faye and Terry was in Cannes at the film festival. In 1982 *The Wicked Lady* was being announced. It was later an invited entry at the festival itself. The film was financed and promoted by two marvellous Israeli cousins called Menahem Golan and Yoram Globus. Before dinner at the Carlton hotel a press conference was given to announce Faye in the movie. Faye and I sat at a trestle table facing a large number of press. At that time the main reception room in the Carlton hotel was divided off by a concertina door, not a particularly strong one, that went across the room and the press who couldn't get into the area of the press conference were waiting behind that screen to come in. So there would be three shifts of press. The press who were in the room were to leave through a side door leading to the back of the hotel.

The press conference was going very well. Menahem and Yoram sat at the side of the room. When Menahem decided it had been going on long enough he went to the front and said, 'Please, everybody, I would like you now to leave through that door [he pointed to the side door] because your colleagues in the press behind the screen are waiting to come in, so will you please now leave to make room for them?' None of the press took any notice of this at all. They kept asking questions. At this point Menahem, who was a big burly Israeli, started to get agitated. This is something he often did. I absolutely adored him. Facing the press he said, 'I've just told you arseholes to get out! I'm telling you now, get out of the room at once! Otherwise I come personally, I grab you and I throw you out of the room!' A gentleman of the press stood up and said, 'I've been coming to the Cannes festival for 20 years and this is the most disgraceful behaviour I've ever seen. How dare you treat us like this?' Menahem went over and grabbed him by the lapels and screamed, 'You fucking bastard. I'm telling you get out or I kick you out!' This had a terrific effect on the rest of the press, who thought, 'Oops.' They scurried out the side door. I was roaring with laughter. I said to Yoram, his partner, who was sitting at the side table, 'I want Menahem to handle all my press conferences. He's absolutely wonderful.' Faye was looking totally terrified. A photograph of us both on the platform appeared in the *Nice Matin* newspaper the following day showing me roaring with laughter and Faye looking extremely nervous as if she desperately wanted out.

Eating with the Editor of the *Sunday Times*

My life on the *Sunday Times* is about as unsocial as you can get. I sit in my house and write my weekly food column. It is emailed in with the photographs and that's it! I hardly ever talk to anybody and nobody talks to me. This is very nice indeed because I don't want to be disturbed, bossed about or anything else.

I was very friendly with a previous editor, Harold Evans, when I started with the paper in 1970 and was very friendly with his successor, Andrew Neil. I greatly admire and like the current editor, John Witherow, but our meetings are limited to one lunch every year. At one of these lunches John made one of the most intelligent remarks I've ever heard. We were at the late and lamented St Alban restaurant, which is now closed, one of the reasons being they wouldn't listen to me and put in a bar and a piano. Some mirrors would have helped as well. For two of the greatest restaurateurs in history, Jeremy King and Chris Corbin, to have a restaurant without atmosphere was very strange. They specialised in atmosphere at Le Caprice, The Ivy, J Sheekey and now the Wolseley, which is as buzzy and terrific a place as you could have. I personally liked St Alban. But I could see why most people I sent there never returned.

Anyway, there I was sitting with John Witherow, the editor of the *Sunday Times*. It was just before my column moved from their 'Style' magazine to the 'News Review' section. John said to me, 'Now you're moving to "News Review", Michael, you'll have a much shorter lead time.' A lead time is the period between your giving in what you have written and the time they print it. With the 'Style' section it was about three weeks. John said, 'With "News Review" you can write it and send it in four days before the paper is on the newsstands. So you can be far more topical.' There was a pause while John thought about that. Then he said, 'That won't make any difference, will it? You only write about yourself.' Outstandingly perceptive man!

Eating with Ava Gardner

Ava Gardner was considered the most beautiful woman in the world. She was listed by the American Film Institute as one of the greatest stars of all time. Her personal life was far more interesting. She married Mickey Rooney, Artie Shaw and Frank Sinatra.

When I met her the marriage to Sinatra had long been over and so had the days of her being beaten to pulp by George C. Scott. She was living quietly in an elegant apartment in a Kensington square. She later played a leading role for me in my horror film *The Sentinel*. To go on the streets of New York with Ava Gardner was to see one of the great crowd pullers of all time. They may not have turned up in their millions to see her movies but she was an icon and a legend.

I described to her my method of making scrambled eggs. This is: take, let us say, six eggs, put them in a bowl, add quite a lot of milk, whisk them up furiously and at the same time have a frying pan (not a saucepan) with butter in it on the stove. When the butter is seriously hot you immediately pour the egg mix into the pan and stir speedily with a wooden spoon. Within seconds you have extremely good scrambled eggs. Ava said, 'That's the way Frank used to do them.' So although I didn't share Ava Gardner with Frank in the conjugal sense, I did share my instinct for how to make scrambled eggs.

On the movie, quite a bit of which was shot in a very large spooky house in Brooklyn, Ava returned one day late from lunch. I am somewhat draconian on the set. If you've got a unit of 80 people and other actors around I expect everyone to return from lunch at the same time and get on with the job. Ava, with her lovely black secretary René, was 15 minutes late. I gave her a bit of a bollocking. She apologised profusely and told me she had been to Peter Luger's Steak House, where she used to go with Sinatra, to relive moments of that relationship.

Sinatra kept her financially after the divorce. Ava was always quite angry that she'd introduced Sinatra to her friend Barbara Marx (ex-wife of Zeppo Marx of the Marx Brothers) and Barbara had nicked him. One famous story of Sinatra and Ava Gardner is that Frank was in a bar in Las Vegas chatting up and about to have a 'do' with a number of prostitutes. A friend said to him, 'Frank, you have Ava Gardner, the most beautiful woman in the world, waiting in your suite and here you are with these second-raters.' To which Frank said, 'Yes, but she's my wife.'

Frank also had another phrase which is politically incorrect but nonetheless very telling. Talking about journalists he said, 'They jerk off and we buy yachts.'

Ava tended to stay in her London apartment, going occasionally to see her friend Charles Gray, who played Blofeld in one of the Bond movies. She was always having rows with him and not speaking and then making up. I remember when Aids came in Ava said to me, 'I go to his parties but I take my own glass now. I'm terrified of getting Aids.' Charles of course was a well-known gay.

Occasionally Ava would come out to dinner with me. I remember once we were dining at Wilton's restaurant. It was a memorable occasion because Ava usually spoke very little about her past. As we had fried plaice and chips she told me how Howard Hughes, with whom she had a long-running on/off affair, had her followed wherever she went, and if any new relationship broke up his people would come up to her and persuade her to go back to see Hughes wherever he was. One time she was in some ski resort in America and had broken up with a man there. She was persuaded to revisit Hughes in Florida. She said, 'I got very quickly bored, because he's extremely boring, and I decided to go to Cuba.' Doubtless in Cuba Ava had some romantic situations ready to unfold for her. Ava explained, 'I booked a ticket for me and René at Miami airport to go to Cuba. It was then I realised for the first time how immensely powerful Hughes was. Because when it came to 10:30am and the plane was due to board for Miami an announcement came over the loudspeaker saying the flight had been cancelled. So I transferred to another flight three hours later. That too was cancelled. And thus it went on throughout the day. I realised that Howard was having various airlines cancel their planes from Miami to Cuba to stop me going there. That made me even more determined to go. The only problem was that my secretary René, being black, was not allowed in the toilets for white people at that time. The toilet for black people was a rather dingy hut a very long walk from the main terminal building in the height of Miami summer when the temperature was well over 100 degrees. I hung on. And it was not until 24 hours later at 10:30am the following day that even Howard Hughes couldn't stop the flights going to Cuba and I went.'

Ava would sit having dinner alone in her apartment doing the *Daily Telegraph* crossword and getting sozzled. She would ring me many, many times. One call I remember particularly because it was so moving. Instead of asking my view of an answer to a clue in the crossword, Ava said, 'You know I've just been watching *The Barefoot Contessa* on television. I wasn't such an ugly broad, was I? I looked pretty good in those days.' I said, 'Ava, you didn't look pretty good. You were the most beautiful thing in the world.' She was so desperately insecure and unsure of herself.

In 1988 I was making an Agatha Christie film called *Appointment with Death*. Ava had had a stroke, but she was very keen to work and get back into real life. She was able to walk, she told me, and the part in the film was that of a crippled lady. So it would not have been difficult for Ava to use a stick. I met her and we cast her in the movie. About five weeks before the movie was due to start, Ava telephoned me and said, 'Can I come round and see you?' I said, 'Of course, Ava, would you like to come for lunch?' She said, 'No, I'll just come and see you. I don't eat much lunch these days.' Ava came round. She still looked very beautiful. She was not seriously incapacitated but she said, 'I had to come and see you personally to tell you that my doctors think the strain of going to Israel to make this movie would be too much for me and sadly I have bow out of it. I don't want you to be disappointed and I'm so sorry.'

Later I made a film with Michael Caine and she said to me, 'Can you get me Michael Caine's autograph? I'd love a photo that he's signed to me. He's one of my favourite actors.' Sadly I never did, although Michael was very chuffed to hear about it.

Ava starred in an enormous number of movies. She was always sad that, as she put it to me: 'You know when I made all those movies, actors and actresses didn't get much money. Not like today. We had no power. We were just shifted from movie to movie. So I never made what I could have done if I'd started out later.'

Ava lived in this luxury flat with photo albums full of pictures of her corgi dog. When her corgi dog died she bought another dog that looked exactly the same and filled more albums with pictures. She used to walk the dog in the park even when she could hardly walk. René came over to look after her.

Ava was a Capricorn. My mother was a Capricorn. Although I'm not a total believer in the zodiac signs I know a number of Capricorns (Faye Dunaway is another one) and the women all have a similar way of life. When they want something they want it at once and they are terrier-like until they get it.

The first time I met Ava there had been a law passed in America that American citizens had to pay American tax regardless of what country they resided in. It was 1pm and I was sitting in her luxurious living room when I told her this. Ava said, 'Wait a minute, please.' She lifted up the phone and called her accountant, who I will call Mr Cohen. I think that was his name but I could be wrong. She said, 'Hello, could I speak to Mr Cohen . . . Oh, Mr Cohen's out. Well, this is Ava Gardner, it's very important, could you please tell me where he is. . . . I see, he's having lunch. Could you give me the name and number of the restaurant please?' I said, 'Ava it's not essential for you to call this man during his lunch at 1pm, you can call him at 3pm or 4pm. The world isn't going to change by then.' 'No darling,' she said, 'I want to get this fixed and clear.' So Ava rang the restaurant and they said Mr Cohen was eating. She said, 'I know but would you please interrupt him and tell him urgently to come to the phone.' These were the days before cell phones. So Mr Cohen comes to the phone and Ava says, 'I'm so sorry to trouble you, Mr Cohen, you're such a wonderful person, but I just have to ask you this. I have a young man here who tells me that the American tax system is changing and I'm liable for tax even though I live in the United Kingdom . . .' When she finished and put the phone down I looked up and I said, 'Ava, are you Capricorn?' She said, 'How did you know?'

Ava had the most extraordinary life. She is blamed for

having actors banned from the Ritz hotel in Madrid because she poo-ed on the carpet in the main lobby. She lived life to the full in the widest sense of that term. When she was going to write her autobiography I said, 'Ava, if you tell the truth about your life it will be the greatest autobiography ever. You married Mickey Rooney, Artie Shaw, Frank Sinatra, you had a long affair with Howard Hughes, you've been with God knows how many other men, you've been through the most extraordinary situations, you must tell the truth.' Ava said, 'Of course I'm not going to tell the truth, darling, I'm going to say things that leave the impression with people that I want left with them.' She never did tell the truth. I found somebody to co-write her autobiography with her. It was benign.

I remember shortly after I first met her, Ava was talking about her first marriage to Mickey Rooney. She said, 'I went to see his mother. We were sitting on a porch in Los Angeles, she was running some sort of home for old people and she said to me, "Don't you realise, Ava, he's only marrying you so he can get in your pants."'

I adored Ava. Perhaps it's salacious of me, but I wish she'd told more stories about her own life, because it was so interesting and most of what happened has gone to the grave with her. After her death, Sinatra's daughter Tina found him slumped in his room, crying and unable to speak. I can understand that.

Eating with Anthony Hopkins

In February 1988 I got together with Anthony Hopkins, who was to star in my film *A Chorus of Disapproval*. Anthony is the most incredible person. He is the only star I've ever met who is a human being first and a star second. Stardom doesn't figure in his personality at all. This is not to say I do not like the other stars I've met, but they are aware that they're stars and they accept, enjoy or revel in the privileges and persona that gives them. Anthony Hopkins is a human being without any of the trimmings of fame.

He went through a confused period of alcoholism and when he knew he was to be in Scarborough with us on the film the first thing he asked me was, 'Can you find the local Alcoholics Anonymous, because I have to go there?'

We were getting his clothes for the film and had lunch in Cibo, a local restaurant in Kensington that I used to use a lot but have since gone off. He was playing a down at heel solicitor in Scarborough so we went to Marks & Spencer in High Street Kensington for his clothes. About 10 outfits were laid out on the counter – trousers, jackets, shirts, ties, the most enormous amount. They filled a very large counter, with some of them lying on top of each other. I said to Anthony, 'Do you mind if I play a little game now, Tony?' He said, 'Not at all.' So I said to the salesman, 'All right, what's the discount?' The salesman said, 'We do not give discounts at Marks & Spencer.' I said, 'Get me the manager please.' The manager turned up. I said, 'You see all that on the counter there? That's the biggest sale you'll have this week if not this year to one customer. I want a discount.' The manager said rather pompously, 'Marks & Spencer do not give discounts.' I said, 'Yes, I heard that from the salesman but let's get into the real world. What's the discount?' The manager said, 'I'm afraid I can't give you one.' I said, 'Look, that's Anthony Hopkins there, that's not chopped liver. He's going to wear your clothes in a film. That has to be worth something.' The manager said, 'I'm very sorry I cannot give you a discount.' 'Okay,' I said, 'take all those clothes from the counter, put them all back, you've sold nothing.'

I turned to walk out with Anthony, who had been watching with some amusement. As we were leaving the manager said, 'Excuse me.' I turned back and said, 'Yes.' He said, 'I can't give you a discount, Mr Winner. What I'll do is, I'll give you three outfits free.' I said, 'Okay, I'll live with that.' I said to Anthony as we left, the wardrobe people staying to pick up the clothing, 'Anthony, I know exactly what he'll do. He's not allowed to give a discount so he'll simply say those three outfits were stolen. Then he gets the report of this big sale on his daily record which he has to send to head office and he puts the others on his stolen sheet which he also has to send to head office.'

When we made the film Jeremy Irons and I stayed in rather a posh hotel in Scarborough and Anthony also had a suite there. But he said, 'No, I'd rather stay with all the other cast.' So he moved to a less good hotel. That was typical of Anthony. He had no ego whatsoever. He is a very rare person as well as being a marvellous actor.

There was one moment where I saw him very worried. He came to me and he said, 'Michael, my ex-wife who I settled with in court regarding alimony has now had her solicitor write to me and say that as I'm earning more money than I was when the divorce was settled, she wants more money too.' I said, 'Anthony, let me ring my divorce solicitor. I'll check on it and get back to you.' The first wife actually was a rather nice woman. She was a secretary to the producer of the film called Elliott Kastner and she was what you call a good respectable girl. But even respectable girls want money when they can get it. I went back to Anthony and said, 'I'm very sorry to tell you that under British law if your circumstances vastly change your wife can go back to the courts and ask for more.' I always wondered when Anthony became even more successful after Hannibal Lecter in his American movies whether the wife went back again – and if so how often!

Eating with Burt Lancaster

Burt Lancaster tried to kill me three times. People reassured me. He only tried to kill his friends.

Burt was as good a friend as I ever had in showbusiness. I met him in 1970 when I flew to Hollywood to talk him into doing a Western I had called *Lawman*, which he did. Burt adored eating, thought he was a very good cook, and as far as I know from what he cooked for me he was. He also enjoyed being a marvellous host. We made *Lawman* in Durango, Mexico. It was typical of Burt that one day he grabbed me by the lapels, shook me practically to death holding me at the edge of a 2,000 foot drop, threatening to throw me over the cliff and screaming expletives at me because he thought I'd given him incorrect directions when he was holding the wrong gun to shoot somebody with. I was right of course. Half an hour after this he said, in that marvellous lilting voice, 'You must come over to dinner with your girl tonight, Michael. I've had some lamb especially flown in from Los Angeles. We're going to grill it.' Of course I went and he did the whole meal, potatoes, lamb, vegetables, all superbly presented with total charm.

Burt was brought up in an Italian section of New York. He desperately wanted to play the Godfather but as we know it went to another friend of mine, Mr B.

On *Lawman* Burt would not eat in the little tent reserved for the stars, he always ate in his caravan with his entourage, a make-up man, driver and a couple of other people. There was one classic lunchtime when Lee J. Cobb, Robert Ryan and I had eaten our lunch in this tent (much to the annoyance of Robert Duvall, who complained to his agent that this was not democratic and fair) when Burt came in and said, 'Michael, I've done some wonderful spaghetti bolognaise, I'm going to bring it in for you all.' When he left the room, Robert Ryan, Lee J. Cobb and I looked at each other aghast. We'd just eaten a large meal. The last thing we wanted was a plate of spaghetti bolognaise, which if we did not eat would annoy Burt enormously and he'd take it out on all of us one way or another. Burt appeared a few seconds later with this gargantuan bowl of spaghetti and meat sauce and put vast portions of it on to three plates for us. It was very, very good. But you really don't need a spaghetti bolognaise after you've just eaten a three-course meal!

Burt is a Scorpio (like me) and loves stirring it up and loves at times being extremely prickly and a bit of a pain. He would use anything when he was in that mood to hit on you just because he felt like it. Please don't get me wrong, I adored Burt and all this went off me like water off a duck's back.

One occasion when we were in Vienna with Paul Scofield and Alain Delon, Burt had asked Paul and me to a restaurant which he'd chosen. This restaurant was absolutely terrible. It was recommended to him by his driver, so Burt only chose it because the driver pointed him there. Obviously the driver was going to be paid by the restaurateur for bringing Burt Lancaster, Paul Scofield and me to the place. There was tomato ketchup on shiny table tops. It was the sort of place that Burt would never normally have gone to. I was absolutely furious that he'd been conned into going there. But Burt would never admit that he'd been 'taken', he had to see the thing through, as it were. So we sat at this table and I was so furious I got up and I went outside to where his driver was and with absolutely venomous fury addressed the driver, 'How dare you bring us to this dreadful restaurant. Whatever tip they've given you will not be worth it. It's an absolute disgrace and we're going to leave.' At which point Burt came and said, 'Come on, Michael, come back in. I think it's going to be very good.' Which of course it wasn't. It was horrific. Burt turned to me after the main course, I can't remember what it was but I remember it was ghastly, and said, 'Well, Winner, what do you think?' I said, 'It's a great pleasure, Burt, to be here with you and Paul. I'm having a very nice evening.' This did not fool Burt at all. He knew that I was saying in a slightly discreet way that the meal stunk. Which it did. So Burt went into one of his marvellous semi-rages, a real rage is enough to go off the Richter scale, but this was semi. He said, 'Well, you see, Paul, what does this bum Winner know about food? Nothing. He's totally useless on food. He goes to Wilton's [a very posh restaurant in Jermyn Street] where all the food is slimy and horrible, and he takes me to Wilton's again and again because he's got no idea about anything.' Paul Scofield quite rightly decided to stay out of it and diplomatically said that he thought it was a wonderful meal. Later I said to Paul on the set, 'Paul, I know you're a great actor, I know you've got an Academy Award, but your performance saying how much you enjoyed the meal last night beat what you did in *A Man for All Seasons*.'

If ever I came to Los Angeles Burt would take me out, mainly to a restaurant called Chasens, now gone, which was famous for its chilli con carne.

Any meal with Burt was a delight, except when he was in a bad mood, which really wasn't very often. I remember once he'd screamed at me on the set because he thought I'd clicked the bullets to go off when he was running along a passageway and I'd done them incorrectly. I hadn't of course. I'd done them absolutely properly. So when I turned up for lunch that day in Vienna Burt was sitting with his stuntman and other entourage. He looked up and said, 'We don't want you here. So go and sit somewhere else.' I may be making Burt sound like a real pig, but he wasn't. He was just very raw and human and 99.9 per cent of the time was the greatest friend you could ever wish for. And there's nothing wrong with a friend who is occasionally snappy. Although you'll find it hard to believe, I can be snappy myself.

I always used to take Burt to lunch when he came to London. I remember once we were sitting in Bibendum at a corner table and a fan came in off the street and started to harass Burt. Burt was very charming and eventually the man left. I said to the head waiter, 'How dare you let that man in to harass a movie star? This is an absolute disgrace. You have a duty to protect your customers.'

And on another occasion I went with Burt to a little local Italian restaurant near me in Kensington. The restaurant manager was an arsehole. But it was quite a good place. And when the manager put on what he thought was charm he wasn't too bad. We ordered our food and Burt was served the wrong main course. Something he hadn't ordered. Well, he went totally berserk. He screamed and shouted and yelled at them. He was quite right. If three people at a table can't order and get what they ordered, then the restaurant is bloody useless. When the right food eventually came Burt liked it. The next day he said to me, 'You know, Michael, I called the restaurant because I wanted to go there again the following night and I couldn't get in. They said they were full.' I knew they weren't full. I knew the manager was such a prick that he thought, 'I was shouted at before so I won't let Burt Lancaster in.' I really murdered the manager for that. Burt Lancaster was one of the most important actors, one of the most marvellous people, and how dare some little pipsqueak idiot who didn't even own the restaurant keep him out? It was obviously immensely valuable for the restaurant to have Burt Lancaster sitting there and for everybody to see him there.

Sadly my meals with Burt Lancaster ended some five years before his death when he suddenly had a stroke and lay totally incapacitated, just grunting and groaning. That was one of the saddest times of my life when I held his hand and saw what he had become. Occasionally he would make an expression for which he was famous which basically said, 'What only I have to put up with.' After his death a biography came out of Burt Lancaster. It was always said that he swung both ways. Well, I saw no sign of it whatsoever, but the biography said that he and Rock Hudson went to a party in Los Angeles with 76 US Marines. I often imagine conversations with friends who are dead. I can hear Burt's voice phoning me when the biography came out saying, 'Did you see what that cocksucker wrote? He said I went to a party with 76 US Marines. There were 79 of them.'

Eating with Sophia Loren

My first lunch with Sophia Loren in May 1977 was particularly memorable. I'd gone to Paris to induce her to star in a film, later made the following year, called *Firepower*. I had a script from Warner Brothers which was one of three scripts they offered to Clint Eastwood each year as a *Dirty Harry* sequel. This one he did not choose. So Warner Brothers gave me what is called in the film business a 'free ride' to set it up somewhere else.

I met with Sophia and her husband, Carlo Ponti, at their apartment opposite the George V hotel in Paris. Sophia was elegant, somewhat cold and very charming. When we later got to know each other I found she was not cold at all but massively human and terrific. On this occasion we went to lunch over the road at the George V hotel. It was my job to explain the script to Sophia, as I hadn't shown it to her. I said, 'Sophia, we have a script which at the moment has your part described as a black lady from Martinique, which she indeed is. She has seven lines of dialogue.' I will never forget Sophia's reaction. She raised an eyebrow and simply said, 'Ooh.' 'But, Sophia,' I continued, 'in a very few weeks this part will be white, Italian, and the co leading role in the picture with the man who will star with you.' Sophia laughed. She went along with it. After all, she hadn't seen the script. She'd make a decision when she saw it. We had a marvellous lunch.

I went back to London. The script was rewritten and then presented to Sophia. In it she was the villainess. She was up to no good at all. Her husband, Carlo, said, 'Sophia will never shoot the villain.' I said, 'Carlo, she doesn't shoot the villain, she is the villain.' Carlo responded, 'She will never play that part, I assure you.' When I telephoned Sophia she said, 'Of course I'll play the part. I think it's very good. I'll enjoy it immensely.' Thus she was cast in the movie.

Sir Lew Grade, who was now making the film, also showed it to Charles Bronson. Lew came back to me and said triumphantly, 'Charles Bronson will star with Sophia Loren in this picture.' I said, 'No he won't, Lew.' Lew said, 'He will. He told me he would and I'm going to announce it with both of them standing beside me at the Cannes festival.' This duly happened. There are pictures of Lew, Sophia and Charles Bronson standing beaming into the cameras, announcing the film *Firepower,* which I was to produce and direct. Lew came back triumphantly and said, 'Well, Michael, you were wrong. Bronson is doing it.' I said, 'No he isn't, Lew. I can assure you he will not do this picture.' I knew Charlie well enough to know that he would never do a movie with a very famous leading actress opposite him. He was too insecure. If you look at his film credits he never did a film with a big female star opposite him. Lew said, 'But he shook hands with me in Cannes. He was with me at the press conference . . .' I said, 'Lew, that means absolutely nothing. Wait and see.'

Sophia was not very enthusiastic about Charles Bronson. Maybe she thought, as I'd made so many films with him, I would favour him above her. Maybe she thought, as she said, that he wasn't a very good actor. This is not true. Charlie was a superb screen actor. She agreed to do the film. She agreed to do it with Bronson. But she had reservations about him. As I absolutely knew would happen, some 10 weeks before the film was due to start, when we were already out finding locations, Charlie Bronson said he was quitting the movie. At this point Sophia, who never liked him anyway, had Carlo say to Lew Grade, 'Sophia's very upset she's no longer in this film with such a big star and as she isn't she wants more money.' That's show business. Lew agreed to give her more money.

Lew was the most wonderful person to have around. He did deals all over the place and never remembered what the deal was. A week before the film was going to be made when he had to give her a contract Lew rang me at 6:30 in the morning, which was his habit, and said, 'What did I agree to pay Sophia Loren? I can't remember.' I said, 'Lew, you raised it from $600,000 to $800,000 because she got more out of you when she learnt she wasn't acting with Charlie Bronson.'

The part was recast with James Coburn, with the third starring role going, by Lew Grade's request, to O.J. Simpson.

Sophia was without doubt the most professional, easy-going, wonderful actress I've ever directed. On her first day in Antigua we were to be on a boat. Her call was ready for 8am to shoot. I came to the pier at 7:15am as it is the director's job to be early and see everything is in order. I said, 'Is Sophia here yet?' They pointed to a bollard about 20 yards away. Sophia in full costume and make-up was sitting on it waiting to start her work. We went on a fairly small boat with O.J. Simpson, James Coburn and Sophia. The sea was a bit rough. It was a couple of hours before we needed Sophia for shooting. She had been on the deck keeping out of the way. When I needed her I couldn't see her anywhere. I said to my assistant director, 'Where's Sophia Loren?' He said, 'She's down in the toilet being sick.

She's not been well at all with the rocking of the boat.' Sophia duly appeared. She made absolutely no comment or fuss about having been ill, and got on and did the work. As far as I'm concerned she's a marvel.

Each day we would have lunch. Sophia, James Coburn, O.J. and myself in a tent reserved for the leading artistes. We bought over an English caterer and the food was pretty good. Sophia announced one day, 'I'm going to make some pasta with meat sauce myself and serve it to you in two days' time.' Indeed she did. She spent a long time doing the sauce at her hotel room and I don't know how she did everything and got the spaghetti but she duly appeared with this fantastic spaghetti, served everybody, including me, herself. It was one of the best Italian meals I've ever had.

I was having dinner one day with Sophia on the Isle of St Lucia in their best hotel, which was called La Toc. It is now Sandals, a mass tourist resort. Sophia said to me, 'You know, Michael, there's an Italian paparazzo arrived on the island. He takes quite salacious photographs. I think he'll try to get photographs of me with O.J. Simpson and intimate that we are having an affair.' At the time, rumours were flying of Sophia having affairs with various people. I have no way of knowing if they were true and nor do I care. Sophia said, 'I'd like him kept off the set.' It's typical that she knew he was there. Sophia is very savvy to what goes on, as all big movie stars are. What Sophia wanted as far as I'm concerned is what Sophia got. After dinner I phoned the chief of police of St Lucia and I said, 'This Italian photographer has arrived. I'm told he's staying at the hotel La Toc and Sophia doesn't want him photographing her on the set.' The police chief rang me back half an hour later. He said, 'Don't worry, Mr Winner, he won't photograph Ms Loren on the set or having lunch with O.J. Simpson or anything like that because we've broken the door down of his hotel room and he's in prison.' So I rang Sophia Loren and said, 'Sophia, don't worry, dear, the photographer has been arrested and he's been put in prison.' Sophia said, 'Well, I didn't want him put in prison. I just wanted him kept off the set.' I said, 'Well, Sophia, he's in prison. He won't be on the set if he's in prison, will he?' Sophia said, 'You've got to get him out.' I said, 'Sophia darling, I just got him in. I'll tell you what, we'll wait until tomorrow when the police chief is coming on to the set with the Prime Minister and his wife and I'll get him out then.'

The next day we were having lunch with the Prime Minister and his wife and the chief of police on a lovely bay called Marigot Bay. At the time it was more or less deserted. Now it's an over-developed yacht car park. The police chief came on the set looking like an old-fashioned commissionaire from a West End cinema. He had epaulets. He had medals. He had badges. He was, as the saying goes, wearing the kitchen sink. I went up to him and said, 'Look, it's terribly sweet of you to put the Italian photographer in jail but Ms Loren would now like him out of jail.' The chief of police said to me, 'We can't get him out of jail, Mr Winner, because we're going to send him off the island. We're flying him to New York.' I said, 'But he didn't come from New York, he came from Rome. What's New York got to do with it?' The police chief said, 'Well, we don't have a direct flight to Rome but we do have one to New York. And that's where he's going. At the moment, he's on the wait list because we can't get him on the plane.' I told Sophia this and said, 'There's nothing I can do, Sophia. Eventually he'll be on a plane to New York. What he does after that I really don't care.'

After the film was over, Sophia rang me in my house in London and said, 'Michael, you don't know what trouble I'm having with this paparazzo who you had put in prison in St Lucia and then had him thrown out. At every press conference I give he stands at the back screaming that I had him put in jail. I was driving along and I was involved in some very minor car accident and he was following me and took dozens of photographs and made it look like the accident was due to me.' I thought that was rather funny. Sophia didn't take it that seriously either.

Another time I was having lunch with Sophia in London and I talked about the fact that she'd been convicted of tax fraud in Italy and was due to go to jail. I said, 'Sophia, what happened? Are you actually going to prison?' She said, 'Yes I am. As soon as I go back to Italy I'm going to be arrested and put in jail. I decided I'd rather see that through than never be able to go back to my home country.' I said, 'Very noble of you, Sophia. When are you going back?' Sophia, picking at a grilled salmon, said, 'I'm going back in the summer because I don't want to go to prison when it's cold because I don't think they'll have very good heating.' That was typical Sophia. Very practical and very reasonable.

You may remember Sophia went back to Italy and was duly put in prison. The newspapers were full of stories that she had a special cell, a television for herself and was generally being very grandly looked after in contrast to the other prisoners. When Sophia came out after four weeks of being in prison I said, 'How was it, Sophia?' She said, 'Absolutely terrible. I can't tell you how awful it was, Michael.' I said, 'I read you had a special cell and you had your own television and it was all kind of luxurious. I read that you had special meals brought in and that you were treated like royalty.' Sophia said, 'Absolutely untrue. I was in a very dingy cell. I did have a television but it was a very antiquated black and white set that hardly worked. The first day I said I wanted to go out and walk about among the prisoners, they said, "You can't do that, Ms Loren, because if the prisoners cut your face, they'll get a lot of attention and they'll be heroes within the prison, so we advise you to stay in your cell." So I had to stay in my cell for the entire four weeks. I never went out and it was quite horrible. But I'm glad it's over and now I'm a free person again.'

The last time I saw Sophia we had tea at her suite in the Ritz when she was visiting England. She had told me on the film set that she was 44 years old and, 'I don't even know where my money is.' As we were having tea I said, 'Sophia, have you found out where your money is now?' She looked at me with a rather wise look and said, 'Yes I have.'

A minor amusing matter is that the first year after *Firepower*, Sophia sent me a printed Christmas card saying 'Happy Christmas from the Pontis.' There was no signature. Nothing personal about it whatsoever. I rang her up and said, 'Sophia, it is very rude to send your friends a printed card without any writing on it.' She just laughed. But from that year on until the current time Sophia has always signed her cards to me and indeed last Christmas (2009) she wrote a long personal note on a piece of paper so everything about it was hand-written. She's an absolutely marvellous person. You don't meet people like that very often.

Eating with Robert Mitchum

Robert Mitchum was far from the wisecracking tough guy, which was the image he put forth and which people had of him. He gave the wittiest interviews ever, but he was quite a troubled person and somewhat schizophrenic. He was half poet and dreamer and half roustabout. I met him in 1977 when he was to star in my movie of Raymond Chandler's *The Big Sleep*. I had always been a fan. We became good friends and stayed good friends until he died of cancer in 1997.

One of the first meals we had, before the film began, was after we went to the theatre to see Sir John Mills (who was also in the film) at the theatre in *Separate Tables*. That afternoon I'd had a photograph taken at my house of topless girls to go on the cover of what was meant to be a pornographic book we used in the film. I was surprised when I went to the lobby of the theatre and Mitchum turned up with one of the nude models, Lindy Benson. She remained his companion throughout the film. At one point she was with Bob in the flat we got for him in Arlington House above Le Caprice when another girl who'd latched on to him knocked on the door. The two girls had an enormous fight in the hall, egged on by Mitchum and his somewhat drunken friends. Lindy

Benson won. The other girl went into retirement in the Robert Mitchum stakes.

There's no question Bob liked to drink. Although he was very professional on the set, he tended to get a bit sozzled in the evenings. Then he became rather incomprehensible, telling stories where he slurred the words and spoke in a very quiet voice. He then got very irate if you weren't following it properly. A lingering situation from that first meal and visit to the theatre was occasioned by the fact that when we got to the theatre the manager gave me my seat and gave Mitchum his. When we checked them out, I was in the royal circle and Mitchum was in the stalls. I said, 'Bob, is that what you want or would you rather sit with me?' He said, 'Of course I'd rather sit with you.' So I said to the manager, 'You may notice that we came together, Mr Mitchum and I, and we'd like to sit together.' The manager said, 'Well, those are the places where Sir John wanted you to sit.' I said, 'With respect, he's on the stage, he knows where he's sitting, we'd like to sit together.' So Mitchum and I sat together. We wondered why Mills had put us separately.

As a result of this I had special notepaper printed, headed 'The Occasional First Nighters Society, Chairman: Robert Mitchum, Secretary: Michael Winner M.A. (Cantab)' and various other strange things to make it look vaguely official, with a West End address that we invented. A letter was written to Sir John Mills concocted by Bob and myself saying something like, 'Dear Sir John, The members of our society are extremely curious as to why you placed Mr Robert Mitchum and Mr Michael Winner in separate seats when they came to see you at the theatre in *Separate Tables*. Our members have made the following suggestions as to why Mr Mitchum and Mr Winner were seated by you in different parts of the theatre. 1: You were afraid that Mr Mitchum and Mr Winner might fart simultaneously thus disturbing your performance. 2: You felt that Mr Mitchum and Mr Winner might gossip throughout the show thus detracting attention from you on the stage. 3: You felt that the sight of Mr Mitchum together with Mr Winner would be too much for the public who would be in such awe of what they saw that they could not properly concentrate on the drama unfolding on the stage . . .' And so the letter went on. The letter was duly sealed in an envelope.

When we were filming a few weeks later on the pier at Margate one of the assistants took the letter over to Sir John Mills, who was sitting on a bale of something. Mitchum and I peered as John opened the letter, looked at it very seriously, folded the letter and put it in his pocket. We were expecting him to come to us and make a joke of it but he didn't. Eventually I went over with Mitchum and I said, 'Johnnie, did you just get a letter?' John Mills said, 'Yes, yes I did. It wasn't important.' I said, 'But John, what was the letter?' John Mills declined to tell us. I said, 'John, the letter was a spoof letter from me and Mitchum.' At this point John didn't think it was a very funny joke and said as little about it as possible.

I was having dinner with Mitchum at Claridge's hotel (before the dining room was ruined and Gordon Ramsay took it over). It was a Saturday evening. Jack Lemmon walked by with some people and sat at another table, having first come over and chatted to us. At the end of the dinner Jack Lemmon came and had coffee with us. Bob Mitchum said to me, 'Where can we go now?' I said, 'We could go to Tramp discotheque if you like.' Bob said, 'I'm not a member.' I said, 'I've been a member since 1966. They know me very well.' At the time Mitchum was not drinking. This was rare. When I asked him why he wasn't drinking he said that he'd been into the Betty Ford clinic to cure him of drinking. I said, 'Why on earth did you go there, Bob?' He said, 'Because my family insisted. My wife was already in there as a live-in patient so I had to go as a day patient.' I never knew his wife, who was very tolerant of his affairs, was on the bottle. But apparently she was.

The four of us (including my girlfriend) went to Tramp. I appeared at the desk. There I am, standing with two of the most famous actors in the world, Robert Mitchum and Jack Lemmon, and the girl at the desk (they were always very haughty and unpleasant) looked up. I announced myself as Michael Winner. The girl said, 'He's not here.' I looked round at Mitchum and Lemmon and said, 'Come on, let's ignore that.' We walked downstairs and went in. After a while everyone came over and apologised profusely and said that the girl didn't understand and thought I was asking about another member and various other bits of drivel. It was ridiculous. Jack Lemmon was drinking like crazy. His head swivelled too and fro as each girl, revealing bosom and more legs, entered the room. He was like a pixie on speed. It was a wonderful sight.

The next day we arranged to go to the French Horn at Sonning for lunch. This is a wonderful restaurant, very much of the old school, where the ducks roast on the spit on an open fire as you come in. Bob Mitchum, Jack Lemmon and my girlfriend met in my house, where Jack immediately had two very large vodka tonics with ice and took a third vodka tonic in an enormous glass with him in the back of my Rolls-Royce as I drove down to the French Horn. Mitchum was still not drinking. I had a Polaroid camera and took a number of photographs of all of us at the French Horn and walking in the village and looking at the church and all that. I was interested that, when we got back to London and I laid them out on the car, Mitchum and Jack Lemmon almost fought over them, they were so keen to have these photographs. I thought, 'This is strange. Here are two stars who are photographed endlessly on the set and off the set and yet they really want these pictures as a souvenir of a day off.'

A week later I took Mitchum down to the Waterside Inn at Bray. They asked me what I wanted to drink and I ordered a Bellini, which was the special of the day. Bob said, 'I'll have that too.' I said, 'But Bob, I thought you'd given up drinking?' He said, 'I've started again.'

Bob was only drunk a couple of times during the film. The first one was when we were filming at the Savoy hotel. We got to the alley at the side where we were going to shoot and there was a very large hole dug by people mending a gas pipe. Around the hole (which had not been there when we visited on the reconnaissance) were barriers and lights and a great pile of earth that had been dug out of the ground. I said to my assistant director, 'I don't care what you do but get this hole filled in. Mitchum and I are going to have dinner in the Savoy hotel and when I come out to start shooting I don't want to see that hole.' So the hole was filled in. The next day, eight Irish labourers came and couldn't find their hole in the ground. The gas board were very good about it. They didn't charge us anything for that. Far worse than the hole was Mitchum after dinner. He'd had far too much to drink. He was rolling about all over the place. There was a German camera crew and he kept screaming at them that they were Nazis and doing the Hitler salute. We did a few takes with him and Sarah Miles and then Mitchum had another scream at the German TV crew and suddenly ran off up the alley and said, 'I'm going home.' My assistant chased him and got him back but there wasn't any point. We did shoot but the scene was unusable, with Bob swaying and forgetting his lines. We had to go back a few weeks later and reshoot it.

The other time I had a memorable dinner with Mitchum, in fact one of the most memorable dinners of my life, took place at a luxury house in Turville near Henley. We were filming there. Just before the dinner break we were going to do a shot of some gentleman's ties tied together that would be set alight and go into the petrol tank of a car that featured in the movie. When the film was shown there would be Mitchum, who had lit the fuse from the bushes, watching the car explode. Then started a big performance with guns and everything going off as he tried to get the villain. As it was not yet dark we erected a tent extension coming off the luxury house, put the car in it on a large gravel space at the back of the house. We were sucking the petrol out of the car. The unit were taking forever doing this. At the time I smoked cigars non-stop. I said to my assistant director, 'Get a fucking move on. We can't wait here forever for this tank to be emptied.' The assistant said, 'I think there's petrol running on to this gravel.' I said, 'Absolute nonsense.' To prove my point I lit a match and threw it on the ground. Whereupon the whole ground ignited. Flames appeared everywhere. The fire shot back into the tent, setting the tent on fire. Did some considerable damage to the camera that was in there ready to do this close-up. The fire nearly burnt the crew to death! They ran out just in time. In the meantime, flames were leaping up at the side of the house as the canvas blazed. At that exact moment three firemen from the Thames Valley Fire Brigade, who were standing by for the shoot-out later, appeared on the scene. I always provide extra food for the stars, stuff made in my own kitchen. One of the firemen was carrying a chocolate cake, another fireman was carrying a pavlova and another was carrying a large cheesecake. Here were the firemen in full uniform carrying these cakes with a raging fire going on a few yards away from them. I burst into hysterical laughter. So did my cameraman Bob Paynter. We fell on the ground crying with laughter. I have a photo of this! The crew were in total shock. The fire was put out. Not by the firemen but by our unit with fire extinguishers that we carried. Nobody could believe that I laughed about it and nobody could believe I did it. Nor for that matter could I. But I did. That's life.

Later I had dinner with Mitchum where we ate the cakes and we ate everything else. Mitchum had been in his caravan so he hadn't seen this fiasco. I described it to him rather gleefully. Then he and Richard Boone, who played the villain, indulged in this enormous shoot-out. By now both of them were drunk. Mitchum was invariably drunk at night. Boone, who managed to stay sober during the day even though he was drinking non-stop, let the drink get the better of him at night. So guns and machine guns were going off at the wrong time. They were shooting into the ground. They nearly shot each other's feet off. I turned to my assistant and said, 'Unbelievable! This is the gunfight at Alcoholics Anonymous. How we'll ever put this together and make a movie I don't know.' But as always happens, things worked out.

After the filming I often saw Mitchum. I'd go to Los Angeles and we would have dinner in various restaurants there and when he came to London I would always see him and we'd eat in London. He came to do a television mini-series called *Reunion at Fairborough* in the mid-80s. They were shooting in the village of Shere, a Surrey village much used by movie companies. Members of the public gathered at the barrier. Mitchum asked an attractive local girl through to his caravan. She was deeply impressed when Bob asked her to lunch the following Sunday. He asked me to join them.

They went to Claridge's, where I'd taken Mitchum before. I didn't want to sit with Mitchum on a Sunday because I knew he'd be somewhat pissed and burbling on rather incoherently. But I did come in toward the end for coffee. By now the girl was in absolute terror. It was one thing to come up briefly to a big movie star in the village of Shere with all the cameras and unit around them and all her friends behind the barrier. Now she was alone in a London hotel with a man who was getting more and more pissed, was quite clearly going to try and seduce her and was old enough to be her grandfather. I stayed a bit and then I said, 'I have to go.' I'll never forget the girl's face. She pleaded, 'Can't you stay Mr Winner?' I said, 'I'm terribly sorry, dear, I've got an appointment.' I thought, 'You got yourself into this. Let it be a lesson to you.' Me and my girlfriend left.

Later I rang Mitchum at the Athenaeum hotel, where he was staying and asked, 'How did it go, Bob?' He said, 'She was no good at all. I had to send her home. How do I get laid in this town?' I replied, 'It's very easy, Bob. You get a magazine called *What's On* (which has since ceased publication) and there are endless adverts for call girls. Phone them up and get one sent round.' Four hours later I rang Mitchum again. I said, 'How did it go with the call girl?' Mitchum said, 'I rang them and they were on ansaphone.' I don't know if that was true but it made a good story. Maybe Mitch was too scared to ring. Maybe he didn't bother. Or maybe he rang and indeed they were on ansaphone. Nothing is impossible with Mitchum.

Eating with Ryan O'Neal

Ryan O'Neal could be immensely charming and could also be a real pain in the arse. I definitely like him. I met him in Hollywood when he was married to an actress called Leigh Taylor-Young. I put him in my movie *The Games* where he played a marathon runner. He was suitable for that because he ran many miles every morning. He had just been in *Peyton Place* on TV. This was his first very big movie. It was a gargantuan film following the path of four individuals to the Olympic marathon in Rome. We shot all over the world – Rome, Paris, Vienna, Australia, London, Tokyo, you name it we were there.

It was my habit, as I have already told you, to have a special tent for the stars so they're out of the way of the crew and the crew are out of the way of them at meal times. On *The Games* there was a bit of a problem. We had a lot of stars, namely Michael Crawford, Stanley Baker, Jeremy Kemp, Charles Aznavour and Ryan O'Neal. There wasn't enough room for all those people plus their girlfriends, wives and hangers-on in one tent. So I decided, perhaps incorrectly, to have just myself, Stanley Baker and Michael Crawford (all English you'll note!) in the tent or private room and everyone else had to dine with the crew. Everyone else included Ryan O'Neal and Charles Aznavour. Aznavour didn't mind at all. He was the most wonderful, broad-minded, non-snobby person. Ryan O'Neal did not like this. Although he'd only been in television he viewed himself as a big star.

After *The Games* he sent me a telegram because Paramount had asked to see the movie as the first example of his work in film and had given him the leading role in *Love Story*, which made him into a gargantuan star. The telegram said, 'Twentieth Century Fox dropped my contract. I lost the part [and he mentioned another film] but I've now, through showing them *The Games*, got the lead in *Love Story*. I owe it all to you. Love Ryan.' About a couple of years later Charlie Bronson gave a dinner at his house. Beautifully done. Wonderful food. Wonderful place settings. His wife Jill Ireland saw to that – she was marvellous at being a hostess. Ryan O'Neal was there. As we left the dining room where everyone had been seated, Ryan said to me with some bitterness, 'If you'd run this dinner, Michael, you and Charlie Bronson would have eaten in the dining room and I'd have been out eating in a tent.' I never realised until that moment how much he resented not being in the main room when we were shooting *The Games*. He got into the private room when Crawford or Stanley Baker were not with us but that wasn't very often!

When he came to London later, he brought with him his daughter Tatum, who was about eight years old. Ryan had to go out for a meal and I was given the job of babysitting Tatum. I took her to an Italian restaurant near my house. She was a very intelligent and bright girl. Sadly, she later went into drugs and God knows what else but then that happens in Hollywood because the temptations are so great.

Eating with Terry O'Neill

The brilliant photographer Terry O'Neill is one of my closest friends. I speak to him nearly every morning at 8am. If he doesn't answer the phone at 8am I become extremely irate. But he always answers by 8.45am.

We first met in December 1962 when I was on location shooting a film called *West 11* at the Eden hotel in South Kensington. The film starred a very famous glamour actress at the time called Diana Dors, among other luminaries. Terry was a photographer on a rather shitty paper called the *Daily Sketch*. He turned up on the set. Normally, in those days, photographers were very docile. There was no taking photographs of celebrities in a funny way or without their permission. Photographers just came, took a fairly standard shot, and left. I looked round for Diana Dors because I was ready to film a scene with her and she was nowhere to be seen. I looked round the corner and there was Diana Dors in a mink coat with a snow scraper sweeping snow while the producer's chauffeur, Mr Minns, held an umbrella over her head. This had been set up by the *Daily Sketch* nonentity photographer. I said, 'Bring that man to me. How dare he interrupt my shooting?' Terry was duly brought over. He had then, and has to this day, the most incredible charm. I saw him from time to time and eventually we became very friendly. He married Faye Dunaway, as I have mentioned.

Terry was without doubt the greatest seducer in the history of the world. There is nobody who came anywhere near him. He has mentioned in interviews some of his conquests, who included Julie Christie, Jean Shrimpton, Ava Gardner, Faye Dunaway, Raquel Welsh and so many more that if I listed them we would need another 26 pages for this book. Terry has now settled down with the most wonderful lady called Lorraine, is happily married, and faithful as anything.

Before the marriage, Terry was famous for some of the greatest remarks I've ever heard. In fact, he's the only person I know who has never said anything to me in the 48 years I've known him which is remotely unintelligent. Actually, he did say something stupid, but only once. That was when he said, 'I'm thinking of buying a house in Barbados.' Two of Terry's great lines were both at dinner parties. The first was at a dinner party given by a mutual friend where Robert Hanson, son of the late Lord Hanson, was at the head of the table and his fiancée Normandy Keith was sitting between Terry and me further down. Throughout the meal Terry would say to me things like, 'Michael, you and I are sitting either side of the most beautiful woman in the world. Look at that face. That is the most wonderful face I've ever seen. Look at the features, the eyes, the nose . . .' He went on complimenting her endlessly. Normandy was very impressed. I drove Terry and the famous showbiz tailor, the late Doug Haywood, back to Mayfair. On the trip I said to Terry, 'What was all that nonsense about praising Normandy Keith as if you were about to seduce her? Her fiancé Robert Hanson was just a few places away.' Terry said, 'Just laying down a marker.'

Another great remark of Terry's was when he was in Hollywood at an evening-dress dinner sitting next to Sherry

Lansing, who was one of the most powerful women in Hollywood. At the time, she was in charge of production for Paramount Studios. Terry said to her, 'Could I please see your ankle?' Sherry Lansing asked, 'Why on earth would you want to see my ankle?' Terry said, 'Because there must be one part of you that is not perfect.' The man's a genius. He was also personal photographer to Frank Sinatra and now does wonderfully well, which he so deserves, with the sale of his prints of stars from the 60s, 70s and 80s – the best-seller being Sinatra.

Eating with the Queen

It is a slight exaggeration. I've never dined with the Queen. But I did host her for two hours when she came to unveil my National Police Memorial in The Mall in 2006. I escorted her to the podium. Then I escorted her from the podium into a large tent where she was to meet wives and families of slain police officers. It was drizzling slightly. The Queen had a clear plastic umbrella so people could see her. She was absolutely marvellous and charming and laughed at my jokes. What more could anyone want? I called her darling four times but either she didn't notice or she decided to ignore it.

We were in this enormous tent where all the families were having tea and cakes and sandwiches. I was taking the Queen round introducing her to various families. After about half an hour I said, 'Would you like a cup of tea?' I could see that the Queen definitely wanted a cup of tea. Being the great professional that she is I could see her also thinking, 'Here I am walking round this group of people and having to shake hands with them all and if I shake hands with them and I'm holding tea in the other hand, will I drop it?' All these things went clearly through her head. I could have held the tea for her but being highly considerate she said, 'No.' So I never got to get a cup of tea for the Queen.

I've been waiting since then for her to ask me to dinner but the invitation must have got lost in the post. Although when I was ill and I later spoke to her private secretary at the palace about something else he said to me, 'You know, the Queen was very concerned about your illness, Michael. She kept asking about it. She doesn't send many people a signed photograph but she sent you one.' I felt like saying, 'Well, it was jolly nice to get the photograph but all it's signed with is Elizabeth R. I'd have liked it to be signed "To my dear friend Michael, love and kisses Queenie".' But it wasn't signed like that. I have it up in a bathroom and it looks very nice.

Eating with Chris Rea

Chris Rea is the most wonderful person as well as being a great singer. He went to the Sandy Lane hotel in Barbados because I reviewed it and he thought the review was positive enough to get him moving from the hotel he used to stay at.

Chris is very benign but can get into a bit of a temper occasionally. One time I remember was Christmas lunch at Sandy Lane. I'd had the Christmas lunch and Chris (who is normally sitting a couple of tables away), when I came out, was sitting on some rather shoddy seating outside. I said, 'Why are you sitting here, Chris?' He said, 'I've been coming here for four years and they haven't got a table for me. They gave my table to some outsider who was just paying to come for lunch.' I said, 'Chris, go in immediately and take my table – I've just left it. I'll come with you and make sure you get it.' I will add, for the record, this was not under the present ownership and management.

On another occasion, which was also before Dermot Desmond and his group took over the hotel and ran it so well, Chris Rea came to me absolutely apoplectic. His family ran an Italian restaurant in Middlesbrough. So he knew a bit about Italian food. He said to me, 'Do you know they have fake Parmesan cheese here. We're paying an absolute fortune for the rooms and the meals and they're serving us fake Parmesan.' I said, 'What do you mean, Chris? I have Parmesan here with the spaghetti all the time.' He said, 'Come and look at it.' So he led me up to the buffet and there was a bowl of finely grated Parmesan cheese. Chris said, 'That's not real, that's some sort of catering product.' I said, 'Chris, you know I'm a food critic. But I was too stupid to notice that. I will get on to the matter immediately.' So I called over the food and beverage manager, who was a Dutchman, very nice person, but obviously working to a budget, shall we say. I said, 'Excuse me, this Parmesan you're serving guests is not real. It's catering Parmesan, isn't it? It's concocted from other ingredients.' He said, 'It is real, Mr Winner, but if you'd like Parmesan in little squares or different type of Parmesan we'll get it.' I said, 'No, no. You tell me this is real Parmesan, I don't believe you. Is it not bought in?' (Bought in means that it comes in from outside which of course Parmesan would anyway). The food and beverage manager said, 'Yes, it is bought in, but it's real Parmesan.' I said, 'Fine. Then I would like you to take me now into kitchen and I would like to look at the packet that this Parmesan comes in and I would like to look very carefully at the ingredients and read what it is.' The food and beverage manager totally refused to take me into the kitchen to see the packet the Parmesan came in, which was proof, were it needed, that the Parmesan was phoney. So after that, they put out squares of real Parmesan. But they still served this ridiculous sort of sand-like fake Parmesan as well.

My greatest dining experience with Chris Rea was on my 70th birthday when I flew 28 people to Venice and took over Harry's Bar for the evening. We had a very long table. Chris was there with his wife Joan and his daughter Julia. Other people included Michael Caine, Roger Moore, Andrew Lloyd Webber and other luminaries. I was sitting at one end of the table with Madeleine Lloyd Webber on my left and Shakira Caine on my right. Joan Collins was nearby. Toward the end of the meal Chris Rea walked up from his end of the table and said, 'How are you, you stupid Jewish bastard then? Are the Jews doing all right up here?' To which Joan Collins said, 'I think that's anti-Semitic.' Now this is the way Chris and I talk to each other. We're very, very good friends. So Chris said, 'Bugger off' and walked off back down the table.

Shortly thereafter, a book was being given around for everybody to sign. The book was by Arrigo Cipriani, the owner of Harry's Bar, and he'd given everybody a copy and all these celebrities were signing the book. So the book from Joan and Percy, her husband, went down the table and Chris Rea wrote something in Joan's book, I can't remember what it was, something about anti-Semitism, which Joan took as deeply offensive. So she looked at the book in fury and turned to Percy and said, 'Look what he's written, go and tell him.' I couldn't hear exactly what she said but she was saying basically to Percy, 'Go and tell him this is a disgrace. Tell him off.' Percy shot up and walked down the table. I said, 'Madeleine, watch this, this will be amusing.' Percy then goes down to Chris and absolutely starts to give him a terrible bollocking. To which Chris says, 'Fuck off, you stupid old fag' in his wonderful Middlesbrough accent. If those were not his exact words they were extremely similar, even though Percy is not gay. Percy came back in high dudgeon and reported to Joan Collins. By now Madeleine and I are in hysterics. Madeleine said, 'Well, you didn't have a cabaret, Michael, if they can spin this out to half an hour it will be wonderful.' I said, 'You're right, it will.' Percy was now telling Joan what Chris Rea said to him. Whereupon Joan shoots up like there's a spring up her arse and roars off down the table to tell Chris Rea what she thinks of him. Chris said something like, 'Fuck off, you stupid old has-been hag', because Chris is known for his directness, to put it mildly, and Joan comes back in absolute rage and sits down. Madeleine and I are now beyond ourselves with delight. We think this is the most wonderful little event.

After that Chris Rea, obviously thinking he had upset me or behaved badly at my party, got an attack of remorse and left the dining room. He'd finished his dessert, he was not going to be with us the next day for the lunch because he was doing a concert in Amsterdam. He simply left the room early and took a water taxi back to the hotel, leaving his wife and daughter at the table.

When we got back to London I rang Chris and he kind of apologised. I said, 'Chris, you don't have to apologise because you're a wonderful person but I do think that what you should do is, you've got this 12 CD album and book out. I think you should sign it to Joan Collins and give it to me and I'll get it to her, because it's always better to have peace than war.' Chris said, 'I don't like her. I don't see why I should.' I said, 'Chris, I'm telling you, you should because it's the decent thing to do and she's a friend of mine and while I don't object to what happened I think you should make up now.' So Chris said, 'Well, she was being silly.' I said, 'Chris, it doesn't matter if she was being silly or she wasn't being silly, sign the fucking album and get it to me. End of story.' So Chris sent me the album and I got it to Joan. I think Joan was quite pleased. They're not actually planning to spend New Year's Eve together or go on holiday together, but I think peace was to a degree restored.

I would add as a finale to this little section on Chris Rea that Chris always told me that unlike most rock and roll singers and musicians he never took drugs, he spent all his money on going to luxury hotels. He married his first girlfriend from his youth and worked his way up from being reasonably poor. And that's how he spent his cash, which

I think was very intelligent. Normally he's extremely well behaved, although occasionally when he was on tour and he came back to a hotel having worked all day and the hotel said to him that he was five minutes late for dinner and they weren't going to serve him, he was known to go completely berserk. Occasionally smash things up in the hotel. I'm sure he doesn't do it now. On the other hand, I've only been in a hotel with him in Barbados and Venice when he wasn't working. If by any chance Chris is ever in court for smashing up a hotel room I'd be very happy to be there as a character witness for him.

Eating with Oliver Reed

I first met Oliver Reed, one of the dearest people I ever came across in life, in November 1961. He came to see me for the leading role in a movie I was to direct called (and about) *West 11*. Oliver was very sensitive. He told me of a short film he'd always wanted to make, something to do with two men in a wardrobe trying to get up a hill.

The producer, Danny Angel, declined to have him in the movie, saying he was a B picture actor. He also said that Sean Connery was a B picture actor and therefore he wouldn't take him. And that Julie Christie, when he saw her screen test, was a B picture actress. As he charmingly put it in front of a large group at Associated British studios, 'Who'd want to fuck Julie Christie?' I said very cheerfully, 'I would.' To which the producer said, 'Well, you're a homosexual.' That was what you had to put up with in those days from the men in three-piece grey suits who drank gin and tonics and ran the film industry. He also thought James Mason was a has-been. Instead of having a film with Sean Connery, Julie Christie and James Mason, we had a film with Alfred Lynch, Kathleen Breck and Eric Portman. Not exactly the same.

Later in 1963, when I'd finished shooting *West 11*, I made the first film where I was the producer in sole charge. That was called *The System* and I gave Oliver Reed the lead. I tried to get Julie Christie to play opposite him but she had made *Billy Liar* (having been rejected originally in favour of a girl called Topsy Jane who became ill) and they all said to Julie, 'You're absolutely terrible in the film. You'll have to go to Birmingham Rep to learn how to act.' I wish I'd kept the postcards Julie Christie sent me from Birmingham Rep saying how awful it was and how much she was not enjoying it. As we know, when the film came out Julie was absolutely sensational and thus commenced an extraordinarily successful career. When Julie Christie got the Academy Award for *Darling* I phoned Danny Angel, the producer who'd said she was a B picture actress, and said, 'Danny, there's been a terrible mistake. A B picture actress got the Academy Award.'

I did six films with Oliver Reed, so that means I ate with him week after week, day after day on the set. But never in the evenings. It was always best to stay away from Oliver in the evenings. He was the most professional artiste and totally sober on the set. In the evening it was another story. When we made *Hannibal Brooks* in Germany and Austria we had to change Oliver's hotel room nearly every day because he'd go into the dining room and throw flour over all the guests, or he would switch the shoes round, left outside the bedroom doors, or he would pee on the Austrian flag and go around doing Hitler salutes. Michael J. Pollard, who was in the movie, was heavily into drugs. Later he went to various cures for drugs and alcohol. I said, 'Michael, you know you've just been nominated for an Academy Award for *Bonnie and Clyde*, you really don't need these drugs, you have a great future ahead of you. You must stop taking the drugs. You don't need them.' Michael Pollard said, 'Yeah, but you don't stay in the same hotel as Oliver Reed.' I said, 'Michael, you've just won the argument. I resign.'

Oliver was very quiet, very demure and very shy. A lot of actors are very shy. That's why they become actors. To become something they are not in real life. So most of our meals were docile and extremely friendly. He was the most wonderful warm-hearted man. I remember once, between movies, I took Oliver to lunch at the Empress restaurant in Berkeley Street which was the 'in' place in the sixties. That is for executives rather than for the swingers. At the time I smoked 15 cigars a day. I later paid the price by having to have open-heart surgery. Then I gave up. When I took a Monte Cristo number one from the tray that was offered (those were the days!) Oliver looked at me and said, 'Can I have a cigar too?' I said, 'Oliver, they're very strong, I don't think you'll like them. They could cause some problems.' Oliver, obviously wanting to be Mr Bravado, said very quietly, 'No, I'm sure it will be all right.' Oliver lit the cigar and as he puffed away it was a very short time indeed before he started to look rather sick. He kept going as much as he could and eventually I said, 'Oliver, this is making you ill you don't have to suffer for me. It's quite alright dear, put the cigar down.' Which he did with great relief.

I remember at another meal with Oliver at the Trattoria Terraza in Romilly Street – an 'in' restaurant of the sixties for the younger set, Princess Margaret, Peter Sellers, etc. – Oliver was ordering champagne. I said, 'Oliver, you shouldn't drink so much I'm worried what will happen to you.' He said, 'I don't drink nearly as much as people say. I only drink champagne.' This of course was total nonsense. Oliver drank whisky, beer, gin, lighter fluid and God knows what else. Actually I made that up, he didn't drink lighter fluid. But he was a very heavy drinker outside of shooting hours.

A meal I remember very well regarding Oliver Reed was one I did not actually attend. On my film *Parting Shots* in 1999 Oliver was, as usual, very sober and quiet on the set.

He had married a then schoolgirl called Josephine to great uproar from the press. Now she looked as old as he did and read him books on the set. One morning my assistant director came to me and said, 'Oliver Reed has come in holding a bottle of Scotch.' Knowing Oliver as I did I knew exactly why he was holding a bottle of Scotch. He had probably been drinking the night before, was hung over, was going to pretend to be drunk (which he wasn't pretending) and wave the bottle of Scotch about. I knew him too well.

I went to see him. Luckily we didn't have to shoot Oliver for three or four hours but he was definitely still a bit pissed from the night before. 'Oliver,' I said, 'this is very naughty of you. I told you I did not wish to employ you if you got drunk and you are drunk.' He said in his very posh voice, 'No I'm not, I'm absolutely sober. I haven't had anything to drink today at all.' I said, 'Oliver, you drank last night and you drank so much you're still feeling the effects of it.' Oliver said, 'I certainly didn't. I went to a Chinese restaurant and we didn't drink at all.' I said, 'Oliver, I don't believe you. Tell me the name of the restaurant.' Oliver gave me the name of the restaurant, which was in Hampstead near the hotel I was putting him up in as he now lived in Ireland. I said, 'Oliver, you drank with that meal a lot. You know you did.' Oliver said, 'I bet you anything you like I did not.' I said, 'Oliver, OK, I'll bet you £1,000 and when you lose you've got to pay the money to my charity the Police Memorial Trust.' Oliver leapt up and shook hands with me on it.

I then telephoned the restaurant and said I was sending a driver to pick up Oliver's bill from the night before. The bill duly arrived. It showed that his party of four had started with three gin and tonics each and then consumed four bottles of white wine and eight glasses of brandy. I showed the bill to Oliver. I said, 'Oliver, if that isn't drinking, perhaps you could tell me what is.' Oliver looked sheepish and immediately gave me a cheque for £1,000. By the time we came to film with him he had sobered up so it didn't matter.

I recall during that movie, which was the first Oliver had done for a long time, he got a telephone call from Ridley Scott's office asking him to come and read for a part in *Gladiator*. Oliver said to me, 'I don't read for parts, I'm a star. You can't have me sitting there and read like a newcomer.' I said, 'Oliver, I told you to go and do television with Ken Russell when you told me you were a big movie star because I thought it would do you good. And it did. I'm now telling you that you need a third act to your life. Ridley is asking to see you because if you're working with me again people must think you're a thoroughly sober citizen because they know I don't take any nonsense. Go and see him.' A couple of days later Oliver said, 'They've asked me again to go and read for Ridley Scott and I'm not going to.' I said, 'Oliver, you go and read for him. That's it. End of story. If you don't go I shall be extremely cross with you.' So Oliver went to read for Ridley Scott and, as we all know, he got the part in *Gladiator* and was absolutely wonderful. He died in Malta just before the end of his shooting. A newspaper rang me. I was in the kitchen. The reporter said, 'Oliver Reed just died.' I literally howled with grief. He'd fallen down in a pub drunk. Heart attack.

About six months later I was in a restaurant and Ridley Scott came over. He said to me, 'You know, Michael, I took Oliver Reed because I thought if he was working with you everything must be all right. We were advised to take his wife and make sure she was with him all the time because she'd stop him drinking.' What happened was, Oliver would be in the pub at around 10pm and say, 'I must go back to the hotel because I'm working tomorrow' and the wife would say, 'Why not stay and have another drink!' Thus a great man passed away. I was always angry when some of the papers said Oliver had a wasted life. He acted with absolute extraordinary talent in many of the most famous films for the previous 20 years. He enjoyed himself immensely. It is true that he was from time to time (to put it mildly) inebriated.

I remember another dinner concerning Oliver Reed which happened in the early eighties. Two people came from Granada (at the time that company made *This Is Your Life*) and said, 'We plan to do *This Is Your Life* live, we normally do it in a studio, and the subject we're going to have is Oliver Reed.' I said, 'You obviously have another job to go to. You wish to leave Granada in a blaze of publicity and scandal. To have Oliver Reed live on *This Is Your Life* is ridiculous. The chances of him being sober are as near nil as you can get.' The producer and director of *This Is Your Life* said, 'No, we've spoken to all Oliver's friends and they say you're the person he most respects in the world. So we're going to tell him that the *This Is Your Life* programme is yours, it's about you, and that he is simply coming on as a guest. Therefore we're absolutely sure he will stay sober. I said, 'That's extremely optimistic of you and I very much doubt if it's true.'

The last time I had seen Oliver was in a Chinese restaurant in Kensington – he was with Ken Russell. He picked me up and threw me over his shoulder onto the carpet. After throwing me on the carpet Oliver had a fight with someone and they went into Hyde Park and Oliver got knocked into the Round Pond. He came back in the restaurant soaking wet with his beautiful suit shrinking all around him.

The shooting was to take place at the Adelphi Theatre in The Strand. A week before it was due to go on I read that the electricians on ITV were striking. All over the place they were going on strike. I rang the producer and said, 'If the electricians are going on strike the one group they're going to strike is you, because you're live and they can do some serious damage. I'm going to be at home having my lunch. You call me 45 minutes before you need me, it only takes me 45 minutes to get to the Adelphi Theatre.' About an hour before I was due to go to the theatre they rang me and said, 'The electricians are on strike, it's called off.' They had Michael J. Pollard there waiting to go in on an elephant. They had everybody there. They said, 'We're now going to do it recorded. We'll send someone to Barbados for you.' So I did Oliver Reed's *This Is Your Life* from the beach in Barbados. I could see when I watched it later that (a) he was drunk and (b) that he knew absolutely that they were coming but he did a reasonable acting job of being surprised.

I didn't cry at my father's funeral. I didn't cry at my mother's funeral. But I cried at Oliver's funeral. I was the only person from show business who attended. I stood in the church in Ireland and his coffin was facing me down the aisle. I walked down the aisle, touched the coffin, said goodbye to him and when I came back to my seat I was crying my eyes out. We then went for the dinner at his house in Ireland in a marquee after visiting the place where he was to be buried. A cortège went through the streets of Ireland with the coffin and various cars following it to the place of burial. This was behind the pub he used to go to regularly in a little village. As the cortège went through the Irish villages, the Irish people crossed themselves. It was like a mini Princess Diana funeral. I was in the car with his first wife, Kate, a beautiful red-headed Irish girl. She still looked very good. We got to the location, left the car and walked down a little alley between the pub and the building next to it. At the bottom of this alley there was the field where Oliver was to be buried. Everybody was saying, 'Oh, look at this field, isn't it beautiful? Look at those towering elm trees. Look at the Irish countryside beyond. Oliver has picked the most perfect place to be buried.' Kate said, 'What a shithouse. What a fucking rubbish dump this is.

Look at it. There's shit everywhere. Flies everywhere. Only Oliver could be so stupid as to want to get buried in a place like this.'

I have imaginary conversations with dead people. The following day I imagined ringing up Oliver and saying, 'Oliver, it was a lovely funeral. This is what Kate said . . .' Oliver would have replied in his very quiet voice, 'She always had a wonderful sense of humour, did Kate.' Well, I never had that conversation. I won't have any more with him. But Oliver is in my mind continually as a great, great person.

Eating with O.J. and Nicole

I did a film called *Firepower* with O.J. Simpson in the late 70s where we shot all over the Caribbean. We were staying at a hotel called Curtain Bluff in Antigua. There was me, O.J. Simpson, James Coburn and Sophia Loren. James Coburn was always in his room screwing Lynsey de Paul. Sophia stayed in her suite with her lady companion.

So O.J. and I would eat from the hotel kitchens. We were not allowed in the restaurant because you had to wear a tie and jacket and, after a full day's filming, we didn't want to do that. The owner let us sit on the terrace of the bar – that was O.J., me and a man called Al Cowling, who was another football player and O.J.'s great friend. Al drove the getaway car in the famous chase when O.J. fled before being arrested and tried for murder. I wish to say at this point that for a double murderer O.J. Simpson was a very nice man. We kept in touch for a long time after the movie.

During one of these dinners on the terrace O.J. said to me, 'I'm going to bring my girlfriend Nicole over. She's very boring, she won't last the movie but she'll pass a couple of weeks away.' He bought Nicole over, who then joined us every night at dinner on the island of Antigua and the other islands we went to. She not only lasted the film she lasted many years later into a marriage and finally became a tragedienne in one of the most famous murders in the history of the USA. I saw her and O.J. many times. We went to the Andrew Lloyd Webber show *Cats* together in London and I dined with him all over the place. He was the most popular man I've ever been out with. I lived my life going out with movie stars but none of them attracted the sympathy and attention that O.J. Simpson got.

A week after the first trial, which I watched with fascination, he phoned me up and said, 'Hi, man,' in a funny voice. I thought it was Marlon. Because Brando always used to phone me putting on strange voices. He was famous for that. I said, 'Marlon, stop using that stupid voice.' O.J. said, 'It's not Marlon, man, it's O.J. I'm coming to England. They've invited me to talk at the Oxford Union.' At this point I was in a quandary. Should I say, 'O.J., I decline to have anything to do with you because I think you're a double murderer?' Or should I just say, 'Hi, O.J., what have you been doing lately'? I decided to say the latter. I was fascinated to meet him after the trial and discuss it with him.

O.J. spent every day with me during his five or six days in London following the trial. At one point I took him to the restaurant Daphne's for a fairly moderate meal and when we came out I was photographed in my Rolls-Royce with O.J. Piers Morgan, then editor of the *Daily Mirror*, printed the picture very large in his newspaper. The headline was marvellous. It read, 'The most despised man in England with his friend O.J. Simpson.' People said to me, 'Isn't that terrible?' I said, 'No, it's extremely funny.' I also took O.J. to Tramp, where girls came to the table endlessly passing him their telephone number. Driving around Hyde Park Corner I was a little careless zooming in and out of lanes. O.J. said, 'Careful, man. If you knock anyone down they'll say O.J.'s killed another person.'

He came to dinner with me about four years ago. When he rang the doorbell I said to Geraldine, 'That's O.J. If he's got a knife throw yourself in front of me.' We went round to the Belvedere restaurant in Holland Park near my house and a rather posh friend of Andrew Lloyd Webber's, dressed in full white cricket gear, came over. I introduced him to O.J. He practically curtsied, he was so impressed. And here was a man, O.J., who was a known naughty person (to put it very mildly!) but he still had some charisma. Although by this time he was hobbling from arthritis and seemed a little worse for wear. I must find out what prison he's in and send him a cake!

Restaurant Reviews

Stately progression after scandalous shortcomings

The worst-run hotel I ever visited was **Cliveden**. I went in June 1999 foolishly thinking, as it was in Berkshire, it would be near Chequers where Tone had asked me to lunch. In fact it was further from the PM than my house in Holland Park. The managing director of Cliveden was John Tam, the manager Ross Stevenson. Mr Tam has thankfully vanished. Stevenson roams from one minor hotel in the Caribbean to another. Cliveden is now part of the Von Essen group run by Andrew Davis. It's gone from disaster to triumph.

In 1999 my tea arrived minus sandwiches, scones or cakes. When they came they were old and tired. A guest said to me, 'You're not going to write about this dreadful aeroplane food, are you?' Ten years ago the room was an astronomical £450 a night. There was dust on every surface I ran my finger along. The breakfast came without toast; Vanessa, my then girlfriend, tried to eat melon with a teaspoon because they'd brought no proper spoon. Your name was displayed on the bedroom door. No confidentiality. The lunch menu said 'Half bottles page 31.' There was no page 31. Vanessa looked at our buck's fizz glasses and said, 'They're filthy.' We walked out and had lunch in Chelsea.

Mr Tam, knowing he was going to get slated, issued a

press release banning me. The *Daily Mail* sent someone down and ran a two-page headline, 'For once Michael Winner got it right.' They found shoddy service, third-rate food, dirty crockery, inedible pastries, no jam or marmalade for breakfast, pan-fried mullet which was raw in the middle, ducks fornicating in the swimming pool. They wrote, 'There are Corsican bandits who relieve people of their money more graciously.' Letters from *Sunday Times* readers poured in. One called it Fawlty Towers revisited, another said that on her daughter's 30th birthday the glasses were all filthy. Present and ex-staff who'd worked in the kitchen wrote describing filth that defied belief. I should have passed the missives on to the health inspector. I was going to, but the *News of the World* took them, promising an exposé, which they never pursued. John Tam, worst hotelier ever, wrote to me, 'We are ladies and gentlemen serving ladies and gentlemen.' Pass the sick bag.

On my recent visit it was immaculate, no dust anywhere. We stayed in the Astor suite, a large, beautifully furnished room, with a grand terrace, and sweeping views of the stunningly kept grounds. The food in their imposing **Terrace** restaurant was a bit fancy for me, but excellent. At the next table people were eating what looked like very good roast beef and Yorkshire pudding. Downstairs they have **Waldo's**, also good. It has a framed sketch of Christine Keeler by Stephen Ward. Cliveden was the home of the Astors. The place where scandalous orgies involving war minister John Profumo, a Russian embassy official and swinging sixties girls Christine Keeler and Mandy Rice-Davies contributed to the defeat of the Macmillan government. Geraldine and I went on a tranquil boat trip up the Thames on a 1911 vessel with a butler serving tea. Superb chocolate éclairs, fresh finger sandwiches, lovely scones, Earl Grey tea. We passed Spring Cottage, where Keeler stayed with Captain Yevgeny Ivanov, assistant naval attaché at the Russian embassy. John Profumo lied to the House of Commons, saying he had no relationship with Christine Keeler. Then the *Daily Mirror* printed love letters he'd sent her on War Office stationery. Those were the days. A taxi driver said to me, 'I think it's wonderful. I thought the Conservatives were all homosexual.' A sex scandal involving our Gord might spice up his poll ratings. A ding-dong with Katie Price, perhaps? Or Ann Widdecombe.

What a difference at Cliveden now from the pathetic John Tam era. The general manager, Sue Crowley, is down to earth, practical, highly efficient, very charming. Her food and beverage manager, Stefan Georgescu, took great trouble to see we were happy. In 1999 some strange German under-manager noted everything I said and did. He was useless. The general manager, Ross Stevenson, was too important even to show himself. I've been to a number of Andrew Davis's hotels. The staff love him. He knows all their names, he's a detail man, he genuinely wants his guests to be well looked after. Not just difficult ones like me. At Cliveden he's about to spend millions on a new spa and a casual brasserie.

Do I have any complaints about the current Cliveden? A couple. Guest names are still displayed on room doors. That's naughty. They should check with guests first. I don't need late-night drunks screaming 'Calm down, dear' or 'Enjoy your dinner, did you?' as I try to get well-earned rest. And they have piped music. That's naff beyond belief. Stefan explained, 'At breakfast time people need waking up.' I'd have thought if they were in the restaurant it's reasonable to assume they were awake. It was lunchtime when he said it. They kindly took the music off to shut me up. That's always wise.

Move over, Rat Pack – Winner's in town

Guess how much a medium-sized main-course portion of turbot, no vegetables, costs at **La Reserve de Beaulieu** on the Côte d'Azur? Do I hear £25? £30? Any advance on £30? Not sold to the reader who said £30. The answer is €84, which equals £76.36.

My bill for 21 nights was . . . You say: 'We don't really care.' Good. I'll tell you: £58,123.69. Well worth it. La Reserve is one of the few privately owned and managed hotels. It's like something out of Noël Coward's *Private Lives*.

At dinner you sit overlooking the bay of Beaulieu and St-Jean-Cap-Ferrat. No high-rise buildings, just the lights of yachts and the distant harbour. A piano and violin play. By day you lie in front of the sparkling Mediterranean. High cliffs to the left, beautiful old buildings to the right. It is one of the great sights. Slightly marred by one of the few mistakes made by the owner, Jean-Claude Delion: very clumsy, heavy white balustrades that block far too much of the view from your sun lounger. Go back to the old, thin wrought iron that used to be there, please, Monsieur Delion.

They've had turbulence in the kitchen. Top chef Olivier Brulard left. A new chef from Switzerland, with two Michelin stars, started just after I departed. While I was there, cooking was handled by sous chef, Dimitri Droisneau. It was spectacularly good. Pricey, but who cares? I was particularly impressed by the freebies. Those bits and pieces you get without asking for them. They were a blend of exquisite tastes. A terrine of carrots (of all things) with lobster, langoustines and herbs was sensational, the lemon soufflé remarkable. I could go on but I can't be bothered to describe the food. 'Why not? You're a food critic,' I hear you say. If you think I'm a food critic it's time for the men in white coats to take you away in a straitjacket.

All the La Reserve staff are superb. Monsieur Delion walks around elegantly checking this and that. I particularly like the chief concierge, Patrick Debuire, and the maître d', Roger Heyd. If you stay 21 nights, however good everyone is, you're bound to encounter some boo-boos. When the lift wasn't working, why didn't Patrick (who's like acting manager) put a sign on the three upper floors telling customers there was no point in waiting for ever, pressing the button, the lift wasn't coming? Why did the wine waiter, Jean-Louis Valla, a great character, when I asked for the white wine, simply bring a bottle and start to open it without showing me the wine list or asking which white wine I wanted?

Monsieur Delion has the title of manager, but he's too grand for me to trouble him with these little drops in service. He should appoint a manager. I nominate his outstanding PA, Josee-Anne Klein. She could be very tough when necessary. In the midst of all this glory one employee stands out as terrible. A scar on the beautiful face of La Reserve. Gerard Lucas, the pool man, is the worst hotel worker I've ever come across. If I had a pound for every guest who's said to me how awful he is, I wouldn't be £6m in debt. Gerard seems permanently angry. Many times when Geraldine was struggling to move the heavy umbrellas to give us shade, Gerard watched and did nothing. My email pal Barry McKay, whom I finally met at La Reserve, was driven to distraction by Gerard's attitude and incompetence. 'Didn't you hear me scream?' asked Barry. I hadn't. But, boy, did I understand why.

A gargantuan moment in the history of television occurred at La Reserve. Shooting started on *Michael Winner's Dining Stars* for ITV1.

Our super-stratospheric boss is the innovative Peter Fincham. We report to a beautiful, dynamic, blonde lady, Alison Sharman, head of factual programmes. There's often conflict between what is laughingly known as 'the talent' and the executives. Not here, there ain't. One thing is odd, though. My show comes under 'reality TV'. Me, real? You must be joking.

* * *

Wikipedia calls itself 'the free encyclopedia.' Free is too expensive. It's the most pathetic purveyor of non-information ever. It even once (possibly twice) printed my obituary. The inaccuracies in my Wiki biography are gross. Anne Diamond, interviewing me for BBC Radio Berkshire, said, 'I see on Wikipedia that you wear a gastric band.' Two journalists came to discuss my forthcoming talk at the Henley literary festival on 3 October. They said the same thing.

Will someone please tell me where Wikipedia hangs out so I can issue proceedings for libel? To say that someone who's written a much-praised book, *Michael Winner's Fat Pig Diet*, and not only lost 3½ stone but kept it off for four years, wears a gastric band is highly defamatory. It also stated I lost weight because I was ill. I lost it before getting ill. I demand a retraction, an apology to be published on the website and read out in the High Court and damages for my charity the Police Memorial Trust. That's presuming I can deliver the writ.

Hard to stay calm when I hear news like this

My friend Peter Wood, boss of esure ('Calm down, dear, it's only an insurance company') is difficult. Correction: he's not difficult, he's very difficult. Second correction: he's not very difficult he's stratospherically difficult. I approve of that. In my *Who's Who* entry under 'hobbies' I list making table mats, washing silk shirts, eating and being difficult. Peter writes outstandingly robust letters of complaint. I wish I'd kept the acidly biting letters of complaint I've written for over 60 years. They'd make an instant best-seller.

Peter is the best employer ever. All our deals for commercials – often for millions of pounds – have been consummated in a two-paragraph letter. He's the only person I know who pays faster than I do. Never mind that Peter's fired me six times. Once to bring in a horrific computerised mouse which spoke with a strange American accent at a speed that made anything said totally incomprehensible. As we sat in **Caraffini**, a blast from the past place in Chelsea, I mentioned the mouse. Peter laid his hand on my arm and said, 'You were right.'

Caraffini's restaurant manager is Francisco Pedre. He remembered me from Al Gallo d'Oro, an Italian restaurant near my house, once owned by a man called Renato. I often saw George Michael, before he came out, sitting with a boyfriend. The place slid from worse to terrible. Renato asked me to do a private critique on it for him. It was damning. I recommended he sell. He said, 'Do you know anybody who might buy?' I recommended it to my friend Claudio Pulze, owner of many restaurants. He tried to buy it, but Renato insisted on staying in charge. So the deal fell through. A few months later I saw Al Gallo d'Oro was closed. Claudio had bought it. He turned it into Memories of China Kensington, which is absolutely terrible. Renato went off with the money from the sale. Claudio acquired a new restaurant. Did either of them write me a 'Thank you' note? No. Did they send a bottle of wine to the unpaid agent? No. The other day Claudio rang, after years of silence, asking me to go to one of his restaurants. He wanted a good review. I stayed at home. 'Er, aren't you dining with Peter Wood in Caraffini?' I hear you ask, 'Why not tell us about it?'

Okay. It's a pleasant, old-fashioned place. It's off the radar. No one I know goes there or talks about it. Except for Peter. The food is early 1970s which is the time it opened. That's fine for me. I ate a faultless gazpacho, an enormous portion of cold poached salmon with potato salad, very good, but too much to finish. Dessert was Cassata alla Siciliana. You don't see that much today. They do a marvellous one at **La Colombe d'Or** in Saint-Paul de Vence. The Caraffinni version was fine, but lacked a band of pink ice cream. I like pink. Overall, a charming meal, well served by cheerful and professional staff.

It ended catastrophically. Peter told me there'd be no esure commercials in 2010. He recently acquired 5,000 rubber figures of me which, when pressed, say 'Calm down, dear.' Peter tested one and it broke. He must have attacked it with an axe. Or got a dud. I was sent two and they were totally indestructible. 'A child might eat one of the parts. That would ruin esure's reputation, my reputation and your reputation,' he warned. I said, 'If someone chokes on a bit of Michael Winner the uproar would be fantastic. I might even become famous.' Send 'em out, Peter, they're marvellous. He's thinking about it. I may do some website ads for him in 2010. Hope so. I'm still £6m in debt. Every little bit helps.

* * *

Those of you with memories (that excludes me) will recall I thought little of the Pinewood Studios Photographic Centre, run by an inept woman misnamed Vicky Joy. After using them for 45 years, many under her marvellous predecessor, Lofty Rice, the printing became so poor I complained. Whereupon Vicky said, 'Go away.' But it's Ms Non-Joy who's gone. Pinewood bosses, coming to their senses, closed their photographic centre. Ms Joy went I know not where. As long as she isn't in a photo-type job, the world could be safe.

* * *

Using Parcelforce to send a package from London to Beaulieu, guaranteed to be delivered five days after posting, I waited and waited. Parcelforce said they delivered on time but no one was in. It was addressed to my hotel. Finally arrived eight days after posting. Next time I'll try a pigeon.

* * *

Here's a joke sent by Londoner Doug Green: Mr Winner walked into The Ivy carrying a duck. The maître d' asked him, 'What are you doing with the pig?' Mr Winner replied, 'You complete idiot, it's a duck.' The maitre d' said, 'I was talking to the duck.'

Hosting a blockbuster birthday bash

I was in the South of France and the phone rang. It was my friend John Cleese. 'Can you recommend somewhere for my 69.9th birthday party?' he asked. 'I'm having the 70th five weeks later, in California.' I recommended the private room at Nobu or the Goring hotel. Putting the phone down, I said to Geraldine, 'He's so generous John. He's just gone down the pan $20m to a lousy cause [grasping ex-wife] leaving him with massively less. Yet he still wants to lavish entertainment on friends.' 'Why don't we give him a party at your house?' said Geraldine.

I don't know what happened for the next five minutes because I fainted. When I came to I phoned John and said, 'I'll do the party, you invite the guests.' This was an extraordinary gesture. The last party I gave was 20 years ago for Arnold Schwarzenegger. He famously said, after my speech of welcome, 'Michael is more than a good friend to me, he's a complete stranger.' We made up later.

I don't believe in entertaining at home. I called my favourite caterer, Johnny Robertson-Roxburgh of the **Admirable Crichton**. Menus were discussed, furniture moved, tables brought in. We had seven waiters for 34 people, champagne and canapés served in my private cinema, a beautifully cooked meal – they bring their own ovens – of beetroot-marinated salmon, chicken and thyme pie, saffron-scented salad of fig, blackberry and red grape with clotted cream, and a birthday cake which was a wedding cake with a bride and groom on top and in icing the words 'Better luck next time'. A photo on the menu was captioned: 'Michael Winner and John Cleese on his honeymoon in St Lucia with Alyce. Right friend. Wrong wife'. Guests included Michael and Shakira Caine, David Hare, Nicole Farhi, Michael Palin and Leslie Caron, whose fascinating autobiography has just been published. I rose to speak. 'I want you to know,' I announced, 'what I say now comes from the heart. This party is a f****** nuisance.' I hate giving parties. Will everyone arrive on time? Will someone drop out at the last minute? Will guests stain my antique furniture? Miraculously, nothing awful occurred.

The food was spectacularly good. I produced historic red wine from my cellar. White Puligny-Montrachet flowed. Johnny rang me before the event and said, 'Have you looked at the quote?' 'I trust you,' I replied. 'Did you notice the garlands round the chicken pot pie?' said Johnny. 'What garlands?' I asked. 'Flowers, herbs, they look very pretty,' replied Johnny. 'Can you eat them?' I asked. 'No,' said Johnny. 'How much?' I enquired. '£32 per person,' explained Johnny. Nobody noticed their plates weren't garlanded. Johnny brought lovely candelabras and lots of bits and pieces that help the luxury look. Add my magnificent house, the beautiful Geraldine – and the only letdown was me. Mind you, John's guests were a load of old scruffs. The best-dressed people around were the waiters. But then what do you expect from a man brought up in Weston-super-Mare?

A couple of weeks earlier Admirable Crichton and Johnny had produced an incredible lunch for three. I was between cooks. Since remedied by the arrival of Lulu. She's great. My guests were Alison Sharman, the dynamic head of factual and daytime for ITV, and her stratospherically important boss, Peter Fincham, ITV's director of television. We had cumin-spiced cucumber mousse, roast breast of barbary duck and treacle tart with poached kumquats, oranges, sorrel cress and yoghurt. One of the best meals ever. Great company. I learnt a lot. As Alison and Peter climbed into my 1966 Rolls-Royce Phantom V to return to work, Peter remarked, 'People will think we're getting married.' I said, 'Dammit, knew I'd forgotten something. The confetti.'

* * *

An apology: it's completely untrue to say John Cleese's guests were a load of old scruffs. They were lovely, elegant, deeply intelligent, refined, witty, brilliant conversationalists – and a load of old scruffs.

* * *

A complaint: that great executive, Peter Fincham, is causing me angst. I'm so upset I can hardly sleep during the day. I read he may leave ITV to head up Channel 4. How dare Peter place job aggrandisement and other self-serving accoutrements above me? If I give you a bag of Smarties and a vanilla ice-cream every day would that induce you to stay, Peter? Not enough? Who do you think you are? Tony

Ball? For the non *au fait* group, Ball's the man offered the ITV chief exec post who said the money wasn't enough.

Decked out for a perfect Italian meal

My idea of a great restaurant is where mama cooks in the kitchen and junior is in charge out front. Thus it is at **Lido di Adriano Gramatica** on Lake Garda in the village of Gargnano, population 1,000. Mama is 74, Adriano somewhat less. 'He's gorgeous,' said Geraldine. I'd like to say that put me off Adriano, but he's so pleasant and the food so good it didn't. The place is right on the lake. It's always full of Italians. Since we're in Italy, this is a good sign. Adriano didn't have fish carpaccio because it was Sunday lunch and he couldn't buy any that day. Anyone else would have put it in the deep-freeze for 10 years and then served it as 'fresh'.

Lake Gargnano is unspoiled by modern rubbish buildings. It's famous for the incredibly good hotel Villa Feltrinelli, once the home of Mussolini. I often sneak out to Adriano for a simple meal. Spaghetti is the only thing he buys in. The rest – taglialini, gnocetti, tortelloni – are all made in mama's kitchen. Her name is Maria Damiani. Never mind yer Gordon Ramsays. She's the best. I started with raw beef sliced with finely cut Parmesan cheese, olive oil and rocket salad. Then steak tartar, then fish from the lake, perch, grilled, seasoned with pesto, parsley, garlic and olive oil and a drop of white wine. It was the tastiest white fish I've ever eaten. Adriano makes the desserts. I had an apple cake, semi-freddo, with amaretto and chocolate cake with pear.

In the same village there's **La Tortuga**, a ghastly restaurant with a Michelin star. Shows what rubbish Michelin can be. Adriano is a million times better and he's not even in the guide. I hate to reveal these gems because you might go there. But my sense of duty is boundless.

* * *

It's a long way from Adriano's simplicity to Simon Cowell's lavish 50th birthday party at Wrotham Park, the stately home where I filmed one of my esure commercials. Four hundred guests walked through the mansion to an enormous marquee where cocktail waiters wore Simon Cowell masks. The catering, by Lucy Gemmell of **Rhubarb**, was superb. Simon's admirable menu was: prawn and lobster cocktail, chicken soup, shepherd and cottage pies or fish and chips with mushy peas, apple pie, bread and butter pudding, rice pudding, custard and fresh cream. That was great. Not so the over-amplified music which prevented me from speaking to the distinguished people on my table. Otherwise it was a terrific 'do' organised by Sir Philip and Tina Green with party professional Julian Posner of **Banana Split**.

When I first met Simon he was so obscure even his mother had trouble recognising him. She's Julie, 84 – the real star of the family. I liked her son Nicholas's speech. Only a much loved brother could get away with it. Simon made a terrible speech at Nicholas's wedding. I know, I was there. Nicholas announced, 'This is my revenge.' Welcoming guests on behalf of the Cowell family, he said, 'Some of you have travelled over water – Battersea, Barnes and many from the Isle of Dogs – and I'm not referring to Simon's past girlfriends. In the 1950s Simon's favourite was Liberace. After the bed wetting stage, at the age of eight, Simon discovered his first true love, Mr Rumbold, the PE teacher. He loved Rolf Harris and would sing "Two Little Boys" over and over again. He still loves two little boys to this day. We lived in the countryside, where Simon was fascinated by elves, goblins and especially fairies. In his teenage years his favourite TV star was Larry Grayson. In the 1980s he favoured the Pet Shop Boys. He had a job as fashion consultant for Top Shop but was fired by the boss's wife for experimenting with the ladies' lingerie. Simon found his first real girlfriend on the web. On the day they met he couldn't believe Terry was a girl's name as well.' Funny stuff. Followed by Sir Philip Green, who referred to Simon's well-known inability to turn up on time. 'I'm getting you a birthday present,' he said. 'Big Ben.'

* * *

Great news from **Sandy Lane**, Barbados. Their dreadful chef, Grant MacPherson, is out. His replacement is Conny Andersson, who's been executive chef at Four Seasons resort hotels. Thus ends a sad era at one of my favourite hotels. It can now return to its former glory. I agree with reader Darren Johns, who writes, 'It's depressing to see Andrew Headley – the undisputed worst restaurant manager in the world – still running Bajan Blue. He'd struggle to run a bath.' I've written about that. Perhaps now Grant MacPherson's gone, management will turn to Mr Headley.

* * *

There's hope for the Winner talking doll. Peter Wood of esure is giving him to a professional toy-testing place. If they certificate me safe, I'll be let loose.

Winner speaks

'A team effort is a lot of people doing what I say.'

The best invisible views in the whole of Wales

I've never comes across a better hotel manager than Joan Reen. But she's nuts. Joan used to own, and sold for millions, a delightful nine-room hotel in Eglwysfach, Wales. She's there at eight in the morning, still going at midnight. A worker beyond belief, exuding charm and hospitality. I was so impressed with Joan, the cooking of chef Shane Hughes and the beauty of the place – the brochure calls it a spiritual retreat – that I'm seriously thinking of going there to live. Forget the army of house staff I need in my London mansion, the builders ever dealing with something, the six cars, the chauffeur. Just rent a few rooms at **Ynyshir Hall** and have done with it. It's pronounced anass-here, in case you care.

'Just a minute,' I hear you say, 'you want to live there, but you said Joan was nuts.' I was being kind. She's totally bonkers. Gone. On a different planet. 'Tell us why,' you mutter. Y-Hall has the greatest view. Lawns, lovely old trees, rolling Welsh hills. The brochure calls it, 'A fairy tale landscape . . . awake to the drama of the view.' You can't. Joan personally made enormous curtains looping from left to right and right to left. They don't open. All you can see, if you kneel down on the floor and peer through the triangular gap at the bottom, is a fraction of the breathtaking view. Geraldine stood on a chair and hooked the curtains up over the pole holding them, so we could see out of the windows.

The brochure shows ruched curtains in the lounge, not hiding anything. Joan removed them and covered the windows with her black-out curtains. 'I suppose we're so used to the view, we don't reckon it,' she explained. 'It's so dark in my room, I have to turn the lights on when the sun's shining,' I explained. 'Have you heard of the book *Bonfire of the Vanities*? You should have a bonfire of the curtains.' I made no impression. Joan is wedded to voile.

Ynyshir Hall is like a friendly country house. There are striking paintings by Joan's husband, Rob. Never saw him. He was probably out buying curtain material. The food is superb. For tea Shane even made the potato crisps that came with fresh sandwiches, fantastic scones and various superb cakes. Breakfast was equally good. Dinner was terrific. The canapés were three-star Michelin. My main course of roast veal sweetbreads, braised marrowbone, spinach and girolles deserved a Michelin star. I also had incredible shellfish bisque and an amazing freebie pea soup. Service was speed-perfect.

Unfortunately the vanilla soufflé was degraded by Shane's heavy, strong and tangy passion fruit sauce, which wiped out the delicate taste of vanilla. Shane explained, 'It's our most popular dessert.' I responded, 'Hitler was the most popular politician in Germany. Doesn't mean he tasted good. Do you think less people would choose your vanilla soufflé if it didn't have that sauce?' I questioned a number of top chefs and restaurateurs. None of them thought passion fruit sauce went with vanilla soufflé. Shane, cut out the sauce. Joan, take a deep breath, a cluster of Valium, and give the curtains to Oxfam. Then you'd have the perfect hotel – and a big problem. I might come to live there.

* * *

Andrew Davis, Chairman of Von Essen hotels, asked me to present Awards for Best Young Chef and Waiter for the British Hospitality Association at the Jumeirah Carlton Tower hotel. Andrew, the most amusing event sponsor ever, greeted me with: 'You must get some new contact lenses for Geraldine. Then she can see what she's had to put up with the last few years.' Later he remarked, 'Do you think Cartier do a wheelchair?' My speech started, 'It's very nice to be here. With the enemy.' Swept away, I personally gave £1000 each to the winning young waiter and chef. A guest observed, 'That's for all the abuse he's heaped on them. He's trying to buy absolution.' I made that last bit up.

* * *

I read fiddling MPs may have to return improperly claimed expenses. No chance of that with me. I don't get any. At my engagement party were the previous editor of the *Sunday Times*, who started me writing about restaurant visits, and the present incumbent. I announced: 'The last year has been the best for me since I started working for the *Sunday Times*. It only cost me £280,000 more to visit the places I write about for them than they give me for the articles.' That's a good job, innit? Minus £280,000 a year. Bet you'd like one of those. Queue up on the left in an orderly fashion.

* * *

PS: It was a sell-out in Abergavenny and Henley but you can still catch my stand-up comedy talk 'My Life in Movies and Other Places' in Canterbury on 19 October, Stamford 25 October. See you there.

Oi, sunshine, you're in my seat

It was very hot for late September. We (that's me an' 'er) drove through picturesque Wales, ending up, as recommended by the Curtain Queen Joan Reen (I told you about her last week) in Aberdyfi (Welsh) or Aberdovey (British) on a pretty estuary somewhere. You want to know precisely, get a road map.

It was 1pm. My lunchtime. Promptly. No delays. The

most interesting place seemed to be the **Britannia Coaching Inn**, overlooking the harbour. Just the place to sit in the sun. The only exterior was a small balcony. 'It's full,' observed Geraldine. 'Let's go and see,' I suggested. 'Why?' asked Geraldine. 'There are no seats.' 'Maybe,' I said. We walked upstairs and on to the balcony. It was indeed full. I stared at a couple who seemed to be near the end of their meal. 'You going?' I asked helpfully. 'We're leaving soon,' they said. 'Let's have a drink at the bar,' suggested Geraldine. 'We'll get the table if I stay and stare at the people occupying it,' I recommended. I did. They left early. It's marvellous how accommodating people are when I become a pain. Only problem was Geraldine, being blonde, hates sitting in the sun. Our table had no umbrella, the next one did. 'Would you mind swapping?' I asked a man who turned out to be Welshman Andy Davies. He swapped. 'The Welsh are very cheerful,' I observed to Andy, 'not like in London, where they're all bloody surly.' 'They have their moments,' said Andy.

Up came Christine Coleman. 'You the owner?' I asked. 'No, sir,' she replied. 'Would you like to be?' I said. 'I love my boss, he's brilliant,' responded Christine. Good for her. Time to stop the small talk and order. I had no great hopes for the food but it was a lovely spot. Geraldine shaded. Me basking in the hot sun. Funnily enough it was boiling hot in Perthshire, Scotland, last week too. That's another story which I may one day relate. Back in Wales (wake up, those who aren't following carefully) Christine assured me everything was fresh. So I ordered 'freshly dressed Aberdyfi crab, large salad, new potatoes and lemon mayonnaise'. Geraldine asked for tiger langoustine. I chatted with Andy, who was (and probably still is) a bricklayer. 'Lovely girl you've got there, Andy,' I said, 'sweet smile, nice manner and attitude.' 'You haven't seen her temper,' remarked Andy. She did have red hair. We know about them.

My crab salad was enormous. Geraldine tried and pronounced it the best crab since she'd eaten one in Brittany, adding, 'Absolutely fantastic.' She was right. This was remarkable. For dessert I chose chocolate fudge cake. Swans drifted by, seagulls did whatever they do. It was idyllic. So was the cake. On the way out I met Christine's favourite owner, Dieter Botchet, a strapping, blond young German, who was cheffing away in the kitchen. I didn't ask what a German was doing running a pub in Wales. Had I done so I'd have breached the Political Correctness Act 2007 ratified with knobs on by the European Parliament in March 2009. I just shut up, paid, and went off a happy customer.

* * *

I get hundreds of requests from readers asking, 'You recommended a place in Venice, can't remember it, could you . . .' I throw the letters away. No offence intended, but I haven't the time or desire to be a one-to-one restaurant advisory service. Now your chance has come. *Winner's Dinners* the book is in shops, flower stalls, burger bars, brothels and other dodgy outlets. It lists over 600 restaurants and hotels, indexed, county by county, country by country. Phone numbers for all. The complete guide for the life you wish to live. It's enlivened with cartoons by my favourite cartoonist. Me. Price is £16.99. If you write I'll send a sticky label signed, inscribed and cartooned to whoever you name. You can get it from the *Sunday Times* bookshop on 08452 712135 for £13.59 including p & p. Think of all the stamps it'll save you writing to me and not getting an answer. 'No post,' you say. Of course there will be. Disputes don't last forever. Unless I'm personally involved.

* * *

I've travelled recently on my ITV1 series *Michael Winner's Dining Stars* to places as diverse as Essex, Solihull and Blairgowrie. I get up 6am, make up 8am, finish shooting around 11pm. The director (like him so far) is Nic Guttridge. TV being a bit cash-deficient, he often quadruples as cameraman, lighting man and sound recordist. He's a disaster with sound equipment. When I told him one of my assistants was leaving, he emailed, 'I will miss Jessica.' I replied, 'Like everyone else Jessica is replaceable.' Nic emailed back: 'Your sentimentality is the thing I most love about you.' Impertinent or funny? Both.

I've always been one for a grand entrance

Not many grand hotels are left. The buildings are there but inside they're so messed about, redecorated and ludicrously updated, the magnificence and grandeur have gone. The Dorchester replaced its old Grill Room with the worst-taste dining room in London. The revamp at Claridge's is undistinguished. The splendid dining room carved up, reduced in size and looking like an airport lounge. The Connaught is the worst. Millions of pounds spent changing elegant period rooms into an over-hyped French brothel. Even the Ritz, far and away the least messed about and best hotel in London, had to change its entrance from the grand, pillared frontage on Piccadilly to a side-door in Arlington Street. It still has the best doormen, while the ones at the Connaught are dreadful beyond belief.

The only untouched, rampantly opulent, marble-pillared, carved-stonework exterior edifice to days of wealth and largesse is the stunning **Hotel de Paris** in Monte Carlo. The lobby is gargantuan, set with turn of the century tables. And occasionally naughty ladies. On the right is the three-

Michelin-starred **Louis XV-Alain Ducasse** restaurant. Gilt everywhere, painted ceilings, a mini Versailles. On its terrace overlooking the main square of Monte Carlo and the casino I lunched with Sir Roger and Lady Moore. There were gold plates, gold cutlery, impeccable service. Never mind what I had, it was all fantastic. For my dessert Rum Baba they brought eight rums and asked, 'Which one do you want?' A question too far for me. I left it to them. I said, 'Can I start my Rum Baba?' Geraldine said sternly 'No, wait until Kristina (Lady Moore to you) has had her strawberries served.' Then she observed to Roger, 'I'm trying to teach him some manners.' 'Too late,' said Roger.

At the top of the hotel is my favourite eating place, the **Grill**. It only boasts one Michelin star, but the food is a delight. Their terrace, overlooking Monte Carlo and the royal palace, is a major place to sit. I took theatrical advertising agent Adam Kenwright, now seriously challenging Dewynters as number one in the field, and his fiancée Nina, daughter of my occasional employer Peter Wood of esure – I introduced the young lovers. If all else fails this could my new profession – matchmaker.

The freebie starter was a superb white bean soup. The excellent general manager of the hotel, Luca Allegri, has relaxed the 'ties must be worn' rule. I didn't know, so I wore one and gave one to Adam. They came from Macro cash and carry. Who says I'm a toff? Answer: nobody. I had baby chicken, crispy skin, wonderful taste. I dictated, 'I don't know what they had done to it.' Served it to me, for sure. The hotel was built in 1864. The waiter said, 'The history of the soufflé was served in this hotel since 1898.' Long time for a soufflé to stand about. My choccie one was historic. I've never seen Geraldine finish a dessert but she had all her hazelnut soufflé and then nicked a bit of everyone else's. Marvellous meal. Great credit to executive chef Franck Cerutti.

One problem: if you sit on the terrace with your back to the view, which almost half the diners do, you look at a tacky cream-painted wall. I told Luca to mirror the back wall. Then people facing it could see both the view and their fellow diners, thus becoming part of the scene. Luca said he'd do it. If I go again and he hasn't, I'll throw a major tantrum. He won't like that, believe me.

* * *

On the flight to Nice (private plane from 247 Jet) was a bottled water called Celtic. I couldn't open it. Geraldine couldn't open it. We attacked it with keys, knives, heavy road drills and finally with dynamite. Nothing. The co-pilot had to come and unscrew it. It wasn't any good anyway.

* * *

A reader was kind enough to suggest that at my increasing age (I was 74 on Friday) and with a depleted left leg, I should be slowing down. In the last two weeks I've flown to Canterbury in Kent and Stamford in Lincolnshire to deliver my talks. 'Gales of laughter' response, as they used to say on theatre posters. Signed 3,000 *Winner's Dinners* books at home and elsewhere. Been to Cornwall and other places for the filming of my ITV1 show, *Michael Winner's Dining Stars*, including one typical 18-hour day where I rose at 6am for work and finished at midnight. My dressing room in the Coronet cinema Notting Hill Gate was a tiny concrete area at the bottom of stairs by an entrance door to the auditorium and beside the ladies' lavatory. Furniture was one ageing, chipped metal chair. People wandered through. No food in 18 hours except one hour off for lunch. My views on that are clear and unequivocal: I'm bloody lucky.

In the court of Winner, they're guilty as charged

'Mr Winner, how do you plead?' asked the judge. 'Guilty, your honour,' I replied. The judge looked over his half-shell glasses and spoke. 'Mr Winner, you have pleaded guilty to the charge of going to restaurants, failing to warn the staff you are going to slate them mercilessly, and then standing next to them for a photograph as if they were your best friends. I sentence you to eat a second meal at La Figa in Narrow Street, E14. 'No, no,' I cried as they led me away, 'anything but that.' The moral of this story is: never trust any restaurant book except mine. *Harden's* London restaurant guide 2009 summed up, via a reader's view, **La Figa** as 'an absolutely stunning local Italian.' Stunning is not the word I'd use. Revolting, ghastly, pathetic and dreadful come to mind.

I was in the East End, yuppie heaven, not my idea of fun, to visit a street in Leyton where PC Gary Toms died in a shoot-out. As founder and chairman of the Police Memorial Trust I'd gone to photograph the spot preparatory to erecting a memorial to commemorate his bravery. I decided to lunch that side of the divide. A mistake. La Figa faces a tedious square which would be a major attraction in Stevenage new town. Nowhere else. David Lean used to live opposite. The last time I was in his house, with a huge garden facing the Thames, was after his memorial service at St Paul's. A deeply moving event. The band of the Welsh guards played 'Colonel Bogey' outside. In the cathedral a 70-piece orchestra was conducted by Maurice Jarre. Peter O'Toole and Omar Sharif spoke, so did Robert Bolt, who wrote *Lawrence of Arabia*. Suffering dreadfully from a stroke, he was assisted by Sarah Miles and shouted in a broken voice, 'I am here, David.'

My friend Steven Berkoff lives in Narrow Street. As does Ian McKellen, who I interviewed for a movie in 1963.

Restaurant manager Attilio Fanciulli assured me they both went to La Figa. Berkoff told me it had gone off. I can't believe it was ever 'on'. Attilio chewed gum as we entered. A poor first impression. The room was devoid of diners, full of grotesque, high-backed, modern chairs looking like art exhibits gone wrong. There were shiny-topped tables and a bar.

I was introduced to the chef, Angelo, who said he'd just made the bread. I took a bit from a large roll. It was heavy and clammy. Bread is obviously not Angelo's strong card. A huge pile of boxes sat on the counter for takeaway pizzas. We were given one. Very average. The bruschetta was at best robust. Too much of everything piled on ungainly bits of toasted bread. All the fish, in my main course and Geraldine's starter, was dry and overcooked. It didn't taste fresh or succulent. I began to realise why Attilio kept saying, 'Have a steak,' when we ordered. If someone keeps on recommending steak, it implies little faith in the rest of the food. In that Attilio was spot on. I wanted cassata for dessert. It was on the menu but our waiter, Lorenzo, said they didn't have any. I settled for chocolate mousse. Geraldine tried some. 'It's not real mousse,' she advised, 'they've added something like gelatine.' It had no particular taste.

All in all a horrendous meal. Only suitable for the yuppies who live in converted warehouses which denude the East End of its old, colourful character. On Sunday lunch there were very few customers. Those that stayed away were lucky.

* * *

I'd like you to know how desperate I am to please. In my pathetic insecurity, riddled with a desire to be loved, not wishing to be an outcast, tarnished by my humble upbringing, I send, at my own expense, by UPS guaranteed next day delivery, all the signed sticky labels requested by you, to Kelly Barnaby of Sparkle Direct Ltd, so that you get, as soon as post permits, these valuable messages to place in your copies of *Winner's Dinners* ~ the book. 'Hello, hello,' I hear you say. 'We ordered from the Sunday Times Booksfirst Bookshop to get their special offer. Who's Sparkle whatever?' How should I know? I just write exactly what you want. The complexities of book distribution are beyond me. Keep ordering on 0845 271 2135, that's all I say. The line-up of presenters for the Winner's Dinners Awards, being handed out at a semi-lavish 'do' at the Belvedere restaurant on Wednesday, gets grander by the minute. Sir Michael Caine will personally present one, so will Joanna Lumley; others aspiring to and approaching such luminosity will follow. Sorry if you aren't invited. You're not important enough.

* * *

Superb **Ritz** hotel doorman Michael O'Dowdall always offers a joke as he opens the Rolls door for me, 'I was reading a book about glue. Couldn't put it down.' Another: 'How do you get a bear out of a tree with cheese? Camembert.' C'mon bear – geddit? C'mon bear sounds like Camembert. Don't think it's funny? Park your own car and sneak in the back door then.

Arnie may have left – but I'll be back

The history of **Planet Hollywood** has moments of take-off speckled with disaster. Branches opened. Branches closed. It went into Chapter 11 US bankruptcy protection. It came out. Now thriving, they have restaurants and a Planet

Hollywood hotel in Las Vegas with 2,600 bedrooms. 'Full every night and movie stars hang out there,' advised Robert Earl, Planet's ebullient boss.

Planet Hollywood opened in London in May 1993. Then it was in Coventry Street, now it's in Haymarket. 'A move of a quarter of a mile and a quarter of the rent,' said Robert. 'We had to contemporise the brand.' He's done well. It's a bright canteen-like room. Gone is much of the movie memorabilia, although they still have the Ursula Andress bikini from *Dr No*. Vast TV screens on the walls show trailers.

I first met Robert in Barbados on the Sandy Lane beach before he'd opened Planet Hollywood. Then he owned the hamburger place Hard Rock Cafe. My girlfriend, Jenny Seagrove, got a gold card entitling her to jump the Hard Rock queue. I went over to Robert and said, 'Jenny doesn't eat meat and gets a gold card. I do and got nothing.' Nothing blossomed into leather jackets, bathrobes, gold cards and other promotional gifts galore.

When Planet Hollywood came here I threw a party for one of its star partners, Arnold Schwarzenegger. 'What'll he do when he stops being governor?' I asked. 'Has he got money?' 'Don't worry about Arnold' said Robert. 'He owns half of Santa Monica.' The menu offers 'A dining experience like no other'. 'That's because you're dining with me,' advised Robert, adding, 'The new hot thing in restaurants is sliders. Have you seen them? They're called baby burgers.'

Trish from Dublin was our superbly charming waitress. The food was amazingly good. If they opened near me I'd go a lot. I had blackened shrimp, baby burgers, barbecued chicken on pizza, tostadas with guacamole and sour cream, spare ribs (didn't like them), mixed fajitas, crispy lemon chicken, a sizzle plate with chicken and beef and tortillas to wrap them in. Some went on my jacket. 'Now we can use it as memorabilia,' said Robert. 'It's cleanable.' The cleaning bill cost more than the meal. Robert told me the average spend was £18 per person including wine. The desserts were sensational. Bananas Foster Cheesecake, bread pudding with white chocolate and whisky sauce and a homemade apple pie. Although I wouldn't call the Planet Hollywood kitchen a 'home' location. Robert asked, 'Do you want to take some away?' 'I've nearly exploded here,' I replied. 'What do I want to explode at home for?'

The place was full at lunchtime. 'Office workers,' said Robert helpfully. I didn't think they came from outer space. The placemats showed 'Hollywood High Class of 2009'. You had fun (or not according to your attitude) identifying photos of today's major stars from their high school photos. Our picture was taken by the Hon. Orlando William Montagu, son of the 11th Earl of Sandwich. Robert's got a sandwich business with him, among many other catering enterprises. I'm glad they're not in London. I'd have to go. Then I truly would burst. That'd give you a laugh.

* * *

I've carried out a thorough investigation into why Sparkle Direct are sending out my *Winner's Dinners* book which you order on 0845 271 2135 from The *Sunday Times* BooksFirst Bookshop. Sparkle Direct is a distribution outfit run entirely by fairies. They sit at tables in an underground tunnel sticking on my personal messages to you, wrapping the books and sending them forth. All the fairies wear little tiaras, their glittering wands leaning against the table, their wings gleaming behind them. I noticed that if a fairy got up to go to the loo, she passed the other hard-at-work fairies, brushing against their wings, thus making a whooshy-whooshy sound as the wings flexed and returned to their natural position. If the fairy was at the end of the row nearest the loo she didn't have to pass the other fairies.

Hence no whooshing sound. The operation is supervised by the Wizard of Wobble, who sits on a raised dais, noting in an enormous ledger, with a quill pen, exactly how many books are sent out. When you phone up to order, I bet you think you're speaking to a librarian-type person with gravitas reflecting the importance of the *Sunday Times*. You're not. You're speaking to a fairy. Only this column offers such valuable information. So stick with me. And buy the book.

* * *

Book launch was a triumph. Everyone was there. Michael Caine, Anne Robinson, Joanna Lumley, the esteemed *Sunday Times* editor John Witherow, Chris Rea, Nigel Havers, Tom Conti, Steven Berkoff. The luminous Alison Sharman, head of factual programmes for ITV, came with their Chief Executive, John Cresswell. Nobody got drunk, fell on the floor or stripped off. Everyone behaved with propriety. You could say a thoroughly boring time was had by all.

Winner speaks

On being offered first greeting from a restaurant receptionist with, 'Do you have a reservation?' I just say, 'Go back to receptionist school.' And walk past.

And the award for the best awards party goes to . . .

Some of you asked, 'Who got the Winner's Dinners awards?' I could say, 'Shut up and buy the book', but being ever helpful I'll reveal some recipients.

Award for best restaurant in London went to the **River Café**. It was picked up by the co-owners, Lady Ruth Rogers and a sadly unwell Rose Gray. It offers, consistently, the best and tastiest food.

Charles Pullan, its restaurant manager, got best restaurant manager even though he once served every course to me not as I'd ordered. A point in his favour was that when a customer claimed (note I say claimed) to have been sick after eating the grilled salmon, Charles responded, 'Did you touch a railing on the way here?' I've eaten at the River Café for decades. Never had so much as a hiccup.

Now I say to Charles, 'I want it on record, I touched no railings on the way to you.' The River Café waiting staff, far and away the best-looking, most efficient and most cheerful bunch ever, got the best waiting award.

Best restaurant in the world went to **Harry's Bar** in Venice, recently decreed a national landmark by the Italian government. Arrigo Cipriani, doyen of restaurateurs and karate black belt, came from Venice to collect it. His food is fantastic. To see his staff weave their way through closely packed tables in the bar area is like watching the Bolshoi Ballet at their most agile.

Best restaurant outside London was Sir Michael Parkinson's **Royal Oak** at Paley Street and the **French Horn** at Sonning-on-Thames. Both magical places.

Richard Caring took best restaurateur. He's the man from nowhere (the rag trade, actually) who bought many of the greatest restaurants and hotels in the UK including The Ivy, Le Caprice and J Sheekey. He created the wonderful new Scott's in Mayfair.

Best UK hotel went to the **Ritz** on Piccadilly, old school in the best sense of the word, and best UK hotel group to Von Essen hotels, owned by the energised Andrew Davis.

The restaurant I go to most award was won by the **Wolseley**. Memorable food under its chef, Julian O'Neill, and the buzziest atmosphere in town. I recently sat next to super-chef Tom Aikens; nearby was multi-starred Hélène Darroze, whose Connaught hotel restaurant looks awful but offers lovely grub.

The Wolseley's suave general manager, Robert Holland, shared best restaurant manager award. Owners Jeremy Kind and Chris Corbin, who could teach everyone a thing or two, came to get their award. I wish they'd put a piano and bar in the nearby St Alban eating house.

Danièle Roux from **La Colombe d'Or** flew in from the Côte d'Azur to accept her best hotel boss personality award. She can kill with a glance. Miraculously, I live.

From Barbados came John and Rain Chandler, whose antique-filled colonial mansion, the **Fisher Pond Great House**, offers giant macaws and an 80-year-old lady pianist for entertainment. Their Bajan food is beyond belief.

Best hotel in Europe was the **Villa Feltrinelli** on Lake Garda, once home to Il Duce. The managing director, Markus Odermatt, came over to pick up the award. Major group of hospitality people. Unique, because they're all genuinely hospitable.

I didn't ask the duds to pick up their 'worst' awards. So no Brian Ward to get worst food, service, attitude, everything award for the **Cliff**, Barbados. No one appeared from the **Athenaeum** on Piccadilly or the **Marriott Grosvenor Square** to admit to the worst meals.

The final award was to my prolific email pal Barry McKay. He started in 2009 saying I was a useless has-been who knew nothing about food, service or anything. Somehow the mood of his emails changed and we became pen pals minus a pen. I now rely on him for at least one smile a day beaming from my laptop.

Lovely gathering. Great people. Excellent canapés from **Belvedere** chef Gary O'Sullivan. An event not to be repeated for four years. By then I could be a ghost.

* * *

I've just sent out 2,100 personally signed Christmas cards. 'Bit early,' you say. My appalling-taste card promotes myself, my books, my television show. I want it on mantelpieces before it's obscured by cards with holly, snow, Santa Claus and other kitsch detritus.

I once thought only vulgar people put their photo on a Christmas card. Mine has six photos and one cartoon of me. This deserves the Guinness World Records award for the grossest display of self-indulgence ever.

My Christmas card list is a disaster. I reckon 20 per cent are addressed to dead people who probably won't get them. A further 25 per cent to people who have since left the address I have for them. A further 20 per cent to people in jobs they no longer inhabit. A further 20 per cent are to people named on my list, but I've no idea who they are. So at the most 15 per cent of my cards go to those I wish to receive them.

I'll have a huge clearout next year. I said that last year. And the year before. For now I'll post my vastly expensive Christmas card to any reader who sends their address. You can sell it via eBay. On a good day you might get 75p. Considerably less than it cost me to print, sign, envelope, stamp and post.

From a serene delight to a cause for alarm

When I cast Faye Dunaway to be the Wicked Lady, her then husband Terry O'Neill said, 'You'll have to fake a first day of shooting because Faye never turns up the first day.' I'd heard on *Mommie Dearest* the only thing to come out of Faye's caravan for the first week were the wigs. They came out of the window, each cut into four pieces. Stories like that never worried me. So even though Terry is a delight (we speak almost every morning at 8am) I said, 'The first day of filming is on the bridge at Ecton in Derbyshire. Alan Bates, Johnnie Gielgud, me, the crew, we'll all be there. So will Faye.' Not only was she there, ahead of her call, I have a photo of Faye sitting on her horse with a see-through plastic bag on her head as protection from the rain. She wouldn't even go to her chair in between shots, let alone her caravan. Faysie (as I called her) was the most hard-working, dedicated actress I ever employed.

I mention this en passant (as they say in Outer Silesia) because I recently visited **Callow Hall**, a hotel which, like Ecton, is near Ashbourne. I was on my way to Wilmslow, a flash neighbour of Manchester, to shoot *Michael Winner's Dining Stars*. Loved Wilmslow. Adored Callow Hall. It's an imposing, ivy-clad Victorian residence, somewhat the worse for wear. I like that. My friend Dame Diana Rigg is a great believer in leaving walls, buildings and I guess people not tarted up. Callow Hall has the mature atmosphere of a real house. There are only 16 bedrooms. It was originally turned into a hotel by the Spencer family who, per the brochure, had been master bakers in Ashbourne since 1724. It also said their 17th-century scones had been baked the same way for generations.

At dinner I was suspicious of my orange juice. 'This comes from a bought-in canister, doesn't it?' I suggested ominously. I got no answer, but my glass was speedily removed and replaced with fresh juice. At tea (excellent) we were given paper napkins. They shouldn't do paper napkins and bought-in orange juice. Dinner was good to superb. The bread, made on the premises, had marvellous texture and taste. Ordering lobster bisque in Derbyshire is a risk. It was hot, fresh and with a fantastic flavour. There were scallops and shrimp with it – all great. My main course was 'bone roast quail, homemade sausage and onion farce, [I think they meant farcie] oven dried grapes, marinated in sweet wine, quail and red wine jus.' More information than I needed. Quail is not the greatest bird in the world and nobody can make it such. This was pretty good. The vegetables were perfectly cooked. The dark chilled chocolate soufflé, summer berry compote, chocolate fudge sauce was historic. Geraldine said her vanilla crème brûlée, poached plum and homemade shortbread was the best ever. For breakfast I'd ordered their famous 17th-century scone. It came without clotted cream. By the time the cream came I'd eaten the scone. Which was fine, but not fully accompanied. Clare Hambleton, Callow Hall's charming manager, was a delight. I enjoyed it and her.

* * *

I've made two disastrous decisions in my life. I bought a Ferrari and installed Chubb Security alarms. The Chubb alarms went wrong even more than the Ferrari. The police were endlessly called on the 'secret' phone line even when the alarm wasn't on. For some 30 years, when turned off, the thing would suddenly beep. Engineers came. They assured me it was fixed. Beeping continued. Sometimes I punched in the code, jabbed wildly at the buttons and it stopped. Other times it didn't.

Recently, beeping rampant, I called the Chubb Customer Service Centre. All I got was music. I found Debbie Yeates,

PA to their UK President, Paul Winnowski. He'd just arrived from America. 'If I want music, I'll go to a concert,' I said. Debbie arranged for an engineer. Before he left, I asked, 'Can I stop this beeping myself?' He advised, 'Put in the code and push the button labelled Stop.' Why hadn't I been told that before? 'But it won't happen now,' the engineer assured me. A few hours later it was beeping again. I called their Managing Director, David Byrne. 'Send someone who knows what they're doing,' I demanded testily. 'The man I sent knew what he was doing,' replied Mr Byrne pompously. 'Then why's the keypad beeping?' I screamed, and slammed the phone down. I wrote to Mr Winnowski, 'The best thing you can do is close the company and give clients their money back.' Two new engineers came and reported, 'The fault's in the keypad by the door. We'll change it.' That had taken decades for Chubb to discover.

Paul Winnowski was now my new best friend. 'It's not your fault. You haven't been here. Get American efficiency to replace the English lethargy,' I suggested. While looking for a flat, Paul is staying at the Kensington Olympia, which faces Shepherd's Bush roundabout. 'That's not very presidential,' I observed. 'We're on a budget,' explained Paul. What do I care? I've suffered for years. Let them suffer.

If you're so clever, Poirot, then go and find us a taxi

I've finished shooting my TV series *Michael Winner's Dining Stars*. Loved the film crew. Well, half of them were okay. Actually, there were two I didn't mind. We filmed in Bruges. As a Bentley whisked me and my assistant Dinah to the location, I saw the director, Nic (pompous – doesn't use the k of Nick), outside Ostend airport, looking worried. There was no vehicle to pick up the film crew. The production manager in London had called a local taxi firm. Not surprisingly, it hadn't turned up. I could give lessons on how it should have been done. Nic called the number recommended on the Call Sheet (the day's working paper); still nothing appeared. Eventually a car was sent from Bruges, over half an hour away, to bring them back. Incompetence like that drives me bananas. It was a showery one-day shoot. The Call Sheet listed seven people with production credits. Yet they couldn't pick up a film crew at the airport. When Nic finally arrived in Bruges, some two hours late, he said, 'I could have done without that lost time.' Maybe we missed a great shot with the sun glistening through trees, rippling on the water, whatever.

So I was not in the best of moods when I entered the hotel **De Tuilerieen**. Which sank further when I saw my gloomy room overlooking the car park. The place wasn't full. Why not a room overlooking the canal? There's a ghastly saying Hollywood film crews use about artistes, 'Bring on da puppets.' I was not infrequently treated like a puppet. 'Do you good,' I hear you say.

The hotel duty manager, Peter Perquy, took ages to explain why the 10 buttons on the phone weren't labelled. How to call room service? Front desk? Men on Mars? Whenever Dinah went to the desk to summon him either no one was there or he ignored her. Peter finally said none of the buttons were programmed for anything. 'I told you to ring 111 for the front desk when I showed you in,' he said testily. He didn't. I made my views known. Peter flounced out in a huff. We went to board our boat on the canal. A worried man arrived. 'Mr Winner, I'm from the hotel,' he said. 'I want to apologise for the way you were treated. Is there anything we can do?' 'Who are you?' I asked. Someone so scruffy I presumed must be the owner. 'I'm the accountant,' he replied. 'Good, I'll have money,' I responded.

Being a Monday evening in Bruges, most places were

closed. In desperation Dinah and I went to restaurant **Den Dyver** next to the hotel. It was fantastic. One of the best meals ever. The owner and host, Philip Vandenbusche, looked like a violinist in a provincial orchestra. 'The preparations we are serving are each time flavoured with beer, that is the speciality of the restaurant,' he announced. I tasted no beer. The black bread was great. A salad with duck, fresh shrimps, black olives and cheese straw appeared (and was devoured) like lightning. Then came cod fish fillet, celeriac, lavers (a kind of herb) mash of sweet potatoes and bacon. Superb. I finished with fig tart, cured cheese, almonds and honey ice-cream. Everything, including freebies, was good as it gets. I recommend Bruges, but (a) be sure you can get out of Ostend airport, (b) go to Den Dyver (c) take the train.

* * *

Actually, I did like all the film crew. Efficient in production matters? Er . . . my lips are (almost) sealed. When I think of the hours I spent on the phone with Stanley Kubrick discussing the minutiae of location filming, of the over 40 location movies I organised, I'm left dazed at what went on. But dazed fades. I've dealt with the bosses of all the major Hollywood studios for decades. One of them phoned me as I was writing this.

Without doubt Peter Fincham, ITV programme chief, and Alison Sharman, in charge of factual and daytime, equal the best of Hollywood executives. They have ability, dedication, charm, professionalism. Peter reminds me of my late friend Lew Grade, founder of what became ITV. They have different backgrounds, very diverse personalities, but share the same enthusiasm and skill for entertaining the viewer. To keep up the bonhomie ('Must have missed that,' I hear you say), I'll recount how, recently, the production staff were seeking a Rolls-Royce to replace my Phantom V, which is acquiring new upholstery. Nic told me they'd come up with cars minor by comparison. I emailed Matt Walton, the oh-so-charming executive producer, 'It's amazing your people didn't suggest a 20-year-old Ford Corsair. That would have been down to normal standard.' Matt emailed back, 'Hello sir, I'm delighted to read you're in your usual high spirits.' I laughed out loud. Anyone who can do that with an email deserves a prime place on the planet.

* * *

PS: For those who don't believe I exist (that includes me) go to Fortnum & Mason in Piccadilly tomorrow. At 4pm I'm signing my literary works. See you?

Sorry, boss, but I think it's back to Square One

At the end of shooting on *The Nightcomers* Marlon Brando made a speech calling us ships that pass in the night. In his autobiography he wrote that my film was the only one he enjoyed making. Marlon and I didn't pass; we stayed together for over three decades. He was a great telephoner. A year before he died Marlon rang and said, 'Y'know, Michael, I've decided nearly all my friends were good-time friends. I reckon I've only got five real friends in the world. I like to think you're one of them.' 'If you've got five real friends, Marlon, you're doing very well,' I responded.

A ship that passes me in the night is Peter McKay, who writes a witty column in a national newspaper. We first met in 1969. Years later we lunched at Assaggi. Marvellous food. Indescribably noisy. Our third lunch was a couple of weeks ago. Three meals in 40 years. Not major bonding. I chose **Kitchen W8**, recently opened near my house. The boss, Philip Howard, has a two-Michelin star restaurant, The Square, in Bruton Street, where he does great food and historic doughnuts. Philip also created The Ledbury in Notting Hill. I hated it. Over-fussed, tasteless, pompous-cooking. When Philip rang to tell me about the arrival of Kitchen I said, 'I hope it's nice and simple.' Philip assured me it would be. The doyenne of food critics, Fay Maschler, wrote in the *Evening Standard*, it seemed very elaborate for a local restaurant.

I had an awful time with a rude receptionist when I phoned to make a booking. The general manager, Eric Handts, ignored us. The head waiter offered a table. We waited and waited. There were only two other diners. Eric walked by right to left ignoring Peter and me. I dictated into my tape recorder, 'He knows we're here. He's a host, why isn't he hospitable? Why is no one taking an order? They do sell food, don't they?' Finally the head waiter took our order. Later Philip's wife introduced herself as 'Jenny'. She was pretty and charming.

The pumpkin and onion bread was cold, tasteless and dreary. My starter of foie gras mousse with raisin purée, fruit bread and Parmesan was highly liquid, served in a steep-rimmed bowl with a fork. Very difficult to eat. Needed a spoon. Not great. My main course was described as 'whole Dover sole with lemon and parsley butter'. It wasn't. They do a fantastic whole Dover sole at Scalini in Knightsbridge. There you get the side juicy bits, the roe, everything except head and tail. The Kitchen sole was trimmed, had no soft, generous texture. It was dry and shrivelled. Eric at last appeared to serve Peter's main course. He continued to ignore me. Four more people came in. 'A rush,' I said to Peter. 'It's still not like Sardi's after an opening night,' he observed. Sardi's is the New York 'in' place, packed to confusion after theatre events. The Kitchen is minimalist, unwelcoming and packed with empty tables. My warm chocolate pudding with hazelnut praline and vanilla ice-cream was good. I dictated, 'Peter says the Christmas pudding was the best he's ever had.' 'The best he's likely to get,' corrected Peter. What's the difference? Lunch cost £113.90. Only alcohol: two glasses of Pinot Noir. Not cheap. Outside the street was being dug up. What street isn't?

* * *

Here's a laugh. I just did *Celebrity Mastermind* for the BBC. No, that's not the laugh, there's another one. As recompense a cheque was to be sent to my charity the Police Memorial Trust. We gave them the address and all details in writing. To send a cheque to a named charity isn't difficult, is it? A trained gorilla could do that. But it's more than the twits producing *Mastermind* can manage. They sent the cheque to the wrong charity at a different address. I pay a licence fee for that idiocy. I was going to suggest the *Mastermind* team be transferred to *Watch with Mother* to 'produce' *Andy Pandy* and *The Flowerpot Men*. But they'd obviously make a mess of that too.

* * *

Staying on the ridiculous, how about the American Express boss Raymond Joabar? He took over a year ago from Ramon Martin, a man so silly he stopped my credit when I was spending over £350,000 a year and paid every Amex bill promptly for 43 years. I had him write to suppliers personally to apologise. In the last 12 months I've spent over £280,000 with Amex. I wanted to redeem my reward points. Always a nightmare. I'd told Ramon Martin that, then Raymond Joabar. Joabar said he'd fix it. He didn't. If you like frustration go to the Amex website and try to locate the catalogue showing what you should be able to get. Then give up and throw yourself out of the basement window.

* * *

I've sent over 600 of my vulgar Christmas cards to readers. First-class stamps. Some to Dubai, Australia, Thailand and other places, where postage is so expensive I'm cancelling my Christmas turkey. Grieve for me.

All I want for Christmas – lunch at the Ritz

I never drank cocktails. But recently I've become infatuated with the Cosmopolitan. I drink it from a classic cocktail glass, thin-stemmed, opening to a funnel. I look like Noël Coward in drag. My addiction to this effete drink is the fault of Yvonne Romain, an actress often bitten on her exquisite bosoms by vampires, wolfmen and other hoi polloi. Not in real life (although I know not what happens in Evie's private world) but in Hammer horror films, where she played the Ruritanian damsel in distress. For years Evie advertised herself in a wonderful manual, *Peter Noble's Film & TV Yearbook*. In 1962 Yvonne's biographical entry was accompanied by a sultry photo of her lounging seductively on a very 1960s chair, no shoes, no stockings, a white leotard and a casually revealing leather zip-up jacket. In her left hand she held aloft a cocktail stick with a piece of cheese on it. In 1964 Yvonne's ad changed to a sensuously posed head shot by famed glamour photographer Ben Jones. She was like a Mediterranean Brigitte Bardot. In 1966 she wore a black top and looked most inviting. A caption stated she'd starred in *The Swinger* for Paramount. The following year Evie co-starred with Elvis in *Double Trouble*. I was shattered to find Yvonne absent from the

1970 edition. She'd married a brilliant composer, Leslie Bricusse, who was with me at Cambridge University. So happy were they she turned down a seven-year contract with Fellini to be with her husband and son. We were in Scott's having dinner with Sir Michael and Lady Caine when I noticed Evie's orange-coloured drink. 'I'll have what she's having,' I said, echoing a famous movie line. I didn't mean Leslie, I meant the drink.

A few days later I took my adorable fiancée for Christmas lunch at the **Ritz**, along with my assistant Dinah, her son Luke, who manages a shoe shop in Covent Garden, and Leslie and Evie. Barman Alan Cook assured me a Cosmopolitan was no problem. Nor was it for me. I drank it. The Ritz chef, John Williams, is a supreme professional. His food is beyond belief good, served in far and away the most beautiful dining room in London. The Ritz is awesome. In a class of its own. I was delighted to learn that John, whom I regarded as the epitome of Yorkshire calm, screamed his head off in the kitchen. When I asked a waiter to take him in some photos we'd shot on my TV show *Michael Winner's Dining Stars*, the waiter went white and said, 'I hope Mr Williams isn't shouting when I give him these.' I congratulated John on the food and on exercising his vocal cords. No gain without pain, I say.

The bread was historic. My bacon brioche was fantastic. The freebie was salad of crab with avocado, ginger jelly and Marie Rose (whoever she is). Then I had ballotine of ham hock and langoustine with artichoke purée, quail egg beignet and fennel pollen. Sounds ridiculous, tasted great. Roast beef, veggies, marvellous roast potatoes and Yorkshire pud followed. Plus pommes soufflés, little fried potato balloons, which only John can do properly. The Christmas pudding was perfection. Beyond historic in texture, taste and flavour. The sweet mince pies were incredible. It was one of the best meals ever. No denim allowed, tie essential. Even for me, well worth it. Service by restaurant manager Simon Girling and his team is exemplary. Outside the dining room the Palm Court serves luxurious tea from 11am. Their manager Michael Kotb is well up to standard. It's fairyland. Tastefully Christmassed up. Pianists tinkle. Harpists pluck. If only all London's grand hotels were as unspoiled.

* * *

I needed names and numbers of bookshop managers who wanted me to come in to sign *Winner's Dinners*. The publicity lady emailed, 'Our sales rep won't give me the managers' names and numbers as they're his clients.' I told salesman David Segrue, who thinks bookshops are part of the secret service. It took us all of 10 minutes to get the bookshop phone numbers and manager names without his help. Then I went to Waterstone's in Kensington, Hatchards, Harrods and Selfridges to sign anything that didn't move. They say in the trade, 'A book signed is a book sold.' Someone should tell Mr Segrue.

* * *

I recounted how the *Mastermind* people sent the cheque for my fee to the wrong charity even though I'd given them in writing the name and address where it should go. Fiona Hamilton, the producer, wrote, 'If Mr Winner chooses to comment on this, the BBC will respond if necessary.' How terrifying. Put on tin hats. Hide in the trenches. Since then the Master-no-minds, having at last got their cheque to me, wrote again to the charity it wasn't meant for, telling them the payment would soon come to them. Unbelievable.

* * *

You can see seasonal goodwill just flows from me. To all my readers, Happy Christmas. Hope the 1,000 plus I sent my card to had fun with it.

Winner speaks

On waiting for my food: 'Please, send a search party to the kitchen to see if they can find my main course.'

The world's most colossal show-off – no, not me

There are people who spread joy and happiness. I'm one of them. Wha'd'ya mean you never noticed? Another is Andrew Davis. When I emailed asking what Andrew did, his PA Sarah responded (a) farms, (b) diamond, silver and art business, (c) property, residential development and commercial development and investment, (d) retail, (e) aviation and airports and (f) hotels. Sounds boring, doesn't it? Snooze time at best. The one thing you'll never do if you're with the ebullient, over-energised Andrew Davis is snooze. That'd be as difficult as getting a word in edgeways.

Andrew owns 29 of the greatest hotels in the world. From Château de Bagnols near Lyons to Cliveden (long lease from the National Trust), Sharrow Bay, the Royal Crescent

Bath, Amberley Castle and so on. He owns more relais and château hotels than anyone else in the world. Has the largest helicopter business in the UK, owns Battersea heliport and the vast new hotel beside it. He's a serious contender to buy the Orient-Express group. I hope he gets it. He's also wonderfully politically incorrect. A cross between Frankie Howerd and Benny Hill on speed, with a perfect foil in his posh, somewhat disdainful, highly efficient PA, Sarah Taylor. He was perfectly described by ex-school teacher Joan Reen, whose hotel Ynyshir Hall he bought for many millions, but who still runs it, as, 'the naughty boy at the back of the class'. At 45, Andrew personifies the gloriously vulgar enthusiasm of the school show-off. Beneath the veneer of lunacy he's a brilliant businessman, a person of great taste, as serious a player as you could meet. He's about to buy two private jet companies. You could say he's acquisitive. Andrew's hotel group is called Von Essen. The name has something to do with an aunt.

We flew in one of his vastly luxurious helicopters – me, Geraldine and his creative director Andrew Onraet – to lunch at **Homewood Park**, Hinton Charterhouse, near Bath. It's a typical Von Essen hotel in that it doesn't look like a hotel. It has the genuine charm of a Victorian house, set in 10 acres of stunning gardens, which happens to take paying guests. The brochure describes the place as 'the perfect environment to do absolutely nothing'. No chance of Andrew doing nothing. He's got 3,000 employees. I've met many of them: they adore him. He knows all their names and all the gossip. He knows where they've been for the last 50 years. Even if they're only 21 he knows where they've been for 50 years. The general manger, Denis Verrier, came over. Andrew explained, 'French, dear. Denis, before he got married, slept with half the female staff of the company. There's a photo of Denis completely naked at the staff party. He's on the straight and narrow now he's a married man with a six-month-old child.'

Andrew switches course, 'We're increasing this to 35 rooms with a new spa. Spend of £2 million. The rooms directed by Andrew Onraet are absolutely fantastic.' Commercial over, Andrew turns to me. 'Geraldine deserves a Nobel Prize, looking after you,' he says. Then to Geraldine, 'He buys you more diamonds because you got him at the wrong end of his life. He's not young, cute and thrusting at the moment.' God, the truth hurts. 'Sarah [his PA] is the great-granddaughter of Sir Francis Drake,' explains Andrew. Sarah says nothing.

I ordered from the set-lunch menu. My caramelised white onion soup was fantastic. I scooped it up with bread, which I never do. The bread was excellent. Then I had Wiltshire duo of pork, braised cheek and chargrilled tenderloin and apple. I was glad I'd eaten a lot of bread because it was a small main course. Andrew tapped me on the right arm. 'Margins, dear, profit margins. You're on the economy menu, not the à la carte.' Andrew bashed my dessert of vanilla pannacotta with a spoon and said, 'Too much gelatine.' He was right.

Andrew has a sweet tooth. All his helicopters are laden with toffees, sweets, chocolates. I used his company PremiAir to get around on my TV show *Michael Winner's Dining Stars*. Miraculously I resisted the sweeties and stayed slim. When you're a star you have to watch these things.

* * *

For the first time in 28 years I'm not at Sandy Lane this season. Geraldine and I are at South Beach, Miami, with Michael and Shakira Caine. I hear the new Sandy Lane chef, Conny Andersson, is terrific. His pastry chef, Claire Clarke, used to work at the French Laundry in California and with my favourite hotel chef, John Williams of the Ritz. Bet she does great mince pies and Christmas pud. No one could last year.

* * *

To celebrate 2010, the year when I become a major TV star, or less, I've borrowed another £3m. I'm now £9m in debt. I'll spend a bit of it flying back from Miami in a Gulfstream private jet. From today, I'm at the Setai, a hotel which I was told is very posh but under-lit. I've taken a torch. Oh, and Happy New Year to you all.

Kicking off the New Year in style

My first words of wisdom for 2010 are illustrated not by a photo of me but of my adorable fiancée Geraldine recumbent by the pool of the **Villa Feltrinelli** in Gargnano, backed by a sliver of Lake Garda. Ms Lynton-Edwards asked me to say she's wearing no make-up. People look better without make-up. I'd greet beautiful and famous movie stars at 6am as they tottered toward their Winnebago motor homes to be made up. They looked fantastic. When they came out of make-up they appeared less than fantastic. Sophia Loren, a marvellous person, always made herself up. She looked orange. For the last scene of my movie *Firepower* I employed a childhood hero, Victor Mature. Greeting him outside the Pierre hotel, New York, I remarked, 'Your hair looks green, Victor.' 'It's normally white. I dye it for you,' said Victor. 'Something went wrong.' 'Marvellous,' I said, 'for our finale I have the orange woman meets the green man. That'll send 'em out laughing.' In front of the movie lights they both looked great. Sophia still does. Victor's not at his best as he's been dead for 11 years. Mussolini, the Italian fascist dictator, has been dead for 65 years.

Il Duce took over the beautiful Villa Feltrinelli and lived there until April 1945, when he and his mistress Clara Petacci, who had a lakeside villa nearby, fled for Switzerland. They were grabbed by partisans, shot and strung up in Milan. The Villa Feltrinelli was eventually bought by an American hotelier who intended to live there, but he remarried and his Oriental wife thought Lake Garda boring. So he sold to a Swiss group. The Villa is now beautifully run by Markus Odermatt. I named it Best Hotel in Europe at my *Winner's Dinners* book launch. The award was handed over by Chris Rea. He'd visited as a result of my recommendation, just as he stayed at Sandy Lane on my advice.

Villa Feltrinelli offers fantastic meals from a young chef, Stefano Baiocco. He writes down the date of every food item that comes into the kitchen. If he thinks it's been there too long (and he allows only a very short time) he throws it away. Markus assured me he kept the kitchen perfectly, 'like a hospital'. Some of the hospitals I've been in were filthy. But Baiocco keeps everything spotless and in order. 'The oranges have to be perfectly in line. He keeps the staff cleaning the kitchen for an hour and a half after service,' explained Markus, 'it's like the surgery of a hospital.' 'In that case I'm surprised I'm not in it,' I responded. I won't bore you with how many operations I've had. We'd be here forever. Nor can I be bothered to tell you exactly what I ate. Villa Feltrinelli reopens on 15 April. It only has 31 rooms. Book now.

Before that be home on 26 February and the next three Fridays. That's when my ITV1 show *Michael Winner's Dining Stars* appears. Get a TV dinner, book a seat in your living room for 9pm and sit transfixed, with amazement, laughter and wonder. If you have to make a cuppa tea, please, do it during the commercials.

* * *

No recession for my staff. They got lovely Christmas presents, a champagne reception in my house with excellent canapés from Gary O'Sullivan of the Belvedere, then dinner at the **Bombay Brasserie**. This year they thought service, food and recent redecoration were poor. My superb cook, Lulu, said, 'I had the fish and the chicken. Both tasted the same.' I said to Arun Harnal, the general manager, 'How is it when you know they're my staff, that they'll to report to me and I'll write about it, that you didn't at least see the service was good?' I've only been once since the makeover. My chicken was mushy. I never went back.

* * *

Eric Handts, surly restaurant manager of my local horror, **Kitchen W8**, ignored me and my guest when there were only two other people there. He also upset a friend, significant in the hospitality game, who was invited to their 'soft opening'. Mr Handts offered, 'Have two glasses of champagne.' My friend accepted thinking they were from management. He was surprised to find them on his bill.

* * *

Richard Swan, product manager of Leica cameras, introduced me to the world of digital photography by lending me their D-Lux 4 camera. It baffled me, so I rang him. 'Read the instruction book,' Richard suggested. 'I'll never understand that,' I said. 'It took me two hours just to get the camera out of the box.' Richard came and patiently showed me how the thing worked. So photos with this column are now taken on my Leica digital. Except this week. That's on my celluloid Leica Minilux with a fixed, non-zoom lens. They're always a bit crisper. Richard says the first digital camera fully made by Leica comes out soon. I'm assured it's a considerable advance and simpler to operate. That means it'll only take me six months to figure out. Watch for the photo improvement then.

A day of dining stars . . . and lunching disasters

As I roamed the country for my TV series *Michael Winner's Dining Stars* dinner was with people who invited me to judge their home cooking. Before that I stalked the streets grabbing locals and talking to them. Got some wonderful dialogue. For lunch we'd drop in locally.

One of the worst meals I've ever eaten was at the **Duke William** in Longridge, near Preston, Lancashire. Strange, because the pub is owned by a local farmer, Martin Carefoot, whose butcher's – Carefoot's Farm Shop – is superb. Everything looked fantastic. I had a sausage roll which was beyond historic. Stratospheric plus. Martin suggested we lunch at his pub, the Duke William. So my hairdresser Dinah May, make-up lady Joan Hills and I sat down for what we expected to be a nice meal. Boy, did we have a wrong number.

I ordered a deluxe burger with cheese, bacon and onion rings. Dinah, chicken curry with braised rice, Joan, a Cajun chicken salad. No one else was lunching except my TV crew. That should have told me something. The sauté potato I took from Joan was poor. I'd been told the chips were made in the kitchen from real potatoes. They weren't brown; I'd never seen an Albino chip. Awful. The waitress hadn't asked how I wanted my hamburger cooked. It came well done. I wanted medium rare. It was flat, skimpy and flaccid. Didn't even look like meat. The ketchup and mustard were in tiny plastic packs. I don't do plastic. Dinah opened them for me. Martin has a fantastic meat shop with pies and cakes and he's serving pathetic hamburgers with packed condiments. I tried another chip. It needed to be fried much longer or at greater heat. The hamburger was inedible. Dinah described her curry as, 'Edible because I'm hungry. The chicken is horrible, absolutely dreadful.' We left most of everything. Realising this was disaster I asked if we could have some sausage rolls brought from the shop. At least they'd been good. They came reheated, slimy and soggy. In the morning they'd been crisp. On the pub menu it said 'Sweets from our blackboard'. None were listed on the blackboard. The waitress said most of them were bought in but the chocolate fudge cake was made on the premises. Another disaster. Tasted as if it had been made out of a packet or a cake mix. Dinah took a bit and said, 'It's revolting.'

The landlord, Dan Horrobin, never greeted us or suggested what we should have. He stuck his head round the corner from a lower-level floor when I was talking and said, 'May I interrupt you?' I said, 'No you may not.' We never saw him again. It was the worst possible example of hospitality, food, ambience. The *Lancashire Evening Post* rang to say Mr Horrobin described having me there as 'a nightmare'. What was he complaining about? He didn't have to eat the food. Horrobin moaned on, 'I think Mr Winner is used to dining in fancy restaurants such as The Ivy.' Horrobin should visit The Ivy to learn. Their hamburgers are superb. His are a disgrace. The Ivy is professional. The Duke William is appalling.

Back on the streets a couple of youngsters said, 'You should be eating local dishes, Lancashire hotpot and Goosnargh chicken.' Goosnargh is a nearby village specialising in corn-fed chickens. Neither was available in the Duke William. Would they had been. Would I'd eaten somewhere else. A Salvation Army hostel for example. If I'm ever in Longridge again I'll check if they've got one. I had my photo taken with the so-called chef, Harry Larter and owner, Martin Carefoot. My advice to Martin: keep the shop, close the pub.

* * *

I flew Virgin to Miami. Their staff are always helpful. Not Richard Marks, Contact Centre Duty Manager. For years his boss, Mary-Anne Coyle, gave me details of those I was to meet, the captain, flight service manager and airport managers. Before that British Airways people gave the same information when I flew with them. Mr Marks refused to reveal anything because airline employees were 'covered by the Data Protection Act'. What drivel! Flight service managers wear a badge with their name on it. So do airport managers. Pilots announce their names on the plane's loudspeakers. They don't work for the secret service. A senior executive of Virgin gave me the information Marks declined to part with. Virgin remains much admired by me. Mr Marks does not.

* * *

My employees didn't like their **Bombay Brasserie** staff dinner. My receptionist Zoe presented her cloakroom ticket on leaving. They'd given her coat to someone else. Arun Harnal, general manager, said they'd pay for a new one. That left Zoe having to look for one, be without a coat and be inconvenienced through no fault of her own. All this, plus the lousy service and food, shows a lack of control at the top. Mr Harnal took over recently from Adi Mohdi, who was very good. I don't think Harnal is up to it. Another restaurant bites the dust. Anyone know a good Indian place?

Nice try, Virgin, but it will be a private jet next time

Geraldine listens to her radio on headphones all night. In the morning I get a breakdown of the news, weather, and other items. On Boxing Day she announced, 'Someone tried to blow a plane up over Detroit.' This was Umar Farouk Abdul Mutallab, who, getting peckish after a long flight, decided to have a roast leg. His own. I was concerned that my 12:30pm departure for Miami on Virgin would be delayed. At 7:30am I phoned Louise Dixon, Virgin's duty manager at Heathrow, for the lowdown. 'You visited my sister's restaurant,' said Louise cheerfully. 'About my flight . . .' I said urgently. 'It's called Delfina, in Bermondsey Street, you particularly liked her mashed potatoes . . .' continued Louise. 'But what's happening to . . .?' I tried to get a word in. 'You said they were the best potatoes you'd ever eaten,' informed Louise. Eventually I persuaded her to tell me what delay she expected on my flight. 'Forty-five minutes' was the answer. Then my friend Steve Ridgway, Chief Executive Officer of Virgin Atlantic, rang. Steve explained all passengers would have a full body and luggage search both at normal entry to the customs area and again just before they boarded. He too estimated a 45-minute delay. Heathrow was chaos.

We went to the **Virgin Atlantic Clubhouse**, an exceedingly pleasant airport lounge, where Louise and Virgin's Premier Customer Services agent, Kirsten Brown, looked after us. I ordered a waffle as the last one I had there was super-historic. This one was good but a little heavier. I got maple syrup on my blazer. Geraldine and I had scrambled eggs. She took coffee with soya milk, I had fresh orange juice. Geraldine's bacon had an excellent honey taste. On the plane I ate a first-rate selection of sandwiches (twice), three cups of tea and some nuts.

By the time we boarded it was 2pm. An hour and a half

after scheduled take-off. The pilot came out, you know the type, tall, deep voice, 'I'm your captain, you can rely on me, I control everything' sort of person. 'When do you think we'll take off?' I asked. 'I reckon 3pm,' said the Captain. 'What planet did you fly in from?' I asked. 'Have you see the chaos out there?' I pointed toward the door. 'There's hundreds of people having every bag unpacked for the second time. If we take off before 4:30 it'll be a miracle.' Know-it-all-Winner was almost right. We took off at 4.17pm. Nearly four hours late.

Much as I admire Virgin, I'll never fly on public transport again. I promptly confirmed a private Gulfstream jet to take Geraldine and me back. Not from Miami airport (that's a total nightmare) but a charming little airstrip nearby named Opa-Locka. No delays, no customs, no immigration. Just turn up, get in, land at Luton after a snack of caviar, Dom Pérignon, chopped egg and onions, blinis, smoked salmon. A snip at £44,000 for what's called an empty leg. That's where you get around 50 per cent off normal price because the plane's going one-way empty. It takes a bit of bottle to lay out that much. As far as I'm concerned, best money I ever spent. Except for Geraldine's engagement ring, of course.

I'd gone to Miami for a change of life after 28 years in a row spending Christmas and New Year at Sandy Lane, Barbados. Christmas Day was at Michael Caine's Surrey house. Brilliantly prepared turkey, sausages, everything. Then to Miami, where Michael and Shakira have an apartment. For New Year's Eve – normally a strained affair but not this time – they took us to Prime Italia, a superb place in Miami Beach. No funny hats, no drunks, no one blowing whistles. Just enormous and tasty portions. A salad full of everything. It would have served 25 people. I had risotto with rib-eye steak, unusual combination, both marvellous. Cauliflower cheese was totally memorable.

Fried zucchini fantastic. For dessert the waiter brought a portion of cheesecake and a portion of chocolate fudge cake. Both so enormous he cut them up and served them to six people. This left enough to fill not so much a doggie bag as an elephant bag.

Myles Chefetz, owner of Prime Italia, has a place opposite called Prime 112. This specialises in steak but does everything. I know of no better restaurant in the world. Stunning. I had sea bass plus some of Michael Caine's prime rib. The spinach (which I normally don't like) was beyond belief. The hashed brown: best ever. An amazing creamed corn on the cob. A selection of desserts, enough to feed 600 people at a wedding, appeared courtesy of the management. Cheesecake, chocolate chip cookies, doughnuts with warm chocolate inside. If Myles came to London I'd be standing in line every day. No I wouldn't. I'd rent a private jet to jump the queue.

* * *

My absence from Sandy Lane induced a short little squirt, chubby, bespectacled theatrical agent, to seek publicity knocking me. Julius Schmulius (not his real name) phones the gossip columns whenever he wobbles. Can't believe they're so silly as to print it.

Glad you've turned over a new leaf, Skye

I know it will surprise you, but sometimes I upset people. And they upset me. Such upsettance occurred at the **Petersham Nurseries Café**, a large greenhouse in a far-flung part of Richmond that sells plants, palm trees, ornaments and food. I visited twice, liked it massively, praised the chef, Skye Gyngell, and was therefore a bit miffed when she was quoted in *The Times* saying, 'That man's bloody well not coming back.'

It followed me writing how much I had not appreciated the attitude of her then restaurant manager, Rachel Lewis. Ms Lewis, when I phoned one Sunday to book a table, was considerably less welcoming than a disembowelled frog. Eventually, as if the effort was killing her, she offered me a table for two. I phoned back and said, 'Don't bother.' Skye Gyngell gave a bizarre account of this incident, saying I'd asked for a table for eight at the last minute. No dear. It was Geraldine and me. We're two people. When Skye told her friend, the wonderful Rose Gray of the River Café, Rose advised, 'You should grow up. We have to learn to play the game. You must always be able to fit people in. It's part of the business.'

I was discussing this with Charles Pullan, the preppie-looking restaurant manager of the River Café, whose wife runs the nursery part of Petersham Nurseries. 'You should go back, I'll take you,' he said. 'They asked me to help find a restaurant manager and Sophia Franc from here has the job.' Sophia is a marvellous restaurant person. Charles, apart from the odd lapse of memory when you order something, is great. He got the Winner's Dinners Award for best restaurant manager at our book launch ceremony. 'What about Skye?' I asked. 'If she comes screaming out of the kitchen waving a sharp knife, will you throw yourself in front of me?' Luckily this wasn't necessary. Skye was all charm.

Her food, as on my previous visits, was totally superb. Fantastic homemade lemonade. Crab cakes of wonderful taste, texture and quality. Guinea fowl accompanied by a tasty, blending-in sauce. To finish I had lemon tart with tulsameen raspberries and créme fraiche. Perfect, old-fashioned, tangy lemon taste, lot of lemon cream on top, more cream and strawberries. Then I dictated, 'Pannacotta very delicate.' I must have nicked a bit from someone else.

Petersham Nurseries Café is as good as it gets. The journey puts me off going as often as I'd like. Move into town, please, Skye. Then you can throw me out from a closer location. As Charles escorted Skye from the kitchen to have our photo taken, she said to him, 'If this isn't a good review I'm going to kill you.' I knew she was dangerous. But boy, can this gal cook.

* * *

You know what surprised and delighted me about New Year's Eve in Miami? I never saw one stupid paper hat, one whistle being blown, crackers, or anyone remotely drunk. After dinner at a great Italian restaurant we went to Michael Caine's apartment, which has an enormous wrap-around terrace, and watched the firework displays all over town. Then we drove back to our hotel down one of Miami's main streets. No one was the worse for drink, no screaming, no shouting, all very constrained and orderly. Not for you? Well, if you want to be an over-dressed lush wearing a funny hat and blowing a whistle, good luck to you. Just keep away from me.

* * *

One of the housewives who welcomed me into their home for my TV show *Michael Winner's Dining Stars* phoned to say she and her family were coming to London for a football match. She and her husband arranged dinner at the **Royal Oak**, Michael Parkinson's pub in Paley Green. Congratulations to chef Dominic Chapman for just getting a Michelin star. For lunch I booked them into the Wolseley. Justine and her daughter came to my house for tea while dad and the rest of the family watched the football. It was a pleasure to pay for all their meals. Justine's story is one of great bravery. It's very moving. She's in my first programme which airs on 26 February. Forget me. Watch it for her.

* * *

Marmite sent me six new cereal bars described as 'Lots of lovely chewy oats, wheat and rice, all wrapped up with the hefty punch of Marmite'. Terrible taste, totally revolting. Product placement people please note: I want no freebies. Send stuff at your peril.

* * *

A clarification: my friends Hymie Pockle, Moishe Pippick and Abe Schwantz wish it to be known they are not in any way associated, personally or professionally, with Julius Schmulius, the pipsqueak, fat, short, bespectacled little squirt, publicity-seeking theatrical agent. Glad to clear that up for you, fellas.

Winner speaks

On waiting for the menu: 'Are you serving food today?'

Red card at the ready in the land of footballers' wives

Wilmslow is footballers' wives territory. As I arrived for my TV show, *Michael Winner's Dining Stars*, a £400,000 Rolls Phantom glided by. It's a dull shopping area enlivened by glittery shops.

For lunch, Rob, a hairdresser at Flannigan's, recommended **44 Bar and Restaurant**. He'd eaten there with famous footballers. I went with Dinah, my hairdresser/ assistant, and Joan Hills, my make-up lady. When you get to my age and you're on telly, you need such support. The waitress, Sophie, aged 19, had a diamond set in her nose. She assured me everything was fresh. I asked, 'Are the French-style peas fresh?' 'They're fresh in today,' replied Sophie. 'Were they actually taken from a pod in your kitchen?' I queried. 'Yeah,' said Sophie, 'they get delivered every day.' I said, 'Now let's turn to the fish and chips with minted peas. These are crushed peas . . .' 'They're purified peas, they get flattened down,' explained Sophie. I said, 'They come in a packet, don't they?' 'They come from a delivery,' responded Sophie. 'So they're not fresh, they're not opened in the kitchen,' I continued. 'No, but they come in every day,' said Sophie. 'They come in prepared.' So of course they weren't fresh.

The conversation with Sophie about various menu items, if fully reported, would be longer than a Jackie Collins novel. Sophie held her ground. But it seemed nothing was fresh except the fish pie and roast chicken pie, which, she assured me, were made on the premises. If so, there's no one in the kitchen who knows how to make chicken pie. The pastry was undercooked and pale. The chicken was shredded and tasteless. Come dessert time and Sophie again informed me everything was made freshly in their kitchen. Somehow I doubted that. I had lemon and lime cheesecake with marinated oranges and vanilla syrup. It tasted bought in. As if it had been in the deep-freeze overnight. The cheesecake part had gone into the base, making it soggy. They took our napkins after the main course and brought no new ones for dessert.

All this was filmed. You won't see it because producing company 12yard (I call them half a millimetre) failed to get a signature authorising filming when we came in. You have to do that otherwise you give them time to think about it, decide the meal didn't go well and decline to sign at the end. Didn't matter, because events we shot in the streets and shops of Wilmslow were hilarious.

* * *

As I rose at 6:30am to be ready for make-up and hair at 8am and filming ended around midnight, I had an hour's rest before I met my housewife hostess for dinner. One rest period was at the **Stanneylands** hotel in Wilmslow. Eight years earlier I'd slated it big time. The Irish manager, Eamonn Phelan, greeted me like an old friend. The owner, Liam Walsh, phoned to check I was all right. I was surprised they let me in. It's a nice hotel, although I hadn't enjoyed the food. It's probably better now.

Matt Walton, executive producer, had booked a suite for the night at the Midland hotel in the centre of Manchester. 'Why,' I asked, 'do I have to drive at least 45 minutes from here through traffic lights and wiggly streets of Manchester, and then in the morning rush hour back to the next location through crowded city streets, when close to here is the M6 motorway that takes us straight to Longridge? I waste one and a half hours travelling, ITV has to pay the driver longer hours. What genius thought of that?' 'The production manager reckoned it was the same distance,' said Matt. 'If it is, which I doubt, the same distance, through a town centre is not the same as driving on a motorway,' I explained patiently. 'Would you rather stay here, Mr Winner,' Matt replied testily? 'Of course,' I said, 'saves time, cheaper accommodation for me, Dinah and Joan, perfectly okay for a night.' So I stayed at Stanneylands. The next day local driver Alan Fitzsimmons had a much easier trip to Longridge. I should give courses on how to run location film shoots. If the series doesn't reach everyone's high expectations I may have to.

* * *

I'd just finished an excellent shepherd's pie at The **Ivy** when I saw coming in the dreaded pipsqueak, fat little squirt, balding theatrical agent Julius Schmulius. He slimed around a few tables. I said to Nicholas Cowell (brother of Simon), with whom we were dining, 'I'm going to look intently at you, Nicholas, because I don't want him to speak to me.' I was doing just that, with my left hand on the table, when a clammy hand was placed on mine. I looked round – a puffed-up face said, 'Julius Schmulius' (not even his real name), and he waddled off. That gave me a turn, I can tell you.

* * *

Joke from the Ritz doorman Michael O'Dowdall: How do you turn a dishwasher into a snowmobile? Give her a shovel.

The right hotel at the wrong time of year

Before I went to Miami, Dermot Desmond, superboss of Sandy Lane, cautioned me to take winter woollies because temperatures there would be six degrees below those in Barbados. If only. Our first week was fine, hot, sunny, on-the-beach weather. The second was the coldest in Miami since 1940. Freezing. We passed an empty shop with a sign: 'Everything you want for the beach.' Geraldine said, 'Fur coats, ski muffs, thermal underwear'. There was a howling, freezing wind. The place was Arctic.

The Seta, where we stayed, is a beautifully run hotel. Fantastic food. The manager, Hans Meier, was the best I've ever come across. Hans is Swiss. But charming. Walked the hotel non-stop greeting everyone. Was always at the desk when I came down, immensely solicitous. The executive chef, Jonathan Wright, was English. He'd been eight years with Raymond Blanc at Le Manoir aux Quat'Saisons.

The food was incredible. The Sunday buffet had about 15 different 'stations', each offering food from diverse areas: Indian, Chinese, Vietnamese, American, British, you name it, they had it. There were three swimming pools each at different temperatures, then a walkway, a strip of palm trees and bushes, then a wide beach facing the Atlantic Ocean. The sand was rather gritty. The enormous sun loungers the most comfortable ever. A fantastic lime pina colada was on offer. The service and staff were perfect. Lot of hands together in praying position, little bow and smiling. As it's run by the Amman group, they were from Thailand, the Philippines, the Pacific islands. I ate everything from sea bass to dim sums to lobster to hotdogs to tarte tartin with Calvados and crème fraîche. All historic or brilliant.

We had an apartment in the Setai Residences, wrap-around terrace overlooking beach, sea and town, large living room, two bedrooms, kitchen. Sweeping views, superb. Richard Caring warned me the place was dark. It was. A guest went into the cloakroom to check her make-up and couldn't see herself in the mirror. The hotel was full of Oriental-type jars on pedestals lit with a mild spotlight. Their website advises, 'Be embraced by the serenity.'

Serenity is not blaring beat music blasted out over the swimming pools. That's tacky. We opted for the beach. Except for the second week, where no one was on the beach or poolside. They were huddling together for warmth. Still, vastly enjoyable. Lovely to be with Michael and Shakira Caine and family. Would I go back? Not at Christmas/New Year, that's for sure. Weather too dodgy.

* * *

Alison Sharman, ITV's head of factual and daytime programmes, spent New Year's Eve on a plane flying Miami to London. On 31 December she came to the Setai for lunch with her two delightful daughters and a husband. Alison is a great worker. All through her holiday and at any time of day, night or weekend she answers emails like lightning. Very rare. She also looks good, keeps in shape, has charm, will travel. I immensely admire the higher-echelon people at ITV. So much so I went bonkers last week and bought some shares. They're well on the rise. Should have bought them for a third as much when Michael Grade was Chairman. His replacement, Archie Norman, is greatly admired by ITV staff. He's on the ball, getting right in and working away. He made a great success of Asda. I told him, when asked, TV is not that different. If you've got a product people buy (or see) en masse, you're ahead of the game. In my few talks with Archie, his choice of words, his attitude, his display of knowledge and desire to learn, were massively impressive. Adam Crozier, who I've also dealt with, is an inspired choice for chief executive.

Archie's predecessor, Michael Grade, was a classic example of failing upwards. I asked a billionaire businessman friend what talent Grade had. He thought for a while and said, 'He's got a good sense of humour.' 'Is that enough for the Chairman of a public company?' I asked. No reply came forth. Grade was massively attacked by Lady Delfont, wife of his uncle Sir Bernard, when he took over Bernie's First Leisure group and saw it disappear in chaos a few years later. He turns up with red braces, a wide grin and a cigar and these deluded TV people line the hallway and clap his entry. It's the emperor's new clothes. Behind his back the same people applaud his departure.

Let's do important matters: me. Don't forget, folks, *Michael Winner's Dining Stars* is only 19 days from its peak time, unveiling at 9pm on ITV1, 26 February. Excitement is reaching fever pitch. Well, it's a millimetre above lethargy. My life is in your hands. Watch and I'll thrive, ignore it and in come the bailiffs.

* * *

Joke from the Ritz doorman Michael O'Dowdall. Man goes to the doctor, says, 'I think I'm a moth.' Doctor advises, 'You should see a psychiatrist.' Man says, 'I was going to but your light was on.'

A decent lunch? Not a ghost of a chance here

I like Shrewsbury. Lot of Tudor buildings, lovely atmosphere. I'm very big in Shrewsbury. It was the only place where we filmed me grabbing shoppers on the street for my TV show *Michael Winner's Dining Stars* and had to move on again and again because crowds of people kept asking for my autograph and following us. Very intelligent people in Shrewsbury. Know a bit of class when they see it.

At lunchtime we were in Milk Street outside **Poppy's Tea Room and Restaurant**. Looked Tudor. Apparently built in 1617. Seriously old oak beams. Dinah, my assistant and hairdresser, thought the carpet was dirty. I was with her and

Joan Hills, my make-up lady. Geoff Meredith, the owner, served us. 'Very nice class of clientele,' I observed. Geoff said he'd got pasta with two Italian sausages mixed with tomato sauce and basil. His menu said, 'All meals cooked fresh to order.' 'What's the pasta, Geoff?' I asked. 'It's mixed pasta,' replied Geoff. 'What do you mean mixed?' I said. 'Does it come from a tin?' 'It comes from three packages and they mix them up,' explained Geoff. 'Now, Geoff, listen to me carefully,' I said. 'I'm going to have the chicken breast and I want a piece of quiche so I can test both items. Dinah is having the English breakfast and Joan the organic panini, green tomato and basil. Rush that through if you could.' 'I'll have it in eight minutes,' said Geoff. He brought me a diet Coke. Obviously thought I was putting on weight. I wasn't.

The chicken was like lead. 'Is it microwaved Geoff?' I asked. He said, 'Yes.' 'This restaurant is very good for the diet because you can't eat anything,' I observed to Dinah and Joan. The quiche was beyond belief awful. The base managed to be soggy and hard at the same time. Joan said her organic panini was hard, too. Dinah said, 'Even my eggs taste funny and I'm hungry. I'm going to buy a bag of sweets or a chocolate bar.' Geoff assured me desserts were made in the kitchen. My Bakewell tart wasn't bad. I shouldn't have asked for it to be warm because they obviously put it in the microwave. Even so it was quite acceptable. Joan did not complain about her damson and apple tart.

'Better than the first course?' asked Geoff, who'd taken away almost-untouched plates. 'You could say that, Geoff,' I replied. He responded, 'Well, you win some, you lose some.' 'He's quite cheerful,' I said to Dinah. 'He's not fazed by any of it.' Dinah was now eating Golden Crunch biscuits. 'This packed biscuit is the best thing I've eaten here,' I observed. Geoff returned. 'Do you believe in ghosts?' he asked. 'We've been told there are six here.' 'Have you seen any of them?' I asked. 'I've felt them,' said Geoff. 'What did they feel like?' I queried. 'Cold,' said Geoff. 'I was working at the bottom of the stairs and suddenly the room went cold and all the hairs on my body stood up. I had a moustache at the time and that went up. Last week a lady was here, she went to the loo and said she couldn't do anything. I asked why and she said, "Because I've just been talking to a gentleman in an 1850 army suit."' Geoff paused for effect. 'And I haven't seen her since,' he said. Could have been the food, I thought. But he was such a nice fellow I didn't say it out loud.

* * *

At **Quo Vadis** in Soho, after a very successful press screening of my TV show at the Soho hotel, I had some fantastic crisp-fried calf's brains. It's a superb restaurant. So is Angela Hartnett's **Murano** in Mayfair. The set lunch is amazing value. As well as three magnificent courses you get freebies – sausages, salami and ham, different breads, *arancini*, which are fried balls of risotto, mascarpone and truffle oil, eight little sorbets and ice-creams and glorious petits fours. All for £27 plus 12 per cent service. The three-course vegetarian menu is £60. Figure that out. I know I've arrived in the important league, because this year Angela sent me a Christmas card.

* * *

If you want to see me in the flesh (an odd sight) then go to the Little Theatre in Leicester next Thursday, 18 February, for my one-man show, 'My Life in Movies and Other Places'. You can even ask questions. For the Oundle literary festival I'm at the Great Hall on 19 March and the Princess Grace Theatre, Monaco, on 27 April. Plus my ITV1 series starts in 12 days. By which time you'll all have had enough of me. Believe me, I know the feeling.

* * *

My assistant Dinah's poodle was 20 years old and very ill. My marvellous PA, Natalie, a bubbly Essex girl, was commiserating. I said, 'The vet's going to put down Dinah's dog, then he's going to do me.' Natalie said, 'Can't he do you first?' Then I'm sitting at the kitchen table with my fantastic and adorable fiancée, Geraldine, when she calmly remarks, 'You're a sicko git with Asperger's syndrome.' Then she returns to delicately sipping her Earl Grey tea. It's a laugh a minute in my house. Luckily, it's being so cheerful that keeps me going.

Cook for me nicely, dear, and I'll make you a star

In five days' time comes the event the world has been waiting for. The unveiling of my ITV1 series *Michael Winner's Dining Stars* next Friday, 9–10pm. All right, the world hasn't been waiting breathlessly. Just the United Kingdom. Well, perhaps not all the United Kingdom. Let's just say there are three people in South Kensington who can't contain their excitement.

In the first programme of four ('Why only four?' you ask) I travel to Wilmslow, world of footballers and Wags, for a trip around the locals, followed by curried goat from a man of Jamaican origin who demolishes houses.

Then on to Longridge, where a Lancashire housewife served rather elaborate dishes. During both these meals I retired, delicately, to another room, where I dictated into my tape recorder what I really thought of what was going on.

To end each show, the two contestants, their families

and guests come to the beautifully restored Coronet cinema in Notting Hill Gate. There they see me on screen dictating my secret notes. Then I ask for their comments. This produces conflict, confrontation, robust ripostes and some very moving results. Finally I reveal if they get one, two, three or no Michael Winner dining stars. I hope you'll watch and let me know what you think. Your usual wit and sarcasm, however clever, are not essential. I seek guidance in case ITV is reckless enough to offer another series.

We now fast-forward to the last of the shows, which we shot in Kingsand, Cornwall. I stayed nearby at the **Whitsand Bay** hotel, Portwrinkle, a once grand, now faded place by a golf course (handy for landing my helicopter) owned by two brothers, John and Paul Phillips.

For dinner I ordered plaice. John told me, 'It was on the day boat.' 'What day?' I asked. 'I imagine yesterday's because we had it in this morning,' replied John. If the plaice was fresh, the chef managed to disguise it brilliantly. It was terrible. It had no succulence, no moisture, rolled up in a silly little display. A miserable course. The rest of the meal matched the standard of the dried-up plaice.

The Whitsand Bay hotel can claim fame for one thing. In it, for the first time, I made a cup of tea in my room. There was a plastic kettle, two beakers and some Tetley tea bags. I put a bit of brown packed sugar in first, but stopped that on realising my mistake. The string on the tea bag wasn't long enough. So I pulled at the label and discovered when you tear off the label the string becomes longer. 'This is fascinating – I'm learning,' I said to myself. The kettle wouldn't go under the tap because the sink was too small, so I poured water from the plastic beakers into the kettle. 'It's now boiled,' I muttered to me. 'I'm pouring the water into the beaker with the tea bag in it.' It wasn't a bad colour. I'd first put in milk from a tiny plastic container with 'Semi-skimmed' written on it. Who said I wanted semi-skimmed? I might not have wanted semi-skimmed. Well, that's what I got.

The tea with its one tea bag looked pretty good. I removed the digestive biscuit from the other beaker and put the tea bag in the second beaker, which I didn't need as Geraldine wasn't with me. I achieved all this without getting a drop of water on the little table. I stirred the sugar in with a spoon, looked out at a rather grey sea, drank a bit. Added a little more white sugar. I placed a small plastic tray on top to keep the heat in and went to pour lager beer over my head (very good for the hair), added some conditioner, combed it out and came back to finish my tea. It was very nice. In future I'll leave tea-making to the staff. But I thought I did pretty well.

* * *

Part of the fun of MW Dinestars (other than seeing the *Sunday Times* being printed, as shown in the opening titles) is that I'm accompanied by my assistant/hairdresser Dinah May and an . . . er, rather overweight make-up lady, Joan Hills. I scream, 'Dinah!' rather a lot. If that doesn't become a national catchphrase I'll eat my 'Calm down, dear' T-shirt. Dinah, who's worked for me for 27 years, is no stranger to TV. She's a former Miss Great Britain, starred on *It's a Knockout*, had a regular role in *Brookside*, acted in movies. On film sets she hairdressed Joanna Lumley, Diana Rigg, Jeremy Irons and Anthony Hopkins. Joan, a marvellous old-timer, goes back to *Chariots of Fire*.

* * *

So far the reviews have been great. Matthew Norman in the *Independent* called it 'cracking television, a riot of both mirth and poignancy'. He said Andrew Neil spoke for everyone at the screening in expressing his pleasant surprise at the quality. Surprised at my qualities, Andrew?

Gosh. The *Sun* said it was 'a hilarious series'. The *Daily Mail*: 'It's funny, confrontational and even touching.' This could go to my head. If it's a hit I look forward to graduating from being difficult to utterly impossible.

Michael's the star of this show (him, not me)

I am not a regular party giver. But I recently screened episode one of *Michael Winner's Dining Stars* in my cinema (hope you enjoyed it on TV) for a few major nobs. These included Archie Norman, Chairman of ITV; Adam Crozier, currently chief executive of the Royal Mail, soon to be CE of ITV; Michael and Shakira Caine; Andrew and Madeleine Lloyd Webber; David and Karina Frost; GP (that's genius playwright) Lucy Prebble, who wrote *Enron;* and Alison Sharman, head of ITV factual and daytime.

When giving a party: keep everything simple. Don't serve canapés that fall apart or drip onto your guests' clothing. I offered caviar or smoked salmon on brown, gluten-free, toast and Dom Pérignon champagne. My brilliant cook, Lulu, knocked the food up, nothing phases her, she's dynamite. I brought in a terrific waiter, Jonathan, from Admirable Crichton. They also provided 17 little gold chairs for my dining table, which normally seats 10. It was self-service from the kitchen – superb beef or chicken stroganoff, brown or white rice, salad. Easy-peasy. Very good quality. Many guests went back for seconds. With dinner the white wine was Puligny-Montrachet 2002, red was Château Lynch-Bages 1982. Plenty of iced water in jugs with lemon. For dessert: cheesecake from the Wolseley, vanilla ice-cream from Marine Ices, which comes in little packets, so you can drop them out a portion at a time. They look a bit like meringues. It's the best ice-cream in London, if not the world. Plus a selection of fruit salads. Afterwards liqueurs and coffee.

Geraldine was the perfect hostess. Dinah and Ruby masterful helpers. At the end of the meal I rose to say, 'I've not had such a distinguished group in the house since the bailiffs came. Now, Michael Caine. I've known you for 47 years. I've dined with you many times. You are a great host but I have consider the full dining experience . . .' and so on as I do in my TV show. Finally – 'Michael Caine, you will go home tonight [pause] with [bigger pause, then triumphantly] three Michael Winner Dining Stars.' Much applause. I screamed, 'Dinah!' and she entered with the stars. Michael was thrilled. He'd been saying to his wife, Shakira, that if his cooking was judged it would get three stars. He's put the award on his shelf at home next to his Oscars, Baftas and Golden Globe Awards. If I could find cooking anywhere in the country as good as Michael does it, and I mean does it, not just supervises, I'd be in heaven compared to some of the strange places I visited.

* * *

In this Friday's show I go to the Highlands of Scotland and to Essex. I just love Essex. Cheerful, bright people, great repartee. Natalie, my Essex-girl PA, is dieting. I asked, 'Have you read my diet book? She replied, 'I ate it.' For lunch I dropped in to **T & J Kelly's Pie & Mash** in Loughton. They offered pie, mash and liquor. The liquor isn't alcoholic, it's a green sauce made with corn flour and parsley. A sign said, 'Gravy now available.' Dinah pointed out the pastry was burnt on top and gooey and unfinished at the bottom. She said the potatoes had no taste. We left nearly everything. Even some eels. There was meant to be apple pie for dessert, but the owner, Bob Kelly, hadn't made any that day. So Dinah went and bought cakes and buns from a nearby shop. They were terrible beyond belief. Clammy, tasteless muck. Not a great dining experience.

* * *

The price of mini-fame is that occasionally you come across a really atrocious journalist. Such as Jenny Johnston of the *Daily Mail*. She greatly upset Dinah by making her look as if she was put upon and exploited when we've been friends for 30 years, 27 of which she's worked for me. Among the careless reporting was that in my cinema were photos of me and Muhammad Ali (never met him), that Dinah lived in my house (she doesn't) and that I nearly married Jane Seymour. I've never met Jane Seymour. It's comforting to know such lousy journalism still exists. Makes me look good.

By contrast a great writer is Charlie Brooker, who reviewed *Dining Stars* in the *Guardian*. He used a very rude word about me many times, but his piece was so funny that when I read it to Geraldine we had to stop again and again because we were crying with laughter. It was overall a good review, in which he said, 'Winner himself plays to the cameras with more knowing skill than anyone in his own films. It's fascinating. In the end I simply admitted defeat and started laughing at and with him.' I hope you do the same with Friday's episode. A TV executive called it 'the funniest hour of television I've ever seen'. Did he miss *Fawlty Towers* and *Some Mothers Do 'Ave 'Em*, I wonder?

* * *

Joke from the Ritz doorman Michael O'Dowdall: I called a pal. He said, 'I can't stop, I'm driving a Toyota.'

Winner speaks

On hearing piped music: 'Turn that din off, please.'

An honorary guest for every occasion

In Solihull, which may be part of Birmingham, the locals told me, when I asked what I should do, to go shopping. I hate shops, except small ones. I'm not even mad about those. The last time I went to a supermarket I was so incensed there were people in front me in the queue for the till, I left my trolley and walked out.

In Solihull, seen on *Michael Winner's Dining Stars* next Friday, I entered a shopping mall and blew up a teddy bear. Not with a nuclear weapon, on a machine. You speak into a little recording device, stick it in the bear and then blow it up with a foot pump. I'd recorded a romantic message to Geraldine inserted in a panda. The bear came out with hysterical calls for Dinah.

At one o'clock we ended up in **Bella Italia**, Unit 52 Touchwood Court, Mill Lane, Solihull, West Midlands B91 3GS. Put that in your satnav if you're planning to go for New Year's Eve. It's quite a jolly place, a poor imitation of a 1950s MGM movie Italian restaurant. Next to us was an 18th birthday party for Rachel Keating complete with balloons. I posed with them for the record – 'What record?' I hear you ask. Our waiter was Matthew Stein, a fey gentleman, not without charm.

Dean Martin sang, sang, and sang as we waited for Matthew to bring some garlic bread. It was six small baguettes with a lot of cheese on top. Dreadful. I couldn't eat more than a nibble. Joan, my make-up lady, said, 'It needs more garlic.' Dinah said, 'Mmm', trying to extract gooey cheese from her teeth. They quite liked it. I'd ordered 'linguine pasta with chicken, mushroom and red onions'. After a long wait, Matthew promised the main course 'in three minutes'. Nothing came. I said to Matthew, 'You told me 15 minutes ago the food would be here in three minutes and another 10 minutes have gone by.' 'You need a new watch,' responded

Matthew. 'I don't need a new watch, I need some food,' I said. 'Go and throttle the chef, Matthew. Pick him up and shake him.' 'Don't walk out, Michael,' pleaded Dinah. She's seen me throw a tantrum or 10. Matthew at last came with the food. 'See this watch which you maligned, Matthew?' I said, 'This a serious white gold Patek Philippe.' 'I believe you,' he said dismissively. My pasta wasn't bad. Dinah's tuna salad got her approval, as did Joan's risotto with roasted hot peppers. For dessert Matthew recommended the 'chocolato Napelano, smooth and creamy milk and white chocolate mousse layered upon a dark chocolate truffle base served with cream'. It was quite good.

They played Happy Birthday through loudspeakers, thus dumping my hero Dean Martin for a few seconds. Matthew came in with a cake. We got up and went back to grabbing people on the streets for robust conversation. As parodied by Harry Hill in his *TV Burp* programme last Saturday.

* * *

For the *MWDS* filmed in Blairgowrie I stayed at the **Ballathie House** hotel in Perth. My room had a great view of the River Tay and two fields, one with sheep, the other bales of hay. My lunchtime club sandwich was atrocious. I understood why the Reserve de Beaulieu, my regular August spot on the French Riviera, charges £50 for a club sandwich which is great, when this one, whatever it cost, wasn't worth eating. Dinah had local fresh salmon and seafood salad and declared it very good. My strawberry pavlova was okay. The shortbread biscuits were excellent, the bread roll dire. Breakfast came speedily but without a cup, saucer, or spoon. Luckily they were in the room with the instant coffee and kettle so I didn't have a fit.

* * *

I recently lunched at **Bibendum** in the Fulham Road, a superb restaurant. The food is simple, the room, in the old Michelin Building, one of the best in London. Comfortable, with marvellous acoustics. The senior sous-chef, Tam Storrar, was on. Couldn't tell the difference from their normal chef, Matthew Harris. The restaurant manager, Karim Mista, is excellent. Another of my favourite restaurants, the **River Café**, lost Rose Gray, its co-owner and chef. She died of cancer last week. Rose was a great, simple cook, a real lady. Her last public appearance was at my Winner's Dinners Awards. I'll miss her.

* * *

A joke: Mrs Cohen is caught shoplifting. The judge intones, 'You stole a packet of 12 asparagus sticks, so I sentence you to 12 days in jail.' Her husband, Hymie, says, 'Excuse me, my lord, she also stole two packs of peas.'

All very quiet on the Western Front

Kingsand, the location for Friday's *Michael Winner's Dining Stars*, is a beautiful coastal village in Cornwall. Fishing used to be its main occupation. Now there's only one fisherman left. He helped me judge the two final contestants before the winner cooked for a genuine celebrity dinner party in my house. So did a lovely 96-year-old lady who'd just finished her home-cooked lunch when I butted in, another man I picked up in a tiny supermarket, my ex-receptionist Zoe who lives nearby, a lady from a café, and the lady who cooks in Kingsand's **Devonport Inn**.

You think I'm picky, watch out for these locals. They were fantastic, clear, lucid, knowledgeable about food – all things I am not. They were also far more critical than I am. In my efforts to find people, I knocked on door after door. What had been village residences were now holiday homes. Hardly anyone about. James Hetreed, landlord and host of the Devonport Inn, has long white hair, a beard and a moustache, a gold necklace and wears a sort of black jerkin. When I asked James if the curry was bought in he stormed off and his wife, Vanda, appeared. 'How dare you say that? I'm deeply offended. You're stupid,' she said severely. Right in all directions, Vanda. She later joined me to judge the contestants' cooking.

Joan, my make-up lady, asked for a dry Sauvignon blanc. She got a screwtop bottle of Willow Glen Chardonnay. Dinah had some other screw-topped wine. 'From Chile,' advised Joan. Dinah lifted her cell phone and said, 'No signal. If I put it on the table it's got a reception of 3.' 'I'll have to lie on the table, then,' I responded. James looked like a 1960s disc jockey. He played a lot of 50s and 60s music. 'I'd like to hear the Best of Johnnie Ray,' I said. James put on 'Walking in Tthe Rain' sung by Johnny Ray, who had one of the greatest singing acts ever. I vaguely knew him. He's warbling in the clouds now. Vanda assured me her curry was not hot. 'If this isn't hot, I don't know what is,' I said. But it was perfectly good. The place had great atmosphere, old posters, the *Titanic*, the Guinness Toucan ads.

Next door was a café, the **Old Boat Store**, where I had the worst Cornish pasty ever. It came from a local bakery. By the time they'd reheated it the pastry was soggy. 'Actually revolting,' I dictated into my faithful tape recorder. To compensate I had a very good lemon cake made by the owner. In another pub two splendid local musicians were playing and in a sea-front café little vials of crumbs left over by famous people were displayed in plastic cones. The main attraction was a Prince of Wales leftover. A museum of the ridiculous. I like eccentricity.

* * *

As my TV series ends I appreciate your largely positive response. I was dopey to shoot my mouth off about how terrible the food was in the North. A number of restaurant owners there reminded me I'd given them a good review. The series producer, Mark Leslie, chose the music superbly. It was melodic, ironic and humorous. The director was good. I greatly liked him. But he had a nutty moment early on and later went bonkers during the editing, when he stormed out, slamming the door on three of the most important executives in television. Then he threatened to quit. If I'd done that I'd never have completed any movie. The greatest joy was getting to know ITV's top brass, meeting people in the street and dining with the contestants. From Hema in Solihull to Justine in Longridge, they were all terrific. Even a group in Scotland who became highly bizarre after a few tipples. This Friday you'll learn who won. It's not exactly an Academy Award but it made one family very happy. I've invited all the contestants to dinner at my house, travel expenses on me. They'll get the same spread Archie Norman, ITV's chairman, got, same as Michael Caine and the Lloyd Webbers. Will they give me any Dining Stars? Who cares? As long as they have fun.

* * *

I was at **McDonald's** in Wood Green, north-east London. Isn't everyone? I ate my first Big Mac in New Rochelle, New York, in 1983. Hated it. Tried again for Sir Trevor McDonald's TV show last year, hated that. Wood Lane's one reached new depths. Soggy bun, bland interior. Their tasteless fried chicken was crusted in unattractive, hard batter. The ice-cream and chips were good. The milkshake machine had broken down. Milkshakes are a prime item. Why can't they have two or three machines? If I was the

American McDonald's boss I'd fire the English chief.

* * *

I've just gone from £6 million in debt to £9 million in debt. As Tommy Cooper said, 'Just like that.' Three years ago, a reader, Edward Cullen, of Barclays Wealth, wrote saying if I needed another loan I should go to him. He persisted. Finally I thought, 'I'll give him a go.' Thus Barclays Wealth acquired a new customer and I got a stash of cash. Wonderful, innit?

Finally I come face to face with a big fan

I like alligators. They look nice, they're very tasty to eat. My knowledge of alligators stems largely from my visit to **Gator Park**, Florida. It's a touristy thing, but I'm glad I went. It involved a trip round the Everglades in a contraption that looked like a school project gone wrong. Some tacky vinyl seats, an enormous fan at the back, and our guide, named Tra, real name Arthur. Art (short for Arthur) spelt backwards is Tra. Geddit? A Russian girl, Elina, showed us to our private contraption and gave me, Geraldine and my friend Adam Kenwright some bottled water. To keep us going, I surmised, if we got lost, until help arrived. 'Are you coming with us?' I asked Elina. 'No,' she replied, 'especially not with this guy.' She pointed to Tra. 'Is he dangerous?' I asked. 'You'll see,' replied Elina. She wasn't kidding.

We floated placidly along a waterway with exotic bushes and trees both sides. Alligators bathed by the banks; white egrets, with long necks and enormous tail feathers, perched and flew. There were lily pads, large iguanas lounged on tree branches. It was idyllic. Then Tra said, 'Hold on.' 'Why's he saying that?' I wondered. We were only going at three miles an hour.

Suddenly everything changed. We lurched forward at 60 mph. The barge skidded and whirred round over the grass; Tra was showing off big time. I clung on to the seat in front as we side-swiped and twirled and roared off again. Health and safety would not have allowed this in England. I waved my hand for Tra to slow down. He said to Adam, 'What does he want?' 'He wants you to go faster,' said Adam. He calls that a sense of humour. It was like the James Bond Everglades chase which featured in one of the movies. Eventually we stopped in the middle of nowhere.

Tra turned from lunatic roadrunner to professor. Indicating the surrounding nature he said, 'They call it river grass because the Everglades is a slow-moving river.' He put his hand in the water and brought out some mud. He thought we needed to see mud. 'The Everglades are 55 miles by 120 miles long,' Tra continued. 'There's a million and a half crocodiles in the Glades. Further south there are alligators. If you take the bottom of the grass [Tra grabbed some] you can peel it and eat it. Each blade of glass is called a glade. You can also let it dry, grind it and get flour.' 'Is it gluten-free?' asked Geraldine. 'What we're sitting in is called an air boat,' added Tra. 'What would you like to do now?' Before I could answer he'd roared off again. I hung on for dear life. I could see the headlines: 'Winner drowned in one foot of Everglades mud.' I fooled 'em though. I lived.

* * *

My other adventures in Miami included a trip to dinner with Michael and Shakira Caine, hindered by the fact that our fat lady taxi driver appeared to be on another planet. I don't know what substance she was on, but the effect was mesmerising. She drove at breakneck speed, then realised she had no idea where she was going. She spoke to her controller in no known language, so now two people were messing up. Finally Adam demanded she pull into a hotel driveway for the doormen to tell us where the restaurant was. She still passed it twice.

It was one of Michael Caine's favourite Italian places, **Gabbiano**. My starter was snails and mushrooms, then porcini ravioli with a fantastic sauce, then what they called a chocolate soufflé but wasn't. It was a chocolate cake, soft in the middle. All excellent. My only advice is: go by bus.

I had lunch at the **Fontainebleau** hotel. This used to be very Jewish. I stayed there the odd night on movie reconnaissance trips when going from Los Angeles to the Caribbean. My friend Terry O'Neill's most famous photo, Sinatra, his stand-in and bodyguards, was taken on the boardwalk by the Fontainebleau. Now they've spent millions on the place. The food was dire. The tuna was horrible; they didn't have chopped liver, instead they produced some inferior foie gras; my spaghetti bolognese was mildly indifferent. The vanilla milkshake wasn't as good as the Wolseley's but not bad. The reasonably good cheesecake lacked finesse.

At **Jerry's Deli** on Collins Avenue the portions were gargantuan. My portion of chopped liver (at least they had some) was enough for six families, crude but okay, the pickled cucumbers severe and salty, the potato pancakes (called latkes) too greasy and not as crisp as they should have been. The grapefruit was fantastic, the water melon without pips had no taste at all. No point in removing pips if the result is that bland.

At **Mr Chow** in the oh-so-fashionable **W** hotel on South Beach the food was marvellous, ambience very buzzy, too noisy. Piped music made it worse. The owner, Michael Chow, was wearing a bright yellow suit. I mentioned that his sister, the actress Tsai Chin, had been in a film of mine. He said they didn't get on. Sounds like my family. Fact of the matter is I'm too good for them. On that cheery and modest note, farewell until next week.

It's perfect, so leave it alone

Andrea Scherz, owner/manager of the **Palace hotel** in Gstaad, depressed me. I was having a Cosmopolitan cocktail in their marvellous lounge. Massive picture windows looked on to snow and the mountains. A log fire. Leather sofas. Like a scene from an Agatha Christie play. On coming down in the morning I always expect to see the body of a newly murdered guest. Then wait to find out who dunnit. Until I was the only one left. So I musta dunnit. I fantasise because the reality of Mr Schertz's remark was so awful. He said casually, 'We're going to redesign the dining room.'

I've never known any hotel redesign improve on what was there before. Look at the Dorchester, Claridge's, the Connaught for scary examples. The dining room at the Palace is wonderful. Comfortable chairs, a dance floor with a six-piece string orchestra alternating with a band with brass and keyboards playing standards. 'Why change it?' I asked. 'People don't like eating in the outer room,' said Andrea. The outer room leads to the dining room. It doesn't have the same view of the dance floor and upper Italian restaurant. Guests feel isolated. 'Well, if you must,' I said, 'do that area quite differently. Decorate it with photos of the many famous people who've stayed here.' They've had everybody, some even more famous than me. The next day Andrea said, 'My father thought it might be considered vulgar to put up photos of our famous guests.' 'Vulgar?' I said in amazement. 'The Splendido in Portofino does it, so does La Reserve de Beaulieu. No one could call them vulgar. In spite of their displaying a photo of me.'

The Palace is triple superb because it's a real, old-style, grand hotel. The food is marvellous. Among things I ate were turbot with champagne sauce, grisons barley soup with dried beef, sole done in two different ways, great desserts. All immaculately served. The restaurant manager, Gildo Bocchini, is the best. The chef, Peter Wyss is outstanding. The food is simple, tasty, charming. Only dud was a spaghetti bolognese served in their Italian restaurant, **Gildo's**. It was the worst spaghetti Bolognese I've ever had. Spaghetti mushy, meat sauce turgid. Peter Wyss did one in the normal hotel area that was fantastic. The Italian one was by a supposedly good chef who did a winter stint there when his hotel in Italy was closed. Sitting on the Palace terrace in hot sun with eight feet of snow a few feet away is one of the delights of the world. Gstaad is unspoiled.

The food at Bernie Ecclestone's **Hotel Iden** is also very good, as it is at the Sonnenhof, perched on the mountain-side. It all looks as Switzerland should. Wooden chalets, fields, towering mountains. Please, Andrea, keep up the standard. If it ain't broke don't fix it. Forget the re-decoration. Unless my photo goes up, of course. I could give you a set of 20.

* * *

For years, out of habit, I used Forever Living products. Creams, toothpaste, assorted twaddle. They're not in shops, but sold through by people who take the order and supposedly see it's sent. The first salesman was useless, kept going away, never seemed to check his emails. I phoned head office. There, Hellen Priest, assured me she was very reliable and would see everything I ordered turned up speedily. I emailed an order later. Hellen was at a sales event. She said she'd be in her office on Monday, four days later, and deal with my order. On Monday she wasn't in the office, she wouldn't be back until Wednesday. I gave up and cancelled everything. My order, music, art, piano lessons, the will to live. These people are paid by twits like me buying product. There's masses of similar stuff on the market, better priced, efficiently distributed. Forever Living indeed. More like Forever Waiting.

* * *

PS: Boots have a couple of creams, No. 7 Protect and Perfect Beauty Serum and Simple Kind to Skin Replenishing rich moisturiser that topped the poll in major non-Boots surveys. Massively cheaper than Forever Expensive. I'm using them. Already I look five years younger. In two weeks I'll look 26 at most.

* * *

I had a spectacularly good lunch at **Mosimann's** in Belgravia, a club owned by the chef Anton Mosimann. The food was not over-complicated. Duck sausage, a marvellous ravioli, good bread and butter pudding. My host, Peter Wood, just bought esure from Barclays Bank. He told me so many people are making false claims, backed up by bent doctors and lawyers, that insurance prices will go sky high. Even more serious: Peter doesn't like the Winner dolls which have apparently passed various safety tests. I'm getting 100. Press my face and I say, 'Calm down, dear' endlessly. I'll give one, occasionally, to our best letter writer. Peter's considering a new commercial with me and my assistant Dinah May. He liked me shouting, 'Dinah!' in the TV show. 'Dinah! Get ready for your close-up, dear. You'll be a star.' If not, too bad. That's show business.

Man the barricades – I'm back in town

I first went to Chichester in July 1992 to see a play by Melvyn Bragg, now Lord Bragg of Braggsville. Jenny

Seagrove was in it. As I sat in her dressing room prior to the performance there were great yells, crashes and bangs on the wall from next door. 'That's John warming up,' explained Jenny. John was John Stride, once predicted to be the next Laurence Olivier. The play was a version of *King Lear* set in New York. It didn't work, showed promise. I said to Melvyn, 'You should persevere, work on it, get it right.' He ignored me. The work is dead, if not buried.

I stayed at **Amberley Castle** in nearby Arundel. I liked it then and I like it now. It's a genuine castle, built in 1103. An American bought it, filled it with armour, spears, jousting poles and various medieval weapons, then came back aged 95 in 2005 and said he regretted selling the place. The general manager, Oliver Smith, told me and Geraldine he'd been there 10 years. Geraldine said, 'You were 12 when you arrived then?' That cheered him up. He looked about 65 to me. Jokey-jokey, not really. More like 64. The fire in the sitting room wouldn't work because the top of the chimney had crumbled. In my house, built in 1870, we pay builders permanently to keep it from collapse.

With my champagne in the castle lounge I had the best canapés ever, a tartlet of homemade rhubarb chutney and a blue cheese Welsh rarebit served warm. The dining room is so posh the plates were designed by Versace. I had a fresh wild mushroom risotto croquette with sauce grabiche – a fried ball with risotto inside. Then maize-fed chicken breast 'poached and roasted', onion purée and spinach. For dessert, mango mousse, pink grapefruit and mint sorbet. There were various freebies of equal flashiness. All extremely good. The chef, James Dugan, is a force to be reckoned with. The lunch bill was £98 for two. Worth it.

The hotel has 19 rooms. If you're lucky you'll get one haunted by me. I'll appear in the night screaming, 'Calm down, dear, I'm only a ghost.' Outside they have white doves and a white peacock. The wine waiter said, 'We bought him a new girlfriend and he chased her away.' Geraldine advised, 'You should have bought him a boy.' If ever I go to Chichester again – I've been a few times to talk at their film festival – I'd definitely stay at Amberley Castle. It's special.

* * *

I'm always disappointed when someone I thought pleasant and sane turns into a twit. Philip Howard is co-owner and chef at **The Square**, a two-Michelin-star restaurant in Mayfair. I've praised him many times. He recently became a partner in **Kitchen W8**, an atrocious place that opened near me. Everything was ghastly, the food, the décor, the ambience, the service, capped by a restaurant manager who behaved like a lobotomised member of the Addams family. My review was not complimentary, although, again, I praised Philip for his culinary skills. When we sent out a flyer about my TV show to many of the people on my Christmas card list, Philip re-enveloped it, restamped it, folded it and sent it back with a hand-written message, 'Don't send me any communications from Michael Winner.' Petty Philip. Silly Philip. Pathetic Philip. Why do some chefs think that anyone who criticises them, or even criticises a distant cousin, should be put down or banned? Would a theatre or film critic be subjected to such silly tantrums? But then most chefs are insecure neurotics. That's putting it kindly.

* * *

PS: Fay Maschler, doyenne of food critics, didn't like Kitchen W8 much either. I wonder if Philip sends her mail back.

* * *

From the ridiculous to the ridiculous. I was recommended the very expensive **Auberge du Père Bise** on Lake Geneva. Never in my decades of booking into top hotels, and well below top hotels, have I met such incompetence. Madame Bise, who runs it, was too grand to get involved. Confusion, confusion, all was confusion. The receptionists seemed to change daily. Other days a recording announced the hotel was closed. We were asked to send copy driving licences, passports, credit cards, toeprints, thumbnails. The final straw was a letter from Marianne in reception 'for rent the car the woman tell me it is necessary to call us for make a reservation and see directly with them'. She gave the car rental phone number. When I called, the lady said she only wanted to be sure I was at the hotel to receive the car. She'd received none of the items we'd faxed to the hotel for her. Why does a hotel dealing with international guests employ a receptionist who can't speak English? Marianne's letter ended, 'I make a maximum for you.' Maximum inconvenience. I cancelled my reservation. Guess where I went instead? Major (well, minor) prize if you can.

In the meantime, please, make a note to watch next Saturday's *Piers Morgan's Life Stories*. It's me being greatly revealed. We're very funny together. Laugh? You'll think you'd never start.

Winner speaks

On having to hold on the phone listening to music whilst phoning a restaurant: 'If I want a concert I'll go to the Albert Hall.'

Arriving in style to find a hidden gem

They say there's no such thing as a free lunch. I don't take 'em so I wouldn't know. But there's no such thing as a free car ride. I decided to do a Jeremy Clarkson and test a car. Not drive it. Not find out if it takes half a second to get from 0 to 163 miles an hour and similar weird information. Just sit in it.

So a Bentley Flying Spur Speed, £175,800 on the road, took me to Oundle for my one-man show. You might think, if you were getting a car to write about, the Bentley PR department who provided it would send details of what car it was and some specifications. I only got those later, after asking twice. You might think they'd give you the name and mobile phone number of their driver. They did. Both wrong. It was said the idiot of the family went into the church. Now the idiot of the family goes into PR. After all, David Cameron was once PR for Michael Green's TV company Carlton Communications.

The Bentley turned up a bit late. The driver explained traffic was heavy. What do people expect when they drive on roads? No traffic? I'm never late because I allow for traffic being greater than normal. As proud owner of a 1975 Bentley I have to admit the 2010 version is sleeker, fantastic road holding, very comfortable and rakish in the appealing way the old Bentleys used to be. The seats were off-white leather, a lot of the rest was black carbon fibre or black leather. It's the perfect car for a very rich young man. Not for a childish retard who's £9 million in debt. If you win the lottery – get a Bentley Flying Spur Speed. Call Jeremy Clarkson to tell you about the technical side.

We drove to the **Falcon Inn**, Fotheringhay, Northhamptonshire. Log fire burning. On the blackboard: 'Fresh orange juice.' I asked Sally Facer, the owner, 'Was that squeezed here this morning?' She replied, 'No. It was squeezed up the road, yesterday.' 'That's not fresh. Sally,' I said, 'Fresh is squeezed when the customer orders it.' Oranges were found in the kitchen. Things brightened. The friendly manager, Dee Chambers, led us to an atrium extension. Faced with dreaded Hildon water I chose Fotheringhay tap. Far superior. It's a very elegant pub.

The bread was exemplary, hot, just out of the oven. I've never eaten better. My rabbit rillette was truly historic. Soft, tasty, fresh, great texture, marvellous chutney. My grilled plaice was thick, juicy, hot. No nicer fish could you possibly want. The pressed chocolate cake with burnt caramel ice-cream was appalling. I switched to the pannetone bread and butter pudding with Seville orange marmalade and ice-cream. That was great. This place is a find.

Fotheringhay is a lovely village, birthplace of King Richard III and where Mary Queen of Scots was beheaded after being locked up for 12 years in Fotheringhay Castle. Historic, you see, in more senses than one.

* * *

Every bit as important as the food are the restaurant staff who supposedly look after you. Hospitality, that much misused word, is sometimes present, frequently not. At the Falcon Inn the good cheer and professionalism of the ladies Facer and Chambers were exemplary. They dealt with everything from reservation to service with immense charm. More than I can say for Jose Torres, assistant restaurant manager at **Le Caprice**. When I phoned to book a specific table he told me it wasn't available and the restaurant was fully booked. So I reserved elsewhere. Then he rang back to say the restaurant wasn't fully booked and I could have the table I wanted. I was already committed to the **River Café**. Best staff in town. Vashti Armit, a perfect manager, my waitress, Melanie Rizzo, smiley and highly efficient. Not like

Kieron Terry at The **Ivy Club**, I find him pompous and unhelpful. Pity, because in general Le Caprice and Ivy staff are superb. I greatly like both places.

* * *

I hope you're coming to the **Belvedere** in Holland Park to dine with me on 11 May. It's a marvellous room in what was part of a Jacobean mansion. If you turn up Melbury Road to get there you'll see my house floodlit with 168 exterior bulbs. Great to deter burglars. Then you'll be greeted by me, my adorable fiancée, Geraldine (I'm trying to persuade her to do a tap dance for you), and the editor of the *Sunday Times*, John Witherow. The room is decorated with millions of pounds' worth of artwork by Damien Hirst and Andy Warhol, part of the owner's private collection. Parking is adjacent and free. The surrounding park is the best in London. I shall be imparting words of wit and wisdom (briefly so as not to upset the chef, Gary O'Sullivan) before dinner. Over coffee I'll perform a potted version of my one-man show and take questions, however saucy. The whole caboodle, pre-dinner champagne and canapés, a signed copy of my *Winner's Dinners* book, a three-course meal chosen by me with wines to match is £150 a head. Call 0844 4122953 to book. I greatly look forward to meeting you.

Some alligator, please . . . and make it snappy

It was Christmas night in the workhouse/and the paupers was having their dinners/and the preacher called from the top of the hall/'Get down on your knees you sinners.' I'm not sure who wrote that, although a number of rock bands have recorded it.

My mind turned to it when thinking of December and January in Miami. The Arctic would have been sunbathing weather by comparison. Unable to lie on my lounger (my main holiday occupation) I rented a large boat for a trip to Fort Lauderdale. The crew was a captain and two young girls who could have come straight from *Playboy*. They were very efficient. The passengers were me, Geraldine, Sir Michael Caine and his daughter Natasha. Michael and I look like a couple of old tarts freezing to death on a bench in Frinton-on-Sea. Actually, I look like an old tart. Michael looks like a distinguished knight of the realm freezing to death in Frinton-on-Sea. The superb Setai hotel manager, Hans Meier, had booked a restaurant but we decided it was taking too long to get there. 'Let's just stop and find somewhere ourselves,' suggested Michael. By now I was going bright blue and my fingers were dropping off. 'Good idea,' I whispered in a feeble voice.

We landed in a little harbour and headed for the **15th Street Fisheries Dockside Café** in Fort Lauderdale, Florida. The menu offered Louisiana Bayou fried alligator, saying, 'It tastes like a cross between chicken and pork, be adventurous – it's great!' We sat on bench seats at a wooden table. I ordered clam chowder and fried alligator. The alligator came within seconds of the soup. The quickest service ever. I said to Michael, 'Try a bit of alligator.' 'I'll be sick,' he said. I dictated into my tape, 'It's very good, there's some dark meat alligator and some light meat. The dark meat is a little more chewy.' Michael said, 'I may throw up just listening to this.' I gave Natasha a small piece of alligator. She said, 'It's just like chicken.' She only took a very tiny piece of a tiny piece. 'I'm eating my fish,' she explained. The excellent chips were made on the premises. The alligator batter was light and top class. To follow I ordered Key lime pie. They had that and a strawberry cheesecake, both done in their kitchen. I liked the Key lime pie. I said to Michael, 'What do you think?' He replied, 'I don't know. I don't even like them. Shakira goes nuts for Key lime pie.' Good for her, I thought. Shakira stayed in the apartment with her mother. Geraldine had blackened fish. 'They call it black in case they burn it,' explained Michael.

Outside, people were feeding huge tarpon fish. It was a thoroughly pleasant experience. All UK restaurateurs should get out with nets, hammers, shotguns, anti-tank missiles and grab alligators. They're a delicacy.

* * *

Back in London, a horrid lunch at **Scalini**. This Knightsbridge Italian is always noisy and overcrowded but the food and management can be good. So why did I receive the worst spaghetti bolognese of all time? It was stringy, thin and hard. The so-called bolognese was like ghastly gravy. The restaurant manager, Valerio, realised this, I think, because he also gave me a plate of meatballs. A strange group sat at the next table, usually reserved for regulars. When Valerio told them they were at the wrong table and offered one next to it, the host snarled. Valerio crumbled. I like to see a manager manage, to feel there's someone in control. That lunch showed quality control was having a day off. I'll have a few days off Scalini. If not months. Maybe years.

The next day I went to **Timo**, in Kensington High Street. Their spaghetti bolognese was immaculate, the real thing. The mozzarella and cherry tomatoes were fresh. The Parmesan squares on the table at Scalini had a 'hanging round forever' taste and texture. At Timo there was space, no overcrowded tables an inch away. The owner, Piero Amadio, could teach Scalini a thing or two, if he was so minded. Which I'm sure he isn't.

* * *

When the **Wolseley** (my favourite venue) first offered chopped liver and treacle tart they were grotesque. Being clever, they got them right. Now they're serving tzimmes, a Viennese dish. It's not brilliant. Lucian Grainge, CBE, tzimmes expert and head of Universal Music, agreed. Tzimmes involves carrots, sweet potatoes, pitted prunes, honey, orange juice, salt, cinnamon. Carrots should be sliced into 'coins' or small squares. They should be soft, but not too soft. Combined with the other ingredients they can produce fantastic flavours. The Wolseley tzimmes lacks taste. The carrots are too solid. I'm sure the chef will perfect it. It's one of my favourites.

* * *

On Sunday 2 May, following a sell-out tour of the UK, America, southern Silesia and Balham, my hilarious one-man show plays at the distinguished King's Head Theatre in Islington. Phone 0844 2090326 to book for the chance of a lifetime.

There were these three Jewish guys in a bakery . . .

A line of dialogue offered in New York on the first day of *The Sentinel*, a cult horror movie, impressed me greatly. My young assistant, whose job was to carry cigars, matches, script, get coffee, etc., greeted me at 7am with, 'How do you feel about bagels, sir?' 'Like them,' I replied. My assistant had a much-loved bagel place near his residence. He brought me some each morning.

I can't say bagels have featured prominently in my life since, nor can I recall why I was in the **Brick Lane Beigel**

Bake one lunchtime. They spell beigel differently to the New York way. Two doors away was the Hot Beigel Shop. Wasn't there a famous song, 'You say bagel and I say beigel . . .'? Brick Lane, in London's East End, used to be very Jewish. Now it's mainly Indian. It's electric on a market Sunday. Marvellous confusion. Litter everywhere. Dress shops, furniture on offer in the street, two drifters selling cacti. Inside the Beigel Bake on the left there's a counter on which to rest your food, on the right a serving counter. Beigels abound filled with smoked salmon, salami, chopped herring, salt beef.

Three owners, Amnon Cohen, Asher Cohen and Shalom Minzley, started it in 1979. Amnon was in charge. He took me into the bakery behind the counter. Very complicated. The dough is boiled first, grilled, then goes into an oven for 20 minutes, then goes on to a board, then the beigels get turned, then back in the oven for 20 minutes, then put on a tray. I've probably got everything wrong. So what? You're not going into beigel manufacturing. However they make 'em, they sell 700 beigels a day.

The cacti seller men from outside were now sitting at the back of the shop offering two fine cacti for £15. That's before negotiation. One said to me, 'You can say you were talking to an Irish Nigerian.' His mate said, 'I'm a Scottish one.' People kept coming over to have their photograph taken with me. It's not just autographs now, it's photos on cell phones as well.

I tried a salt beef beigel. Geraldine said, 'The salt beef is dry,' She wasn't even eating it. 'It's not dry,' I said. 'Looks it,' said Geraldine. Then she tried it and said, 'Yeah, okay.' They had big éclairs. The one I tried was heavy, not the best. Then I got a Swiss roll. 'Very creamy,' I said to Geraldine. 'How do you eat that? It's all cream.' 'Just shove it in your mouth,' she suggested. It was very good. 'Try a cheesecake,' said Geraldine. She wants to blow me up, I thought. The cheesecake wasn't very tasty.

I went back into the bakery to get Amnon for his photo. The beigels were now floating around in water and he was scooping them with a fish slice. Probably a great art to that. Then they went on to a board and were cooled down with water spray. An enormous urn was going round, turning over the beigel dough. 'I know you're a big star in beigel-world, Amnon,' I said, 'but I need you for a photo.' Fiona, a lovely, blonde Irish lady who served us, took over laying out the beigels. Amnon wouldn't take any money so I whizzed back in and gave Fiona £60 for the staff. As I got to my car a man came up and said, 'I'm trying to sell the *Big Issue* but I'm not doing very well.'

* * *

Following a recent ghastly lunch at **Scalini**, we revisited **San Lorenzo**. This has lasted over 40 years with a standard which I find remarkable. Sadly Maria Berni, hostess with the mostest, is too unwell to attend. This leaves a gaping hole in the ambience. But it's still first rate. Our table had marvellous crudités on it, very freshly broken pieces from a superb Parmesan, quite unlike the stale-tasting little squares at Scalini, which had the feel of being bought in. The pasta with bolognese sauce was memorable. The chocolate ice-cream stupendous. San Lorenzo's unsung hero is chef Gino Gianelli. He's been there 30 years. The restaurant manager, Giancarlo Saba, looks lugubrious, but is a great professional. I shall return.

* * *

I'm told the *Sunday Times* 11 May **Belvedere** Dinner with Winner is sold out. I never believe anything, so phone 0844 4122953 in case of a cancellation. Adding to the cornucopia of things on offer, I'll personally give diners a signed copy of my best-selling autobiography and a surprise biggie – a raffle for three Winner talking dolls. Should be more but Peter Wood, boss of esure, has gone completely nuts. He's destroyed, dunaway with, demolished, extinctified 4,750 Winner dolls. He didn't like them. The world is now denied this artistic masterpiece. I got 100 before the axe fell. His publicity boss, a bright man called Chris Bowden, purloined another 100. Roger Moore has six, Michael Caine one. Henry Wyndham, Chairman of Sotheby's, three. The rubbish dump 4,750. Who says life is fair? Here's how to make it fairer. If you can't get to the Winner-Dinner (or even if you can) call the King's Head Theatre in Islington on 0844 2090326 to book for my unexpurgated, very funny one-man show, 7.30pm on 2 May.

Not my choice of lifestyle, but a great destination

When I told people I'd abandoned the Auberge du Père Bise after their incompetent reservation procedures, and was going to Dubrovnik, they asked 'Why?' The charming PR lady of the **Excelsior** hotel, Nikolina Vicelic, said, 'We want to make Dubrovnik a lifestyle destination.' No chance, dear. But it was a marvellous place, I had a great time. The old town is large, unspoiled. In spite of being warned of dreadful food I had a historic meal in Dubrovnik and two outside. Plus some shockers.

The Excelsior does not personify top-class luxury. It's practical. The dining room seats 600 people, there are conference rooms, one for 500 delegates, it does a lot of Irish and Spanish weddings. It's a typical communist blob built in 1970. My Dubrovnik guide said, 'It looks like a fist in the eye. When the Serbs shelled Dubrovnik we all hoped they'd demolish the Excelsior.' If they had, another monstrosity would have risen in its place. Our suite was superb. Enormous, nicely furnished, with a vast terrace and a stunning view of sea and the old town. The hotel interior is well designed in a practical way. A lot of fine rugs enliven the marble floors. A great thing about Croatia is the people. They're immensely pleasant, smiling, willing. The fact that the coffee was cold every morning, the croissants and breads inferior, the jams horrendous is kind of incidental. The bathroom was so complex you needed a 100-page instruction book. The bath water never left. The taps resembled bollards with knobs on, the shower a spaceship. Simplicity was not rampant.

There's a fantastic dining terrace where I had my first (and only) hotel lunch. Two cut-up pieces of John Dory fish, one so salty it was practically inedible, the other overcooked and dry. I ate one dinner at their sushi restaurant. My soup was watery, the fish heavy, the desserts on both occasions okay, but surrounded by cheap catering cream from a plastic container. A lifestyle experience? Not exactly. Strangely the bread I ate at lunch was warm and wonderful. At dinner it was like rubber. I tried to pull it apart and it stretched endlessly. Geraldine thought her sushi was superb.

In the suite the TV channels didn't correspond to the printed list. There was no instruction how to work the safe. The concierge said, 'Your room key opens the safe.' Why not tell us in advance? The room key is knocked off in plastic at the desk. So the safety element of a code or lock combination, which you normally choose, is gone. In spite of these few (okay many) quibbles I enjoyed myself. The hotel owner, Goran Strok, and his wife, Renata, were supremely hospitable. They showed us round. If they didn't the delightful hotel manager, Jasna Durkovic and the PR Nikolina did. I suggest you visit Dubrovnik before it goes. New buildings are raising their hideous heads. It'll look like the Costa Brava soon. Now it has great atmosphere and architectural beauty beyond belief.

We had a terrific meal in **Nautika** by the walls of the old town. It's owned by a jolly local, Mato Djuvoric. The marinated scampi with goat's cheese were incredible, fresh from the Adriatic. The medallions of young veal, Prosecco, sweet raisin and white wine sauce with a mousse of peas and potato cone – magnificent. Like the castle on a rock, rising from the sea, where Daniel Day-Lewis performed *Hamlet*. My dessert was Skoropa, described as cream cake with butter, eggs, almonds and lemon zest. Another triumph.

To unbalance that I had one of the worst meals ever in **Gil's**, a ghastly restaurant owned by a Russian and run by Gilles Camilleri, a surly, arrogant, inhospitable ghoul. There's a phrase 'everything but the kitchen sink'. This dump was so appallingly over-decorated the kitchen sink, metaphorically, was ever present. To add to the horror, they played discotheque music, loudly. I had tasteless cod with tagine. 'Nothing in it to light you up,' I dictated. Renata Strok had John Dory with pork. Big clumsy bits of both. Ridiculous. My starter was 'buratta cheese, beetroot, ginger apple, watermelon granite.' The waiter said, 'Be sure to eat all of it together'. Later, faced with an equally miserable dessert, 'Gil's cube, light, milky ganache in an emulsion of lime of violets', the waiter instructed, 'Start at the top and work your way down.' I dictated, 'Thank you very much. It's my plate of food. I bought it. I can eat it how I bloody well like.' The Gil's experience was horrific. See Dubrovnik. Avoid Gil's.

* * *

At a Dubrovnik cashpoint I tried to withdraw 2,000 krone (£270) on my Amex gold card. 'Transaction refused.' When asked, Raymond Joabar, UK boss of Amex, who'd personally arranged the facility, said my maximum withdrawal was £200 a week. I spend some £300,000 a year with Amex. Why wasn't I told of this ludicrous restriction before? Mr Joabar explained if I went from gold card to platinum I could withdraw £285 a week. But that would cost £300 a year. The words 'Bloomin' liberty' come to mind.

Chef's table? Don't lead me up the garden path

I hate chef's tables. That's where you're seated in some gloomy room that wouldn't be good enough to store dead cats. Even worse, you're faced with screens exhibiting kitchen staff at work. Who needs that?

I was shown the most ghastly chef's table ever at an otherwise splendid hotel, Lewtrenchard Manor in Devon. Jason Hornbuckle, chef and general manager of this beautiful Jacobean mansion, pointed with pride to a long, narrow table facing three TV screens. You could only talk to people on your immediate left and right. Mr Hornbuckle intended to tell us, from his personal TV, what we were being served. Please, just shut up, Jason, stay in the kitchen and dish it out. Preferably at great speed. This, to his credit, is what he did.

Re-seated in a marvellous panelled room with leaded windows, the set dinner flowed like a torrent. Artichoke with sautéed scallops, sea bass with curry, venison with liquorice sauce, rhubarb fool, hot chocolate tart, coffee and homemade fudge, all came at the speed of an express train. Possibly influenced by my presence and that of the hotel's owner, Andrew Davis. Mr Davis specialises in country house hotels. They remain extremely un-centralised. Each has real, welcoming character, an individual atmosphere. Unfortunately, the bread, which I was assured was made every day, didn't get to me. Neither did the water. 'They didn't serve me the water, now they're not serving me bread,' I complained. Andrew said, 'Geraldine needs a Nobel Prize. I'm going to model myself on you in future.' His assistant Sarah remarked, 'He'll never complain about me again.' Andrew, the most politically incorrect person ever, does a double act with the prim Sarah that is hilarious. They'd have been a wow closing the first half of the variety bill at the old Chiswick Empire. In an hour we'd had six triumphant courses, the only dud being a caramelised orange and cardamom ice-cream. Geraldine loved it. Andrew and I had ours replaced with vanilla. I don't think chefs should be too clever with ice-cream.

Andrew, who has dozens of hotels, including Cliveden, Sharrow Bay and the magnificent Château de Bagnols near Lyons, started out as a property developer, converting old mansions into flats. He bought the Mount Somerset hotel in Devon, went there to close it and the phone rang. It was the Yves St Laurent company booking a large group in for £20,000. Andrew thought: I'll have the £20,000 and keep it open another week. Thus he got into hotels and thus I fled from the chef's table in a room absurdly named the Purple Carrot. I was told a scrap-metal dealer took my place when I declined. 'Just the sort of person who should be there,' I commented with disgraceful snobbery.

* * *

I just managed to reach Nice recently, after the Icelandic ash fiasco. Planes were grounded. Now we learn the ash was never more than 20 per cent of the real danger level. I congratulate Wee Willie Walsh, the British Airways chief, for annihilating the credibility of the Met Office and other 'experts' by flying into the ash with no bad results. I was desperately trying to get to the Côte d'Azur by Eurostar with the help of their charming PR lady, Lesley Retallack. First to Paris, then a flight to Nice or on the TGV fast train, just before Willie proved the skies were safe. Thanks to him my private jet could perform. The public were denied the delight of travelling with me. You'll be glad to learn Nice airport has a posh new reception area for private jet passengers. They were putting down a red carpet. Not, amazingly, for me, but for some nob who was going to open it.

We stayed at the magical **La Colombe d'Or** in Saint-Paul de Vence, a walled medieval village on a hilltop. Picasso, Braque, Bonnard and other famous Impressionists left examples of their work to pay for food. In the dining room hang some £75m of paintings. The expressive Danielle Roux, who owns the place with her husband, François, was being quizzed on the phone by a prospective guest. 'What size is the room? What's in it?' Eventually she said testily, 'This isn't a Hilton, it's an antique hotel.'

The prices are antique, they're so low. The three course set lunch, as good a meal as you'll get, is 30 euros (£26). For dinner with a cheese course added it's incredible value at 35 euros. The chef, Hervé Roy, and the highly efficient restaurant manager Filippo Donata, have been there 23 years. It shows.

We had the best bouillabaisse ever at **Tétou**, in a hut facing the sea in Golfe-Juan. One portion of fish soup with white fish and half a lobster costs 124 euros (£108). They only take cash. I never have enough. Currently I owe them 79 euros. I'll pay when I go again this summer.

* * *

PS: I told you of my amazement at finding I could only draw £200 cash a week on my Gold Amex card. On my Coutts Gold Mastercard – used massively less than my Amex – I can draw not £200 a week, but £1,000 a day. That might just cover lunch for two at Tétou.

Winner speaks

On not getting service, when someone eventually turns up: 'Are the staff on strike today?'

A fling with Zing rekindles my love of Indian food

I waved goodbye to the **Bombay Brasserie** because my staff Christmas dinner was mishandled and the food was poor, as I'd found it to be earlier. The general manager, Arun Harnal, isn't up to much either. Nor is the redesign of the restaurant. My ex-receptionist Zoe had a lovely coat. When she went to get it they'd given it to someone else. Mr Harnal apologised and paid for a replacement. But Zoe had to leave in the cold, find a new coat and be highly inconvenienced. A bunch of flowers for fifty quid wouldn't have been inappropriate. Nor would her meal being removed from my bill. Mr Harnal did none of that. Although, later, when I wrote about it, he suddenly offered freebies galore. Not accepted. Instead I sought advice from *Sunday Times* readers.

Peter Willsher, Jonathan Robinson and Richard Price recommended **Indian Zing** in King Street, Hammersmith. Geraldine and I dropped in for Saturday lunch. Place was empty. Not a good sign. All changed. It's amazing. The greatest Indian food I've ever eaten. Don't take it from me (although why not?). When I took Shakira Caine (she's Indian, in case you didn't know) and her husband, Sir

Michael (he's not Indian, in case you didn't know) they were equally ecstatic. Shakira declared it best ever and she knows. She cooks that type of nosh. The owner-chef, Manoj Vasaika, blends flavours and tastes and textures like a genius artist. Everything is perfect. The décor is simple and welcoming. They have a menu headed 'Relaxed weekend lunch, £12 for two courses, £15 for three courses'. Only downer is Hildon water. Awful.

I had, in no particular order, onion bhaji, a vegetable bhanavai 'first baked and then griddled in the authentic Maharashtrian way', green peppercorn Malai tikka (that's chicken cooked in a clay oven), lamb Rogan josh 'cooked in a traditional Awadh way with a unique flavour of rogan (tinged flavoured and spiced oil) and josh a strong punch of knuckle juice and marrow'. I nicked some of Geraldine's Karwari fish curry, lemon and ginger rice, unbelievably good poppadoms and chapattis, saffron-flavoured rice, tandoori scallops with onion and tomato relish . . . I could go on. I dictated, 'Everything is beyond belief tender, effective, sensational blend of whatever he's blending.' Geraldine kept muttering, 'Incredible.' Indian desserts are usually terrible. I had a splendid organic multi-seeded bread and butter pudding and a sweet lassi.

Later I took Michael and Shakira Caine. Can't remember what we had but it was all fantastic. This place is more than a find, it's an Aladdin's cave of taste-bud enlightenment. Before she died Rose Gray, co-boss of the River Café, used to get takeaway from here. I'm not sure they do that massively, but Shakira was definitely planning to have some. It's near enough my house that I can go and eat it straight from Manoj's kitchen. It was most efficiently served by the restaurant manager, Rahul Kulkarni. Eat your heart out, Bombay Brasserie. This is Indian food as it should be.

* * *

Good news: Richard Caring's Ivy-Caprice-Scott's group of restaurants is abandoning Tufa water in favour of Malvern. Malvern and Evian are the best. Tufa, Hildon and Blenheim the worst.

I had a superb lunch in **Le Caprice** the other day. It was full of Saturday boys. That's a marvellous phrase I've just learnt to describe Jewish men. Because they go (in theory) to synagogue on Saturday. My friend, hotelier Andrew Davis, said, 'I can do business with him, he's a Saturday boy.' Thus I was educated.

I also ate very well at **Scott's** in Mayfair. Lovely group there: Eric Clapton, Terry O'Neill, Bernie Ecclestone, Michael and Shakira Caine, Joan Collins, Carol Vorderman, Andrew Neil. Scott's is a favourite of mine. This visit was unique. I ordered a starter and a main course. I got them. But neither was what I ordered. I asked for seafood cocktail to start and got asparagus. I ordered a risotto to follow and got seafood cocktail. They were both so good I didn't even mention it. Joan Collins ordered a Cosmopolitan cocktail, got something entirely different. Not important.

There's always a rare day when even excellent staff make a bit of a mess. Happened at the **River Café** when I ordered salmon and the restaurant manager, Charles Pullan, who'd taken the order, brought lamb. A way round this is for me to order things I don't want on the basis that I'll probably get something else.

* * *

Winner's Dinners at the **Belvedere** was massively over-booked as was my one-man show at the King's Head Theatre a week earlier. I met 96 charming and interesting readers. Introducing the meal I said, 'I asked the chef Gary O'Sullivan what he could do. That produced a 20-minute silence finally broken by the words 'Beans on toast.' You'll have to stretch a bit beyond that, Gary, I responded.' He did, superbly.

* * *

PS: I'm on TV's QVC next Friday at 1am and 1pm flogging signed copies of my Winner's Dinners *and* Fat Pig Diet *books for an amazing price: two books inc. p&p for £17.88. Should be a laugh.*

A hissy fit followed by an island of tranquillity

You'll find this hard to believe, but occasionally I throw a tantrumette. She (that's me) stamps her little feet and flounces about something terrible. It's a right performance. Varda, varda.

A recent flappette was in Dubrovnik. The object of my displeasure was a marvellous man, Goran Strok, who owns three big hotels there. The schedule provided listed a visit to his **Dubrovnik Palace** hotel. 'Why should I want to see that?' I demanded of Nikolina Vicelic, his excellent PR lady. 'I don't want new buildings, I've come to see old Dubrovnik.' In a moment of stupidity when Mr Strok said, 'I'm taking you on a boat trip, my Palace hotel is on the way, would you drop in for coffee?' I agreed. So there I was in a car with Geraldine and Nikolina, travelling through boring Dubrovnik streets. 'It seems a long way to the boat,' I remarked. 'We're going to the Dubrovnik Palace,' explained Nikolina. 'But,' I protested, 'I didn't want to go there.' 'Mr Strok wants you to,' said Nikolina. I became all a-tremble. 'I will not enter the place,' I said, tantrumette building. 'I'm paying my way, this is a holiday not a hotel inspection. How dare he do this to me?' 'It'll only be for a moment,' said Nikolina. 'I won't even get out of the car,' I said, now in full floodette. 'You get him and we'll go to the boat.'

When we reached the hotel I was in such a state I rushed out. So did Nikolina. Mr Strok came toward me, smiling in the vast lobby. 'How dare you drag me here?' I yelled. 'You know I didn't want to come. I've been driven forever through rubbish. I'm getting straight back into the car.' Nikolina followed, giggling like a schoolgirl. 'Did you see his face?' she asked. 'I'll never forget his expression when you shouted.'

We proceeded to Goran's boat. When things had calmed down, he said, 'But you agreed to drop in for coffee.' 'You said it was on the way to your boat,' I responded pleasantly. 'It may have been on the way to Alaska. It certainly wasn't on the way to your boat.' Massive credit to Goran Strok that he remained a perfect host. With his wife, Renata, we set off for the islands around Dubrovnik. These are marvellous beyond belief. Untouched. Just a few old buildings, hardly any population. 'Oh dear,' I thought when Goran pointed out one on which he was to build a hotel. Having been a racing driver, Goran was obsessed with speed. 'We're doing 45 knots,' he announced. 'Look at the water rising from the propeller.' At the back a great spray. Who cares? We reached Sipan Island. Extraordinary. Wonderful old houses, peaceful, hardly any people. Soon it will be tarted up by millionaires. Now it's bliss.

We pulled into the village of Sipanska Luka. Sitting outside in the sun, the owner of restaurant **More**, Baldo Svijtkovic, served focaccia and bread with pumpkin seeds, both warm from the oven. Best I've ever tasted. Then a very light cheese with garlic. Great olive oil. I dictated, 'I've got like an octopus hamburger now, freshly fried, soft, it's historic beyond belief.' With it was wild asparagus picked on the island and hard-boiled eggs. Exquisite. Then came gregada, a fish stew which they cook for three hours. The fish was all local –

gregada grouper, lobster, a fish they call red devil, sliced potatoes. The taste of the fish soup was incredible. To end, a yellow sponge cake with icing and another with almonds and walnuts. I've never had a better meal.

The chef is a young man called Vatroslav Sevlina. He's one of 400 people living on this island. Never mind yer Gordon Ramsays and yer Heston Blumenthals. Vatroslav knocks them all into a tin can. If you're in Dubrovnik, rent, steal or borrow a boat and go to restaurant More on Sipan Island. Whatever it costs to get there, it's worth it.

* * *

From sublime to ridiculous – **Gil's** restaurant, Dubrovnik. I wrote it was ghastly beyond belief. Its manager Gilles Camilleri responded, 'At your age I understand you had difficulty distinguishing the genre of music playing.' I said annoying, intrusive discotheque. Gilles calls it Buddha bar lounge music. That's a joke. He says I was arrogant asking for it to be turned off as other people might have liked it. When I asked there were no other diners there at all. It was turned down. Very few people came in anyway. Gilles (surprisingly) objects to my calling him surly and inhospitable. Exactly what my dinner companion, local hotelier Goran Strok, thought. 'My three hotels must give him many clients,' said Goran. 'He hardly even bothered to greet me.' Gilles says I shouldn't have objected to his waiter telling me precisely how to eat my meal because, 'It is commonplace in restaurants so the client may experience the full flavour of the dish.' Flavour? I didn't notice any. What planet is this man from? I've been going to top-class restaurants for decades. No waiter ever told me how to eat the food. You must go to very strange places Gilles, None more bizarre than your own.

Feed me, Ramsay, and I'll forgive you anything

Poor old Gord. Had a bit of a caning recently. Restaurants collapsing or being given up. Two outlets chucked out of the Berkeley. Announced he had to sell his Ferrari to pay the debts. 'That's a laugh, Gordon,' I said when we met. 'I had a Ferrari. If you get £5.80 for a second-hand one it's a result.' 'I bought a new one,' said Gordon. 'That's why I got rid of the other.' Long may Ramsay be rich enough to do that. He never stops insulting me in public, but I like him.

So I felt it appropriate to visit his new London gaff, **Petrus** in Belgravia. I arrived with my assistant Dinah, who was to take our photo. We sat on red banquettes in a little bar. I asked for champagne and orange juice for me, champagne for Dinah. The only thing that arrived was a glass of orange juice for me. I pointed out the error. They came back with champagne and orange juice for me, nothing for Dinah. 'Serve the lady first,' advised the restaurant manager, Jean-Philippe Susilovic. They brought Dinah an empty glass. 'That'll teach her,' I thought most unfairly because she's very good. With the champagne we got two types of popcorn in paper funnels. Absurd. Popcorn does not complement champagne. Bits of it disintegrate in your fingers, putting nasty stuff all over the place. Jean-Philippe proudly told me they were fully booked that lunchtime. Then a man arrived and said, 'I haven't reserved, can I have a table for two?' 'Yes, of course,' replied JP. 'So you're not fully booked,' I pointed out. 'We need to be flexible,' responded Jean-Philippe, adding, 'I took a Prozac this morning. I know why.'

My guest Adam Kenwright, theatrical supremo, entered. We proceeded to the dining area. I'd already been there on a planning trip. It's a bizarre room with an enormous floor-to-ceiling wine container in the middle. This cuts the place up so you gaze at wine bottles instead of the theatre of a full dining room. That's particularly odd, because when I went to L'Atelier de Joel Robuchon in Covent Garden, Gordon Ramsay said how ridiculous it was their first-floor restaurant was divided by a large counter with pots on it. Now he's divided his own place. I had trouble finding a good table. Jean-Philippe offered me one near the kitchen. 'That's the best table,' I said, pointing to another, 'but it's too small.' 'We'll move a larger table there,' suggested Jean-Philippe.

The food, under chef Sean Burbridge, was very good indeed. Sean was sous-chef at Gordon's restaurant in Versailles, when he owned one. We started with a freebie white onion velouté soup. Totally superb. I had the set menu lunch, £25 ex service and coffee. My starter of crab and salmon cannelloni was delicate, well prepared. Adam started with pigeon from Vendée. That's rare. Most restaurants serve pigeon from Bresse. My main course was boiled beef cheek with root vegetables and cardamom consommé. We both liked everything. Even the bread was warm and spectacularly good. My dessert of orange meringue pie with clove ice-cream was incredible.

'This has been an excellent meal,' I dictated into my tape, 'and not too fancy.' 'Would you like coffee or tea?' I asked Adam. 'No, I'm saving you the £5, dear,' he replied. Petits fours arrived. Some were ice-cream covered in chocolate with dry ice smoke swirling about. All we needed was Gordon coming through the mist trying to flog us a used Ferrari. I'd been told he might turn up for our photo. Jean-Philippe rang to check, came back and said, 'He's stuck abroad somewhere.' 'Abroad is probably his home in Battersea,' I observed. I put my 1966 Rolls Phantom V in the photo instead. Stick Ferraris up your jumper, Gordon. That's a proper car.

* * *

The food is horrible at **La Petite Maison** in Mayfair, the staff grotesquely rude. I saw them give away the table of one of the most renowned chefs in England. When he arrived and asked if they knew who he was, the receptionist snapped, 'No.' Recently the wife of a famous movie star booked in her husband's name for five people at 8pm. The star's daughter and husband came early. They asked for the table for X-X. The arrogant employee replied, referring to an actor known worldwide, asking, 'How do you spell the name?' They were informed the table would not be available until 8pm even though, as they told me, 'There were five or six big tables free.' As the bar was full the daughter asked if they could wait at a table. 'They're all booked,' snapped an employee. Daughter went to the manager. He ordered, 'Wait outside.' It was very cold.

So daughter cancelled the table, phoned her parents, and the group diverted to **Mr Chow**, where they were courteously treated. None of this surprises me. London's Petite Maison is owned by the rudest man I've ever met. He asked me to join him for pre-dinner drinks at a French Riviera hotel, then went into a diatribe which left Geraldine and me open-mouthed. I often tell the story. As they say: fish rots from the head down.

* * *

PS: The Nice original is owned by Nicole Rubi. She's lovely and a great host.

Landing in style to enjoy the height of good taste

My friend John Cleese loves the city of Bath and Jennifer Wade. Possibly in reverse order. I'm very happy about this, as John went through emotional and financial hell in the divorce from his grasping ex-wife Alyce. She was living in a council flat when the relationship started. After a 15-year marriage she ended up with more of his money than he did. A psychiatrist friend of mine who met Alyce recently said, 'She's got all that money but she's got nothing.' John, on the other hand, has a tall, lovely blonde for whom he bought a Maine Coon cat which Jenny named Monte. John wanted to call it Schopenhauer. Face it, in no relationship do people see eye to eye on everything. John says the cat will end up bigger than a dog. Not a St Bernard I hope.

We lunched at **Ston Easton Park**, a sensational Palladian hotel outside Bath. John came in his little-used 1986 green Bentley. 'Only worth £7,000,' he observed wryly. I arrived in a rented Sikorsky S76 helicopter. Costs a bit over £8.5m. That's in case you feel like buying one. In times of austerity it's always cheering to spend money. While waiting, I had coffee, flapjack and a chocolate biscuit in the library. Exceptionally good. I dictated, 'Geraldine burped.' Although I'm not sure that was fully relevant.

Ston Easton is marvellously grand. In the main salon is a Nollekens bust of Pitt the Younger, taken from his death mask. I have one. It faces me as I write, resplendent atop a 19th-century Dutch commode, surrounded by 15 teddy bears, and a police helmet presented to me by the City of London constabulary. When I acquired the bust at auction I was grabbed by the curator of Hampstead's stately Kenwood House. He said, 'I was meant to buy that. Will you take a profit?' I declined, putting beauty before money. Although beautiful William Pitt is not.

For lunch, I started with asparagus, more al dente than I like, sitting on a bed of spinach with a soft-boiled egg. John and I had lemon sole; John asked for hollandaise sauce. He took my tape and dictated, 'About the lemon sole, I'd forgotten that it has quite a savoury taste. Right at the end of the taste there's something a tiny little bit bitter, so I asked for a slightly sweet sauce with it which made it perfect.' That's more food detail than you've ever read in this column.

I like Jennifer Wade. Marriage could be on the cards. 'She brings you down to earth,' I told John. 'You think I'm not down to earth?' asked John. 'You're from another planet,' I replied. 'A planet so distant it isn't even in the known universe.' That shut him up for five seconds. Jennifer does a line in jewellery which is sold at the Carlton Tower hotel in Knightsbridge. She flogs it herself at the Chelsea Harbour Club. 'You should go on QVC,' I suggested. 'I could sell ashtrays to non-smokers,' observed Jenny. I believe her.

The perceptive among you may have noticed I was not on QVC recently as I'd told you I would be. Little drama-ette there. I stormed out. They were wrong and most graciously sent flowers to me and my lovely PA Natalie. So I may be back.

To finish lunch I had 'apple tarte fine, Bramley cream and five spices.' That and the homemade fudge petits fours were superb. I chatted with the talented chef, Matthew Butcher, when I arrived. Then he said, 'I must get back to the stove.' I said, 'I agree, Matthew, I think you should have gone two minutes ago.' As ever, I'm all charm.

* * *

Next week I'll give my largely positive view of the newly re-opened very posh hotel **La Mamounia** in Marrakech. Now I'll relate incompetent and devious hotel employee behaviour that drives me mad. A short journey you might say.

The old chief concierge was the marvellous Abdelkrim Temsamani. Very efficient. He's replaced by Taoufiq Aitelhaddad. Not efficient. I asked the general manager and the operations manager to see I got a private plane from Marrakech leaving on Friday at 10am for Taroudant, a town over the Atlas Mountains. They passed this on to Taoufiq. When I got the flight plan on Thursday I saw I was to leave at 11am. When asked why, Taoufiq told me that was the only available slot. Nonsense. No such things as slots for a short local journey. I went berserk. Within 20 minutes the flight was changed to depart at 10am as I'd originally requested. When I asked why he hadn't told me of the earlier departure before I saw it on the flight plan, Taoufiq said, 'I came to the pool but you were asleep, so I told Geraldine.' Totally untrue. Taoufiq come to the pool only once when he handed Geraldine a typed list of different planes I could take for the journey and the prices. I hadn't even booked the flight so how could he have told her it was to leave one hour earlier? This is not top-class hotel service.

* * *

PS: Did you know that when concierges recommend a local restaurant they aren't offering what they think is the best, they're guiding guests to places that give them the greatest 'commission' on your spend. Think that's cynical? Learn.

Finally – a revamp that improves on the original

They closed **La Mamounia** in Marrakech, Morocco, for over three years to spend £180m-plus tarting it up. The old manager, short Robert Bergé, was like a minor French consul in the Tropics. He'd walk round the pool with his chubby Jewish wife, greeting guests. They were warm and wonderful. The new general manager, Didier Picquot, is tall and rather terrifying. His wife is Karin, Baroness von Stempel. A new order indeed.

My suite used to be small, with a bathroom so tiny you risked injury every time you entered. The rooms are much the same size now, with the most beautiful architraves, dado rails, furnishings. Exquisite. But lumbered with a pathetic, complicated electrical system. The bathroom is large, with a harsh marble step down they don't warn you of, another step down to the balcony.

Picquot serves white sugar cubes each wrapped in see-through rubbish which is tricky to get off and then litters the classically perfect breakfast table. When I objected Picquot explained, as if to a recalcitrant child, that health and safety had hotels wrapping sugar to stop dirty finger contamination. Hasn't Mr P heard of sugar tongs? I've known people die from tripping on hidden-trap steps, not from eating sugar. No hotel or restaurant I could find served wrapped cube sugar, including the Plaza New York, the Dorchester, the Ritz, Chewton Glen, Scott's and dozens of other top-class places.

La Mamounia was designed by Jacques Garcia, king of gloom. Windows in the corridor outside my suite used to reveal delightful vistas of Marrakech. Now they're all curtained. 'This is creating mood,' explained Picquot. 'It's the way Garcia sees it.' Obviously Garcia prefers material to views.

In the French restaurant, a superb offshoot of L'Apicius, a two-Michelin-starred place in Paris, there was piped music. 'Do you know of any major restaurant that has piped music?' I asked Picquot. 'It's revolting.' 'That's an opinion,' he replied, as if dealing with a retard. 'Does Jean-Pierre Vigato have piped music in his Paris L'Apicius?' I asked. 'I don't know,' said Mr P. I've got news for him: he doesn't.

When I suggested we lunch at the pool Mr P said, 'But that's a buffet', as if it was beneath him. 'But it's your buffet,' I responded. 'You'll have to get up all the time to fetch food,' said Mr P. 'Better than relying on waiters,' I said. Mamounia's Moroccan pool lunch is the best buffet I've ever seen. Fantastic quality, amazing selection and a lovely setting. They also have an Italian restaurant, an offspring of two-Michelin-starred Don Alfonso near Naples. This is staggeringly good. I ate some of the best Italian food imaginable.

Their Moroccan restaurant was always brilliant. The food still is. But it's now housed in a newly built riad away from the hotel. It rains quite a bit in Morocco. Not great for an exterior walk to dinner. 'We provide umbrellas,' explained Mr Picquot. The old restaurant used to be bright: you could see the whole room. The new one is nice but low-key. You sit in little alcoves. All you see clearly is the other table in the same alcove.

Nevertheless, a hotel with four fantastic-quality restaurants is rare. Oddities include a new spa where Geraldine, treadmill expert, was glad to see TVs on the machines. The TVs didn't work. They had a marvellous horse-drawn carriage. Gone. 'Horses died,' explained Picquot. Why not replace them? One day I was told they had no strawberries or raspberries for breakfast. Morocco produces both, and very good they are. I mentioned this to the excellent executive chef, Fabrice Lasnon. 'I heard you'd ordered. I told them to send you strawberries, we had them. Didn't they ring and offer them?' 'No,' I said. 'But I told them,' said Lasnon.' 'Do you ever get the feeling people aren't listening to you, Fabrice?' I asked. 'All the time,' he replied.

Garcia redesigned the pool, beautifully. When I was there it was closed for five days to regrout the tiles. Operations manager, Gerard Madani, explained the builder used salty sand from the beach in his cement, so it cracked. I asked if resort guests, minus pool and pool restaurant, got a discount. 'No,' he said. 'But we told them.' So why did reader Howard Winston email me that he was shocked to find the pool closed when he'd not been warned? Also, the pool, finished only six months ago, was tiled in marble mosaic. Marble is porous. So it all has to be retiled in August. Jacques Garcia may be a famous designer but he obviously hadn't heard of quantity surveyors.

There are other funnies I could list about La Mamounia. But that wouldn't be fair. I liked Picquot: he's very professional, elegant and a great host in a senior way. The Baroness is a total delight who knows all about local shopping. This pleased Geraldine. The hotel in general is a terrific, refined, successful reconstruction. Unlike most hotels which mess it up. The Moroccan staff are charming, cheerful, fantastic. The chefs and restaurant managers exemplary. It's a definite recommendation. Go there.

Winner speaks

When I got baked beans instead of mushy peas with fish and chips, to the waitress: 'You see, dear, these are beans, not mushy peas. Mushy peas are green. Baked beans are orange. Doesn't someone here know the difference?'

Let sleeping dogs lie – but not sloppy websites

A large chocolate-coloured Labrador dog named Tickle obstructed my triumphal entry to the Elms hotel in Abberley,

Worcestershire. He lay there, just inside the hall, uncaring that guests had to come in and out. The general manager, Adam Salter, negotiated a way round Tickle as if to go close would set off an explosive device. As far as I know this was not a suicide bomber-dog, just a lethargic Labrador. 'All Von Essen family hotels have a dog,' explained Salter.

If the Elms is a family hotel, it's for those who won the lottery. The grand Queen Anne mansion is exquisitely furnished and decorated, as if Queenie was actually living there. Enormous grounds, old fireplaces, oil paintings and . . . what's that? I don't believe it. DVDs and loudspeakers. Lucky nothing's playing. I'd have gone nuts. How tacky in a place of such style.

To revive myself after this horrendous discovery, we had some tea. The best scones I've ever tasted, light with a crispy exterior. Could have been a bit warmer, but I'd ordered them, then walked around inspecting, and returned. Gave them time to cool, perhaps. Geraldine had gluten-free cake. 'I'm glad they didn't offer me another, because it's so good I'd have accepted,' she remarked. This girl keeps trim. Our bedroom was very elegant, slightly marred by Wenlock Spring water. That's unfair. Wenlock may be marvellous. I didn't try it because they'd got Evian in just for me. A reader pointed out Evian spelt backwards is naïve. That's me. A simple country boy.

I was frightened at dinner by two balloons rising from a corner table with the numbers 21 on them. Drunken revellers coming, I surmised. Wrong. The young couple were demure and delightful. We waited far too long for the bread to arrive. When it came after 30 minutes (ridiculous) it was warm but didn't taste good or fresh. We got a freebie starter – cream, cauliflower and Oxford blue cheese velouté (soup to you) and a beignet (fried doughnut to you), both superb. My first course, Brixham crab tian, was impeccable. To follow: 'pork three ways'. This was a famous Marco

Pierre White dish which he did brilliantly when he was an exciting chef rather than the total bore he's become. I got a rolled boneless bit of pork, a pork cheek and a tenderloin of pork. Perfectly good, but nothing could compare to Marco's. Can't be bothered to tell you about the desserts, but both mine and Geraldine's were excellent.

The chef is Daren Bale. The decoration, which didn't look like decoration – the highest compliment I can pay – is by Von Essen's executive designer, Andrew Onraet. When we left Tickle was no longer on duty as doorkeeper. Having a kip somewhere else, I suppose.

* * *

Mirror, mirror on the wall, who is the rudest of them all? Not me, silly. Many readers nominated staff at Mayfair's **La Petite Maison**. 'What a dreadful place,' wrote Erica Worth. 'Staff arrogant and rude,' said Brian Green. Some picked Nicole Rubi, who runs the Nice original. I always found her to be a fantastic, charming, professional. The French government agrees. I was recently invited to see Nicole receive the Légion d'Honneur, one of France's highest awards. Didn't go. But I'd gladly turn up to see Arjun Waney, owner of the London version, get his award for rudest man ever to enter Winner world.

* * *

Wikipedia has printed my obituary. Twice. The second time they were right. It's a grotesque organisation. Idiots galore can add nonsense to any biography, true or false. Wikipedia just print it. Newspapers silly enough to rely on it, repeat it. To sue you have to find the person who originated the inaccuracy. We had them remove the libellous allegation that I wore a gastric band when my diet book rightly shows how brilliantly I dieted and kept the weight off. When we objected, a Wikipedia rep, Joe Daly, complained that we wrote to him in capital letters. That's a joke, innit? They're printing rubbish and he's concerned with typography. Recently a 10th-rate comedian, Dom Jolly, proudly boasted in a national newspaper he'd 'tweaked' my Wikipedia biography. He'd added a host of untruths to amuse himself. Get a life, Dom. We wrote once more pointing out 10 further inaccuracies. Another Wikipedia 'genius', Guy Chapman, again complained we'd written in capital letters. Oscar Wilde said, 'Believe nothing of what you hear and absolutely nothing of what you see.' He was surely referring to Wikipedia.

* * *

Ninety-year-old film director Lewis Gilbert (*Reach for the Sky*, *Alfie*, *Educating Rita*, many Bond movies) has written a terrific autobiography, *All My Flashbacks*. This recalls his days in music hall and as a child actor with Laurence Olivier. His account of how we met is totally inaccurate. But he's a great man. Read his book.

Who can outdo my 70th birthday? Me on my 75th

Marlon Brando's remark to me on a late-night telephone call that he only had five real friends in the world and would like to think I was one of them, came to mind as I planned my 75th birthday party. This is to be held not on 30 October, my real birthday (then I'll be in Venice with real friend John Cleese because it's his birthday too), but on 9 and 10 October when JC is performing his one-man show in Denmark.

For my 70th I flew a group of 30 people to Venice. This

time, assuming I'm still alive, I'm taking over Europe's best hotel, the **Villa Feltrinelli** on Lake Garda, for 11 couples. They're not all real friends in the full sense of the word. I'd say four of them are, including my very special fiancée, Geraldine. The others I greatly like but couldn't rely on if poo hit the fan. Add Cleese and it's five. We'll private jet out on Saturday morning, dine in the Feltrinelli and on Sunday cruise the lake to **Locanda San Vigilio** before returning on Sunday from Verona.

San Vigilio is a splendid restaurant which featured in my TV show. A stunning location, lovely old building, great views. When I went with the TV crew, there was a hiccup. The visit had been arranged by Markus Odermatt, boss of Villa Feltrinelli. The receptionist, Emma Simonelli, viewed us as criminals intent on nicking the cutlery. To get the TV people in I had to phone the superb general manager, Adriano Girardi, who was with his family in Venice. Family above me? Ridiculous. Then, with his blessing, we proceeded to the lakeside terrace. Only four people were lunching there. The TV director asked if Geraldine and I could sit where they were. The difference was about three feet. Both tables were adjacent. I suggested the waiter, Aliv Zilbehar, please ask this group to move. He looked at me as if I'd ordered the murder of his mother, father and children. So I spoke to the diners myself, a delightful Austrian family led by Dr Heber from Innsbruck. They'd all seen and loved *Death Wish*, were totally pleasant and didn't mind swapping tables. I gave them a bottle of champagne. We chatted throughout the meal. Zilbehar thawed from hostile to neutral.

The food, from the chef Giorgio Tomasini, was, as always, fantastic. The starter, a courgette pudding on a bed of tomatoes, was soft. It featured cheese plus pasta or chicken. Geraldine said haddock. 'It's white, that's all that matters,' I said, dictating, 'This was absolutely outstanding.

A revelatory new experience.' We followed with lavarella, a fish from the lake. There was, mercifully, no attempt to lay out the veggies in decorative precision. 'What's this?' I asked Geraldine. 'Sweet peppers,' she answered. 'They go very well with the fish because the fish is white and the sweet peppers red and orange. It's called colour contrast,' I reflected. Dessert, white mousse surrounded by peaches, raspberries and other berries, was perfect. The chef then produced his speciality, ice-cream inside kumquats, walnuts, greengages, everything. Just extraordinary. A spectacularly good meal. Chef Tomasini is a hero.

* * *

My movie *The Jokers* just played at the Edinburgh film festival. The programme described it as 'Using comic dexterity to hint at the era's underlying distemper. Michael Winner divines magic from a restless script . . . effervescent and breathless.' On top of that it still earns me Universal Pictures profit cheques. It's at the National Film Theatre in 2011. I'll try and remind you in time.

The film provided a memorable meal in 1966. While filming in Curzon Street Michael Crawford, not a big spender, invited Oliver Reed, me and that great actor Harry Andrews to lunch at the nearby 'in' place, the White Elephant. 'Michael won't turn up,' I warned Oliver. As lunch approached Michael Crawford vanished. I saw a distressed Oliver running up the concrete back stairs of the office complex above the Curzon cinema, searching for Crawford. 'Don't worry, Oliver, I'll pay,' I said. The lunch took place minus Crawford.

That night Michael and Oliver wore evening dress for our shooting in Trafalgar Square. As Michael Crawford came on the set Oliver rushed up, grabbed him, and held him above one of the fountains. 'Pay up for lunch now,' he said, 'or I'll throw you in.' 'Oliver, no,' I begged, 'we have to shoot, you'll ruin Michael's clothes.' Michael paid and stayed dry. He now makes jam in Kerikeri, New Zealand. He's a great talent. Oliver's acting in the sky. I miss them both.

* * *

I may be getting a big, multi-million-pound offer for my house. 'If I take it,' I told Andrew Davis, owner of Von Essen hotels, 'as it's owned by my company, the tax will be enormous. I'll have to live abroad.' 'No country would take you,' said Andrew. 'They only let you stay here because they don't know how to get you out.' God, the truth hurts.

All fine and dandy for my day back on set

My acting talent never received the acclaim it deserved. You'll recall my important role as Sir Randolph Spence in *For the Greater Good*, a TV film written by G.F. Newman, where I was cast by director Danny Boyle who later (he owes it all to me) won an Oscar for *Slumdog Millionaire*. So impressive was my performance that my scene with Roy Dotrice illustrated the proceedings when the show was launched at BAFTA. My co-stars, Rachel Kempson, Martin Shaw, Julian Fellowes, to name but a few, were in awe of my dramatic skills.

Amazingly, further acting work failed to materialise. I am consoled by my outstanding performances on *The Kenny Everett Show*, for Steven Berkoff in his movie *Decadence*, a comedic gem in *Hotel Babylon* and, trifles though they were, my skill as farceur for Reeves, Mortimer, Al Murray and others.

I like to think Hollywood director John Landis, who made

Trading Places and Michael Jackson's *Thriller*, chose me for his new film *Burke & Hare* because he'd heard of my on-screen charisma. More likely it was because he started his career as a stuntman on my movie *Chato's Land* in 1970. It took 40 years before he contacted me again, this time to play an English nobleman (no stupid reader remarks please) whose carriage Burke and Hare cause to crash over the cliffs at Dover. There's thanks for you. I start the Landis career and 40 years later he hurls me over a cliff. Why he gave the leads to Andy Sirkis, Simon Pegg and Tom Wilkinson I can't imagine. I was available. I turned up as requested shortly before 12:30pm at the movie base in Luton Hoo. The Rolls Phantom deposited me at my caravan dressing room, where I was told they weren't ready for my close-up.

It was suggested I lunch at nearby **Luton Hoo** hotel. John's wife, top costumier (*Raiders of the Lost Ark*) Deborah, said to my assistant Dinah, 'It's just as well he's not eating here because the food's terrible.' As I drove off Barnaby Thompson, the producer, observed, 'Sorry you won't be eating here because the food is very good.' 'That's not what the troops are saying,' I replied.

Hoo, a Saxon word, means a hill. The hotel is magnificent. It's a major stately home in the Cliveden league, restored by Robert Adam in 1771. Capability Brown laid out the gardens. The courteous manager, Matthew Long, showed Dinah and me through the vast hall. I turned left to see the Russian chapel where ladies were lunching prior to a fashion show. One of them asked, 'Are you going to be a model?' That left me speechless. We lunched in a dining room only beaten in grandeur by the Ritz in Piccadilly. Tapestries, wall paintings, gilt, massive chandeliers, pillars, a view of stunning grounds and a lake.

Food was very good. Foie gras terrine followed by pan-fried sea bass. 'And for your dining pleasure this afternoon,' said the waitress as she and a colleague lifted our cloches in unison to reveal the main course. All went splendidly until dessert, which took ages to come. I was having a mixed chocolate thing, Dinah cheese. 'It's cold food,' I said to the waitress. 'Why have we waited 20 minutes?' 'Desserts are on the way,' she responded. 'That means nothing to me,' I said.

Back with the film unit, the make-up lady stuck a couple of sideburns on me, then said, 'That's it.' 'What do you mean that's it?' I asked. 'You don't need make-up, you've got a lovely skin,' she replied. I recently sat next to Jemima Khan at David Tang's Chinese restaurant at the Dorchester. She said, 'You've had botox.' 'I have not,' I responded indignantly. 'Wiggle your eyebrows,' commanded Jemima. I did. 'You're right,' she said. 'No botox. I don't know how you do it.' Clean living is the answer, dear.

* * *

In last Sunday's Culture interview with Jeff Goldblum, shortly to open in *Prisoner of Second Avenue* in the West End, he joked that his first movie role as the chief mugger in *Death Wish* was referred to on the cast list as Freak One. Paramount was adamant I didn't have too many black muggers (a permissible word in those days) in case they objected. So at mugging auditions seven actors at a time raped a chair. Best chair molester, no inhibitions, was a tall, skinny fellow. I said to Charlie Bludhorn, boss of Paramount, 'Don't worry, our chief rapist is a Jew. They won't mind.' 'Who is he?' asked Bludhorn. 'You've never heard of him,' I replied. 'Name is Jeff Goldblum.' Jeff was in my horror movie *The Sentinel* a year later. Lovely person. Superb actor. Glad he's done well. He deserves it.

* * *

An email from Wikipedia follows my complaint of vast inaccuracies in their information about me and that anyone can write any lies into any Wiki biography. Twice Wiki printed my obituary. Joe Daly said they have a new 'software update' which means edits by 'a certain class of users must be approved by a trusted user before they go live on the article. This feature has been activated with regard to Mr Winner.' Figure that out. I'll be watching. Daly adds that he's soon getting married. Congratulations, Joe.

Lock up your grannies, I'm in town

I didn't intend to be in Llanidloes. I was meant to be on the A487 taking a wobbly-way to the toll gate at Penmaenpool for lunch at a pub I'd been recommended. By mistake I went right on the A470. When my error became clear I'd gone from page 63 of the roadmap to page 52. In order to get back I had to turn right at Caersws down the picturesque B4509 Roman road.

We ended up in Llanidloes around lunchtime. The Mount Inn looked pretty. Outside little flower boxes, inside ghastly beyond belief. Didn't matter because it was 1:50pm and the chef had closed the kitchen. We cruised Llanidloes main street. On the left a fish and chip shop which also did Pukka pies in an olde worlde building, then the Bengal Brasserie. I was in Wales I wanted local produce. The **Travellers Rest** restaurant sign indicated 'Open'. Geraldine checked, put her thumb up and said, 'You'll like this. It's little old ladies and youngsters serving. Very sweet.'

As I entered an attractive blonde girl gave me a kiss. I'd gone into the kitchen which was next door. She was the chef-owner, Margaret Owen. 'Are you a good cook?' I asked. 'Brilliant,' was the reply, 'been doing it for 11 years.'

In the real restaurant were four lovely old ladies and a chubby waitress. It's nice to see overweight waitresses. I assume they enjoy the food they're serving. Wooden chairs, shiny-topped tables. On to ours, local server Sarah Mills, dressed in black, put a Coca-Cola with ice and a slice of lemon.

For £6 I got roast beef, Yorkshire pudding, carrots, mashed and roast potatoes, broccoli, carrots, cauliflower and peas. 'Unless that's inedible it's bloody good value,' I dictated into my tape. It was inedible. Stringy, thin beef, watery veg, soggy carrots, soft no substance broccoli, diabolical Yorkshire pud. Geraldine had a baked potato with onion and cheese. She greatly liked it. Sarah told me she'd made the sherry trifle that day. There was also blackberry and apple pie from a local baker. The pie was okay, the sherry trifle full of catering cream, not great.

Behind me three Welsh ladies spoke in lilting voices. They were having tea with toasted teacakes. I purloined a teacake. It was absolutely marvellous. In front of me were the four white-haired old ladies whom I'd said hello to when I came in. Cheerful, lovely faces, very animated. They all seem so positive these Welsh ladies. I paid the bill for the four old ladies. Also for the three people I took the teacake from. It was like a Western movie when a man says, 'Drinks are on me,' and everyone rushes to the bar.

Was it a good meal? No. Did I enjoy myself? Greatly. News flash: the Travellers Rest is now for sale. Probably because when I came in Margaret reckoned it was time to end her life in catering.

* * *

At the **Cipriani** hotel in Venice redecoration, supervised by Maurizio Saccani, Vice-President of Orient-Express in Italy, was superb. He's now upgrading two hotels the group recently bought in Sicily – the Grand Timeo and the Villa Sant'Andrea. The Cipriani's charming manager, Giampolo Ottazzi, should tighten up his staff. Five hours after leaving my suite housekeeping had done zilch to clean up. There were other funnies, also.

The new **Fortuny** restaurant manager, Emiliano Milza, messed up our reservation. He's all talk, little action. Why give written and verbal notice that guests require jackets in his dining room when I saw seven men in shirtsleeves? If you say it, mean it. If not, shut up.

The hotel's lagoon restaurant, **Cip's**, overlooks St Mark's Square and the church of Santa Maria della Salute. It's fantastic. No jackets required. The chef, Roberto Gatto, produces historic food. The best Bellinis. Extraordinary cannelloni with meat sauce. Adamello Bianco, the manager, is marvellously experienced. He should give lessons to his colleague in the main restaurant.

Greatest of all is the giant swimming pool set in large gardens. There the **Porticciolo** restaurant faces the San Giorgio church and the distant Lido island. As at Cip's you dine inches from the water. These are the two best restaurant views I've ever come across.

* * *

My favourite caterer, Johnny Robertson-Roxburgh of the **Admirable Crichton**, became a restaurateur for Art Antiques London, an exhibition in a tent by the Albert Memorial. He produced an elegant room and menu. The food was delicate and tasty. Johnny was asked to do an encore at other fairs and events, but declined. 'Not enough money in it,' he told me. I was surprised to see no tuna in Geraldine's salade niçoise; interested to see his staff, unequalled at catered events, fumble when not serving a set meal. The waitress declined to use a pad and returned endlessly to check what we'd ordered. Plates of food arriving from the kitchen were held up at the pay-desk, where everyone seemed to be voting on which table they should be given to. As usual, I'm being over-picky. It was massively the best dining experience I've ever enjoyed at a glorified boot sale.

Go in shrimp-sized and emerge as an elephant

I was in Homestead, Florida, looking for somewhere to eat lunch. Homestead Branch Library on my right, Mavericks High, whatever that is, not many buildings, lots of fields. I was hoping to find a lovely little place run by mom and pop with a mesh door to keep out the mosquitoes, a counter, a few tables. Mom in the kitchen baking apple pie. Pop behind the counter pouring milkshakes. As it was in Ossining, New York, when I first visited the USA in 1953. With me and Geraldine was the theatrical biggie Adam Kenwright.

He spotted **Sonny's Real Pit Bar-B-Q** on South Dixie Highway, Florida City. A town we'd entered without realising. Its sign read, 'All you can eat chicken $7.99'. I hear you mutter, 'The same sign says Happy New Year. Are you reviewing a restaurant you went to over six months ago?' 'Why not?' I respond vigorously. 'I have copious notes on what occurred. Last week I phoned our waitress, Melissa, who told me Sonny's is still there, serving the same food, not redecorated or mucked about. What else do you want, elephants?' So here's my incisive report on this important chain offering American cuisine throughout the Southern states.

It's quite a big space, booths, piped music. Four people were getting the most enormous plates of food. A woman said it was one of her favourite places. Her husband added, 'It's not so far from Key Largo. We go shopping at Wal-

Mart, then we come here for lunch.' Next to our booth were Phil and Sue Metzoler. Phil suggested the pulled pork. 'They pull the pork apart so it's shredded.'

Up came the waitress, beaming. 'I'm Melissa, I'll be your server today.' She speedily brought an enormous glass of Coca-Cola, another of ice and a big bowl of lemon slices. Very efficient. 'I'm going to have the barbecue pulled pork . . .' I announced. 'Wait a minute, darling – I want the lunch favourite barbecue pulled pork. I'm going to have some barbecue beans and macaroni cheese with it . . . . I haven't finished, Melissa. I'm going to have signature baby back ribs and also cornbread and garlic bread. I'm having both so I can taste them.' It was to Melissa's considerable credit that she didn't fall asleep or die of boredom as I droned on.

I can't tell you that any of this was marvellous. I'm not booking for New Year's Eve. But it was all pleasant. Geraldine went to the salad bar and described the result as 'fantastic'. Then I had Sonny's signature dessert: double chocolate brownie bliss topped with a scoop of ice-cream and a drizzle of hot fudge whipped cream and a cherry. Melissa said the dessert of the day was Key lime pie. I ordered that too. The brownie was okay, the Key lime pie rather good. Adam didn't like it. Geraldine said, 'It's got gelatine in it.'

The bill for three people with drinks was $52 (£34). It was a jolly place and exceptional value. Go there. What do you mean it's a bit far? Not if you live in Florida City it isn't.

* * *

For my 75th birthday I'd planned to fly friends by private jet to the hotel **Villa Feltrinelli** on Lake Garda. The next day taking them by boat for lunch at **Locanda San Vigilio**, then to Verona for the flight home. All that is cancelled. Just back from the still-superb Villa Feltrinelli, I realised if rain came it would be a fiasco. I'm considering the YMCA Epping and other locations.

On Lake Garda I met Massimo Callestrini, whose restored 1926 sailboat I was to hire. Massimo owns a crocodile farm. From their skins he makes handbags that sell for 5,000 to 20,000 euros and jackets up to 100,000 euros (£83,000).

At the Villa Feltrinelli, the best hotel in Europe, there were wobbles. I hate waiters who, faced with still and fizzy mineral water, don't check, just pour. Twice I got fizzy instead of still. I pointed this out to the restaurant manager, Peter Eisendle. He assured me it wouldn't happen again. An hour later, at lunch, the waiter didn't ask, just poured fizzy water. A guest's laptop was blaring dreadful disco music, shattering the peaceful lakeside atmosphere. I told Eisendle, who'd totally ignored the din, that this was not appreciated. If he wanted guests to provide music I'd bring my tape recorder and blast back. I think paying £1,200 a night for my room I deserved trouble-free meals. The excellent general manager of the Feltrinelli, Markus Odermatt, should discreetly dump Eisendle in the lake.

* * *

You may remember Julius Schmulius, the creepy-crawly theatrical agent whom I find quite appalling. Julius waddled over at a function to apologise for upsetting me. I should have let bygones be bygones. But Schmulius was wearing a white suit. Grossly overweight people should not wear white. Had he been wearing a dark grey suit I'd have accepted and made up. As it is, I'm thinking about it.

* * *

Ashley Fox of Maidenhead wrote that I was an extra in the movie *Burke & Hare*. How dare you, sir. I played an important cameo role. Spoke at least 10 words. Brilliantly. Stardom awaits me.

Winner speaks

On being shown a table: 'I'd like that table moved there, and those chairs taken from there and put at my table.'
Restaurant manager: 'We don't do that.'
MW: 'Doesn't mean you can't. I'll help you. Grab that side of the table.'
When it's done, MW: 'See, no one rioted. We're not under siege. Thank you.'

Heading back to school to award an A for effort

Skye Harris, seven, wrote asking me to sample a meal from her school's new kitchen. Geraldine and I went down Earls Court road. Opposite the police station was **St Barnabas and St Philip's**, a Church of England primary school. Red, white and blue balloons fluttered from a railing. No 'Welcome Michael' sign. Although Skye observed later, 'It's like a royal visit.'

As we approached the locked gate a pretty blonde girl in

a red gingham dress appeared. I screamed, 'Let me in.' It was Skye who rushed to press the button, releasing the door. With her was an elegant young pupil, Junsang. 'Don't you need a cardigan? You're going to be cold,' Geraldine said to Skye. 'No, I'm boiling,' replied Skye. A teacher called us back. 'You have to sign in and take a badge.' 'I'm always getting something wrong,' sighed Skye. They gave me a yellow badge saying 'Visitor'. 'I don't think they'll mistake me for a student,' I observed.

The head teacher, Christopher Doyle, appeared. Very tall, smart, no jacket. 'I can go and get a jacket if you'd like me to wear one. It's been very hot recently,' he offered. 'Cold today,' I pointed out. Junsang asked how old I was. 'Nearly 75,' I replied. That got a laugh. A noticeboard in the corridor read: 'Learn to write a letter to a famous person and get them to respond.' Replies were displayed from Buckingham Palace, signed by a lady-in-waiting with an unreadable signature. From Downing Street, signed by some nonentity. Blah on behalf of Jamie Oliver. Genuinely signed letters from J.K. Rowling, Gordon Ramsay and me. Amanda Vasey, Skye's teacher, explained, 'One wanted to write to Samuel Pepys, another to Michael Jackson.' 'Take a while for them to answer,' I observed. Then to the classroom.

'They're all very polite,' observed Geraldine. It's a mixed-race school, no fees to pay, incredibly friendly atmosphere. Everyone seemed to like everyone. All immaculately turned out in red uniforms. In the high-ceilinged dining room was a large mural of a tree.

Self-service lunch, dished out by the cook, Howa Mansary, offered roast beef, roast potatoes, Yorkshire pudding, beans, carrots, macaroni and gravy. 'Is the food good?' I asked Skye. 'Yes,' she said. 'Good as your mother does?' I continued. 'Not really,' responded Skye. I sat on a low bench at a shiny-topped table. The supervisor suggested, 'Sit over there, the chairs are higher.' The head teacher said, 'Don't worry, he's all right. Leave him there.' I was practically squatting on the floor. They didn't have napkins. 'Major de-merit,' I announced. 'Should have brought my own.'

Junsang wanted to be an inventor when he grew up. I thought Skye said she wanted to be a food critic so I suggested she write a review of meals she ate out. Later Geraldine pointed out she'd said film critic. Ignore what I advised, Skye. Write a review of every film you see. If it's one of mine praise it.

'On a scale of one to 10, Skye, how much did the food improve when you got the new kitchen?' I asked. 'Lots,' she replied. 'It was always freezing, now it's hot.' Two girls appeared. One wore a badge reading: 'Have you had a drink today?' The other girl was labelled 'Water Monitor'. 'They're encouraging the children to drink more water,' explained Amanda. 'It's very good for their energy levels and their brains.'

The main course was pretty good. This is Kensington's first school to serve only organic food. The dessert, fruit and a custard tart, I liked very much. Amanda said they had 15 different languages in her class. When there's a birthday they sang in all different languages, including Latin. 'A lot of children go to Latin classes after school,' she advised. 'Why?' I asked. 'Because they want to,' was the reply. Skye told me she did ballet at school and out of school Irish dancing and swimming. She was very composed, a marvellous host.

After lunch we toured the playgrounds, lovely murals, happy children everywhere. No one knifing the teacher or beating up fellow students. What is the world coming to? 'We believe in community,' explained Amanda. 'Have I done all right?' I asked Skye. She made an open-arm gesture as if she wasn't sure. Then she rushed for the gate-release button to let us out. That's the sort of school I never went to. Organised, cheerful, orderly. I won't go into my education. You might cry.

* * *

At last I can operate my new Leica X1 camera. Anything more than an on/off button confuses me. The image quality is extraordinary. It's the first digital compact camera approved by the prestigious Getty Images library, which supplies photos to the media. Boots were fine printing negative film. Not much good with digital. I now email pix to Lee Gribbin of Harrison Cameras in Sheffield. Takes forever. You should be able to email a photo in a second. By the time that happens I'll be photographing Marilyn Monroe with the Almighty.

It's taken the palace only 40 years to invite me back

Geraldine lay at the bottom of the grand staircase in my house, crying, badly bruised, bleeding and shaken. She'd crawled there from the basement where . . . I'll tell you later.

Now: Her Majesty the Queen. In an envelope stamped Buckingham Palace was an invitation: 'The Lord Chamberlain is commanded by Her Majesty to invite Mr Michael Winner and Ms Geraldine Lynton-Edwards to a Garden Party at Buckingham Palace'. I first went to one of those in 1968, a second in 1970. I thought I behaved impeccably. Obviously not, as it took 40 years before I was asked again.

I'm a great fan of the Queen. She sent me a personally signed photo. I hosted her for two hours when she unveiled my National Police Memorial in the Mall. I was flattered to be told by a Private Secretary that the Queen asked after me more than once when I was ill. I admire true professionals.

None greater than Her Majesty, the greatest bargain our nation possesses. She doesn't interfere in business, doesn't foist her personal views on to other countries or UK authorities. She leads by example, very aware of the path she should tread in a confused world. The fact that Her Majesty asked some 7,500 people to the same tea party as me I bear bravely. A private cuppa with a bun and six butlers was, I suppose, out of the question.

The Royal Garden parties are a lesson in organisation and good taste. Apart from my being included. One of two military bands played robustly as we sauntered in. Geraldine's leg was swollen beyond belief, bruised and with open wounds. She had to wear trousers, not the dress she'd planned. Walking was difficult, standing even worse. We sat briefly on the lawn, where I met a mayor from Gwent. Our tickets were for the Diplomatic Tent, next to the Royal Tent. There we managed to find a table, sharing with a Lebanese embassy first secretary and a Hungarian.

The tea itself was historic. A massive credit to the caterer, Charles Boyd. All the sandwiches tasted fresh, the sponge cake with jam and cream was fantastic, the ginger and fruit cakes beyond belief, and, greatest marvel of all, the coffee éclairs extraordinary. Any éclair that goes in the fridge comes out massively degraded. Charles explained the humidity in the fridge melts the icing on top, called fondant. He wraps plastic round the tray in the fridge, then opens the plastic bags two hours before serving. To further reduce humidity he turns off one of the motors, making the fridge a cooler only. Charles has a restaurant, **Boyds**, in Northumberland Avenue. 'On a scale of one to 10, how posh is it?' I asked. 'Five,' said Charles, 'but the building's nine.' A lovely Korean lady whose husband, John Hope, once organised Royal Garden parties said, 'When I see you on television I always laugh. You're far more handsome in the flesh.' That shows the high intelligence of royal guests.

A burst of 'That's Entertainment' from the band. Sixteen Beefeaters appeared the other side of the lawn and formed an avenue. 'The Queen's gonna come out dancing,' I thought. 'That'll be nice.' 'She won't be in view for 15 minutes,' explained John Hope. As we were standing at the rail facing the lawn, I looked round for our chairs. They'd gone. I said loudly, 'Never seen a room with so many chair nickers in it.' This embarrassed at least one elegantly dressed guest. A pretty girl, Caroline Reed from Windsor, brought some chairs over.

The Duke of Edinburgh (one of my all-time favourite people) walked by. Then the Queen crossed the lawn in pale blue, looking delightful. Geraldine said 'She recognised you. She looked, saw you, went on, then looked back.'

The written instruction said no photos should be taken in the palace. As we were leaving the front forecourt was full of guests photographing each other. I thought, 'If they're doing it why shouldn't I?' Jim, my chauffeur, manned the Leica. A palace official said, 'No photographs.' I pointed out cheerfully, 'Behind you 30 people are taking photos. Better get your running shoes on.' The official said, 'All right then, but be quick.' As we finished it started to rain.

* * *

Geraldine was walking at 4mph on the Precor treadmill. She does this regularly. Suddenly, without warning, the speed increased to around 30mph. She fell on to the rotating rubber, which gouged into her skin, then she was catapulted on to the doorframe and hard surfaces of my gym. She could have been killed. That was two weeks ago. She's still suffering.

Precor behaved poorly. Two executives came and said they'd never heard of such a thing. I spoke to accident lawyers who'd dealt with similar cases. Precor examined the machine, but could find no fault. They took it for further inspection. When it was last serviced no word of caution was given. Neither did any concern for Geraldine emanate from Precor, until the threat of litigation appeared. Then they offered sympathy galore. This show will run and run. Geraldine will never go on a treadmill again. I don't blame her.

Crazy names, crazy clothes, great food

Goran Strok, Croatian hotel owner supreme, took us at ludicrous speed in his BMW up the winding mountain roads behind Dubrovnik. Goran used to be a racing driver and he can't forget it. Even on the way down, after a big meal, with his wife, Renata, pleading, 'Go slower,' Yorrie lurched on.

Away from the bastardised coastline of Croatia you can find gems. We ended up in a tiny mountain village, Velji, near Cavtat. Neither of which you've heard of. Nor do you know the restaurant **Konavoski Komin**. That's why I'm on the planet. To tell you about such places. This one is a magical 300-year-old stone farmhouse with terraces overlooking a valley. During the war the Serbians used it as their army HQ. The owner is an old man, Vigo Siljug, the chef Stepan Martinovic. Vigo's daughters Maria and Smiljan help out. Love those Croatian names.

We started with local herb grappa. Fantastic. Went on to prosecco with cheese. Then the best prosciutto I've ever eaten, served with little onions from Vigo's garden. He takes three months to prepare the prosciutto. It's hung up in another stone house with a fire to smoke it and a draught to get the smoke out. Main course was young lamb and veal baked on charcoal for four hours under an iron bell. Historic beyond belief. The potatoes, cooked in the juices of the lamb, were fantastic too. To balance this, the bread was rubbery, the apple strudel horrific. Tasted as if it had been sitting about. Should have come straight from the oven. The daughter Maria was wearing Dalmatian costume. There's a website where you can buy those. The daughter in grey only works there occasionally.

Now to the **Taverna Bota Sare** in an old building in Mali Ston. We got there after a depressing coastal drive. Ugly, large new hotels going up. Nasty, nasty. The restaurant manager, Jerko Radic, moved our table into the road overlooking hills and the sea. A driver going by couldn't believe five people were eating in the road and crashed into a bollard with a bang. I haven't eaten an oyster since Barbados four years ago, when one, from the warm waters of the Gulf of Mexico, did my left leg in. If you ate an oyster from the Gulf of Mexico now you'd get 60 miles to the gallon. I tried Croatian oysters, some fried, some not. I lived. Then sensational bread, black squid risotto, sea bass. Dessert, which dated from the 15th century, was made of pasta, nuts, apple, cinnamon, chocolate, almonds, lemon and dates. Very heavy. Everyone was watching so I ate more than I wanted.

My final Croatian exposé is **Kamenice** in a beautiful old square in Dubrovnik. Locals go there. The serving ladies looked like they're running a communist prison, but they were efficient and charming. Terrible bread. Excellent scampi in tomato sauce. Small fish called jerite which tasted like whitebait. The only dessert was crème caramel so I had that. Pretty good. Lovely setting. Not expensive. A million times better than Gil's, Dubrovnik's 'in' place, which looks and tastes like a 1970 fiasco gone wrong. Far and away the best is **Nautika**, which I told you about. I mention it again in case you forgot.

* * *

Chef Jonathan Wright is a man of taste. When he owned the Gousse d'Ail restaurant in Oxford he ran out of the kitchen screaming and threatened to kill me with a kitchen knife. I met him again last Christmas when he worked at the **Setai** in Miami, a marvellous hotel with amazing food. Jonathan was a delight. A changed man. He's just signed to be executive chef at **Sandy Lane**, Barbados. I wish him well.

Had to laugh at a press release from Gordon Ramsay about October's reopening of the **Savoy Grill**. It said, 'Main courses will include Lobster Thermidor and Beef Wellington from the trolley.' In an interview Gordon once said the trolley was the enemy of good food, it dried out meat. He'd never have one. I wrote that this was a load of cobblers. Some of the best meat I've ever had was served to me from a trolley. I asked Gordon to comment on his change of mind. He declined. Nice to see, as blabbermouth approaches old age and penury, he's come round to my way of thinking.

* * *

Lunch at home: outstanding grilled plaice, major melon to start and a superb pavlova (meringue, fruit and cream) from my wonderful cook Lulu. American guest was Paul Winnowski, newish UK and other areas boss of Chubb alarms. My 40 years with Chubb have been a nightmare. Paul is sorting them out. Boy, do they need it. Only when he arrived and sent some top staff was it divined my alarm going off endlessly was due to a faulty box. Then the main unit suddenly emitted smoke. It was practically red hot. It had recently been replaced. Electricity was going in but nowhere else. It was cooking. My builder disconnected it. Why, I asked Paul, did they let me encase it in a teak box which, had no one spotted the smoke, would have caught fire and maybe burnt the house down? He was as shocked as me. Get rid of 96 per cent of your employees, Paul. Then start again.

Slow snails in the sunset, lovely teddies, odd potatoes

I missed the World Snail Racing Championships 2010. Had I known about it I'd have entered. With a fair wind I might have come second. The event is held in July at the Congham Church Fête.

If you book for 2011 stay at **Congham Hall**, a Georgian mansion set in parklands, orchards and gardens near miles of Norfolk's sandy beaches. That's what the brochure says. It also announces upcoming additions including a spa. So you can go snailing, sailing, trailing and wailing. Not that there was much to wail about. Except for the roast potatoes. They were dreadful. I was most upset, because when I met the chef, James Parkinson, he said, 'I can't stay and talk, I have to make sure the roast potatoes are up to standard.' 'You'll have a problem beating Sir Michael Caine's,' I said. Michael's are top, James's well below. They had no crispness on the outside and didn't appear to be properly roasted. You'll get a better roast lunch when you go there, because James doesn't normally cook. He's Von Essen group's executive chef, who appoints staff, oversees and administers. Congham's real chef is David Hammond. Hopefully a roast potato genius.

The Norfolk trip started badly. I forgot my camera. Luckily the helicopter pilot (you should have one) lent me his. Otherwise I'd have had to put in a large photo of me, thus destroying your Sunday rest. It's a beautiful hotel, not overdone, very discreet, clients a nice class of elderly gentlefolk. An ex-RAF lady of 84 sat alone with a drink. 'It's the champagne that keeps me going,' she announced. They sell teddy bears in the lobby. For those, like me, in their second childhood. If I didn't already possess 56 teddy bears I'd have bought a Congham one. I was dining with the marvellous Lord Waheed Alli. We're plotting a new TV show. He said, 'You're 75, Michael, but you behave like 19.' 'Not 19, Waheed, 17,' I remarked.

At Congham we sat in a bay window for drinks, got some fantastic canapés. 'The lounge is yellow,' I dictated. 'Sudbury yellow,' the manager, Julie Woodhouse, informed me. 'The dining room's pink,' I dictated later. 'Old rose,' advised Geraldine. It's little details like that which make life worth living. I had very good warm rolls, followed by a historic tian of Cromer crab. My roast beef was overcooked and cut too thin. Not a patch on the Wolseley, which has the best roast beef in London. To compensate, Parkinson's carrot purée and red cabbage were memorable. I tried a pleasant Bakewell tart with vanilla ice-cream, Geraldine a baked apple from the garden. She pronounced that and her Cromer lobster 'a triumph'. So it's executive chef a strong 7; Richard Gilderson the pilot 9, for lending his camera; Geraldine 10 and me off the top of the scale for being a blessing to mankind.

* * *

My new hero is Jean Barnard, the US tourist who sued Qantas airline because a three-year-old boy screamed so loudly that her ears started bleeding. She required hospital treatment. Jean wrote to her travel agent, 'I guess we're fortunate that my eardrum was exploding and I was swallowing blood. Had it not been for that I would have dragged the kid out of his mother's arms and stomped him to death.' I'm with you all the way, Jean. I'd like you in restaurants when screaming kids destroy the pleasure of my meal. If I made a noise like that I'd be told to shut up or leave. Restaurant managers are terrified of pointing out that yelling monsters upset other customers. Just as that silly restaurant manager Peter Eisendle at the Villa Feltrinelli on Lake Garda saw nothing amiss when a diner put his laptop on the serving counter and blasted out rock music. Jean Barnard achieved a 'confidential agreement out of court' with Qantas. Whatever she got she deserved. Maybe I'll wave a few writs at restaurants where my culinary enjoyment is battered by noisy kids.

* * *

I never thought a London mayor could be worse than Ken Livingstone. Boris Johnson beats him by a million light miles. Traffic is moving slower than ever. World War II was a blessing compared to what Boris is doing to our capital. The worst traffic jam in London is going east through Admiralty Arch at the bottom of the Mall. The lights are on red for a minute, on green for eight seconds. To make things worse Boris has cut the two lanes down, by reserving one for cyclists.

Cycling should be banned in all cities. Instead Boris floods London with rent-a-bikes. Concrete an area north of Golders Green and let them ride round it to their heart's content. On real roads they're a menace. My Award for Dopey Remark of the Year goes to Boris for: 'Cycling – you can enjoy God's fresh air.' Where's he cycling? In the Outer Hebrides? In London you can suffocate from the pollution. Doesn't he realise most of us have cars? Why can't we get a bit of consideration?

* * *

Old jokes are best. A flasher pulls open his coat in front of Mrs Cohen and says, 'What do you think of that?' 'Nice lining,' she replies.

Dining Stars take a bite of the unknown

Throw a stone into water – there are ripples. Throw Winner: there are shock waves. When I made *Michael Winner's Dining Stars* for ITV most of the critics realised I was playing the wicked pantomime villain, described by some as the panto dame. A few thought I was just being rude. 'Reduced contestants to tears,' all that sort of claptrap. Truth is I remain friends with them all. I had them to my house for dinner. I speak a lot to the series winner, Justine Forrest, a housewife from Longridge near Preston who dieted and lost 14 stone. I made Justine famous for her brownies. Now she's selling them to local shops and via a website which is grander than mine. Not difficult, as I haven't got one.

Dean Lewis, the Jamaican who wanted to kill me because I hated his curried goat (his father agreed with me that he'd done it all wrong) has given up his job as demolisher of buildings. He and his wife Sophie, now, own **Mango's Café Bar**, serving Jamaican food in Failsworth, Manchester. Dean asked me to come for the opening. I declined but sent a signed photo. I asked the other day, 'Is my photo on the wall?' 'No,' he replied. 'Why not?' I asked. 'Because it's you,' said Dean. He's a laugh. I wish him well.

Particularly memorable was taking Justine to Bruges. Lunch was at one of my favourite restaurants, the **Gouden Harynck**, Golden Herring to those not speaking Flemish or whatever the jargon is in that area. Michelin-starred chef Philippe Serruys cooks, his wife, Maryke, manages front of house. Philippe was in his kitchen showing Justine how to cook pommes boulangère. She said, 'I don't do it that way,' as if hers was better. Terrific. Lancashire to the fore.

I loved my lunch. Scallops with puréed chestnut, a second course of langoustines with cabbage and some delicious sauce. Main course: pan-fried partridge with a vine leaf on top, buckwheat on the side, and chutney. For dessert, apple tartin with vanilla cream. 'What are you having?' I asked Justine. 'The mango thing,' she replied. At a nearby table my assistant Dinah and make-up lady Joan had sea bass. Both said it was the best ever. Justine left almost everything. Too twiddly-diddly for her.

There we were in this lovely 17th-century building, beautiful room, a fire burning, lovely flowers, all water off a duck's back to Justine. That's what I like about her. She is what she is. Go to her website, order chocolate brownies. She sent me some, the container wrapped in white paper with red hearts on it. People ask me why I cried when giving judgement on her cooking. Her 13-year-old daughter, a stroke victim, said in a slurred voice, after I'd not been kind about her mother's meal, but referring to how thrilled Justine was to be on TV with me, 'I want to thank you for all you've done for my mummy.' That tipped it. A marvellous, loving family. Her nine-year-old son Christopher has half a heart. He's undergone many serious operations. He's still at risk.

I also speak regularly to Hemma Chauhan, a lovely Indian contestant. She gave a dinner party to celebrate her husband Dillip's recovery from cancer. I proposed a toast to his continued well-being. The cancer's returned. Doctors say he won't live. Peter, the lively Essex boy, will just miss me in the South of France this summer. They're all part of my life now. I like that.

* * *

Be on red alert. Buy nothing for Christmas (a mere 124 shopping days away, as I write) because my new book, *Unbelievable! My Life in Restaurants and Other Places* is out in October at £14.99, less from *Sunday Times* Books. It contains very funny stories (I'm doing my own book review) about my dining with movie stars and other biggies. It's a great addition to last year's *Winner's Dinners* book, because it contains all these columns to bring the information right up to date. Plus new Winner's Dinners Awards. The first five off the press will be given, fully signed, dedicated and cartooned by me, to the letter writers whose work is published in the *Sunday Times* nearest to the date of the book arriving on the planet. Please, hold the applause until you've read it.

* * *

I'm not going to **Sandy Lane**, Barbados, this Christmas/ New Year. With my depleted left leg I can't get in or out of the sea because there's a shingle drop that had me yelling for help anyway. The beach slopes so much I can't handle that either. As last year, Geraldine and I will have Christmas Day lunch prepared by the world's greatest cook, Sir Michael Caine, aided and abetted by the wondrous Shakira. We'll New Year it at the **Palace** hotel, Gstaad. I have secret plans to visit a different Caribbean location early in 2011. You'll be the first to know. Possibly the second. Maybe the 105th.

* * *

I haven't written lately about Moishe Pippick, Abe Schwantz and Hymie Pockle. They're mourning the closure of Bloom's kosher restaurant in Golders Green. I told them Rubens in Baker Street was better. But they're inconsolable. Some people are never satisfied.

Winner speaks

On waiting for food: 'I was hoping to eat this meal before I died of old age.'

Confused information, amazing grub

I'm the world expert on Kensington High Street. I should have chosen it as my *Mastermind* subject. Whoever sets the questions would have been hard-pressed to think of any. I moved into a flat in my present residence (later turning the house into one unit) in 1946. The High Street was a few yards to the south. My first ever published article, on 8 September 1950, was about the child star John Howard Davis (Oliver in David Lean's *Oliver Twist*), who lived nearby. I was 14 years old. My peak writing period.

I also wrote about Trevor Bowen. 'Who's that?' you ask. He was boss of Barker's, the High Street's biggest shop. The war delayed the building of its second tower. It turned into Biba. Now like all the big High Street stores it's broken into iddly-piddly little units. A national newspaper has offices where once ladies' lingerie ruled. Their employees often go to **Côte**, a newish restaurant just south of the High Street. My lovely receptionist Ruby loved their Soho branch. I thought, 'A Winner receptionist and a gaggle of hacks, wadda they know?' I was wrong.

Côte is fantastic. It's a Richard Caring enterprise, he who imports schmutter from the Far East. Richard also owns many of the classiest restaurants and hotels in the world. Old-timers in the hospitality industry scoffed when he arrived. Today they're ridden with jealousy. Outside, before eating, I was with the chef, Alex Scrimgeour and the charming manager, Louise Hill. I asked Alex, 'Do you work here?' 'The answer to that is yes and no,' he replied. I asked again, 'Do you work here?' Alex said, 'I'm the executive chef.' 'Do you work in this branch?' I persisted. 'Sometimes,' said Alex. Eventually he let on (deep secret, should only be known by MI5) that he worked at the group's head office.

Once inside I asked Alex, 'What should I eat?' 'We're known for our steaks,' he responded. 'Which one should I have?' I asked. 'Rib eye, sirloin, fillet, all of those,' Alex declared. I dictated into my tape, 'He can't give a precise answer, this man. He's got a problem.' I continued patiently, 'Of the three, Alex, suggest one.' He chose the rib eye. Alex was executive chef at the Wolseley after Chris Galvin. I thought he improved the food greatly. The grub at Côte is amazing and remarkably inexpensive. From Monday to Friday, 12 noon to 7pm, they do a two-course meal for £9.95, three courses for £11.90. It's now my staff's favourite. The food is tasty, fresh, beautifully prepared.

The room is spacious, tables generously spaced. Service a bit slow for my main course, otherwise exemplary. I started with fantastic goat's cheese tartine. Followed by steak and very good chips, they call them frites. Geraldine thought my béarnaise sauce incredible. 'It's just like a French bistro,' she said. Pity about the piped, boom-boom beat music. If it's trying to be French why not have Charles Aznavour, Jacques Brel and Edith Piaf? My dessert was crème caramel, Geraldine's chocolate mousse. Both superb. We even got a freebie melon liqueur.

For the grand finale, Alex changed his title. 'I'm food and beverage manager for Côte Holdings,' he announced. Information ain't his speciality. Luckily, food is.

* * *

I hate phone calls from people trying to sell something. Most are just a recording, 'Hi there . . .' I guess when ordering on the internet I foolishly gave my phone number. My friend Robert Mitchum said in an interview, 'I don't see why any bum with two cents should be allowed to intrude on my life.' He and my pal Victor Mature were the best interviewees ever. They're gone. My acquaintance, Hugh Grant, is alive and good. Sadly, he's stopped being interviewed.

I also hate packaging. It's all plastic or processed rubbish which defies tearing, knifing, hydrogen bombs, killer dogs. I tried to open a carton of organic goat's cheese the other night. Ended up hitting it with a hammer, attacking it with a chisel, throwing it against the wall. Then Geraldine came in, and with a flick of her wrist it was open. Wha'd'ya mean, 'Why are you eating organic goat's cheese?' For dinner, to keep weight down, I eat practically nothing. Two glasses of tomato juice is a big meal for me. Strange really, when I write a column called 'Winner's Dinners'.

* * *

Moishe is in the desert standing behind trestle tables, selling ties. A Taliban staggers up and says, 'You Jewish bastard, I should shoot you. But I need water.' Moishe says, 'Water I don't do. I do silk ties, wool ties, here's a nice one, blue with white spots.' The Taliban says, 'Gimme water, you pig.' Moishe says, 'You want water, go over that sand dune there. Turn left. Walk a mile, take a right, go over two more sand dunes. There you'll find a restaurant. They do water.' The Taliban lurches off, returns two hours later, parched, tongue cracked, in a terrible state. 'I'll have the blue one with white spots,' he says. 'You, I should slit your throat. I get to the restaurant and your f****** brother says he won't let me in without a tie.'

Waitresses R Us, hooray

I don't know how you can make money on a hotel with only 11 rooms. But as I'm not an accountant, tax inspector or financial wizard, it doesn't matter what I think.

The Samling, an exquisite Edwardian hotel in the Lake District, is set on its own 76-acre estate. That makes seven acres per room. So guests such as Tom Cruise and David Beckham could have cavorted in their very own space. Since I was there nothing's changed except the manager. It's no longer Claire Pollock. She was temporary and now works in the Cotswolds. The restaurant supervisor is Kerry Maguire. The hotel manager is now Andrew McKay, who, with verve veering on total insanity, offers guests a refund if it rains during their stay. 'Even if it drizzles,' he announced to the press. Mind you, he didn't say how big the refund would be.

When I was there I complained bitterly that I was given tea bags instead of loose tea. Not good enough for an exclusive hotel. Claire said she'd put it top of her agenda to get loose tea. She didn't. She left. They still serve tea bags. Black mark, Andrew. Deal with this. Other than the tea bag problem the rest was fine. They even provided butter as well as jam and cream for the scones. Not many places do that. The brochure calls it a hidden gem, which is more or less true. There's a great view of Lake Windermere. At dinner, the waitress, Londi, came over and said, 'I've got some canapés here for us.' I said, 'For us? Are you going to join us?' She didn't.

They served Blenheim water, along with Tufa and Hildon – 'bottom three world,' as the actor Bruce Dern used to say regularly about almost anything. 'Pigeon parfait, soft egg, shallot purée, that's my starter,' I announced. For my main course I got a couple of bits of duck that were red and a couple of bits of lamb that were red. I'd never have known which one was which if I hadn't been told. Sounds odd, but they were fine. The starter was very good, too. Then the waitress appeared and said, again, 'Here's a pre-dessert for us.' 'I don't why she doesn't sit down at our table if it's for us,' I dictated. Londi declined to join 'us' for what was described as orange marmalade, lemon and lime sorbet, tequila jelly, lemon and lime zest. That's more information than I need to know. But it was very pleasant. So was my real dessert, which Londi did not suggest was for 'us'. Had I offended her? It was pink grapefruit jelly, honey, ginger and granola biscuit.

The chef, Nigel Menham, did well. He'd have done better if he'd blown up the piped music supply. I got them to turn it off, but really. A marvellously understated old place, beautiful rooms and piped rubbish. What comes over these people? Don't they think punters can live with just their own conversation? I find my dialogue fascinating. I could talk to myself for hours. Often have to, because no one else is interested.

* * *

Investigations continue to find a venue for my 75th birthday party. We looked at Princess Margaret's apartment in **Kensington Palace**. They're doing great things at the palace, but not to Margaret's place. It resembled the DHSS office in Beckton. The only toilet was like a 1970s council flat gone wrong. The **Wallace Collection** museum is grand beyond belief. Too corporate. My favourite caterer, Johnny Robertson-Roxburgh of Admirable Crichton, came round to help. We considered Chiswick House but it closes at the end of October for restoration. I needed it on 30 October for 24 people. I've hired a superb harpist, Nicola Broke, to play during pre-dinner drinks. But where? I suppose McDonald's, Kensington High Street, is out of the question. I'll keep trying. Only eight weeks left. Must make more effort.

* * *

My marvellous PA has quit after a year. 'Because you're a bad-tempered git,' I hear you remark most unkindly. Er . . . no. If this isn't the most extraordinary reason to lose a PA, what is? The lady in question was an unmarried mother living in Essex. Seeking a new companion, she went to a website called sugardaddies.com. Within seconds the man she met had given her a £35,000 diamond ring, followed by other jewellery galore, followed by a new 4x4 BMW, followed by a half-share in a multi-million-pound house, followed by . . . it matters not. The lady bade farewell to me, I couldn't compete. She's a great gal. I wish her continued happiness. I'm £9m in debt. When I need another couple of mill I know where to go.

* * *

Mrs Cohen goes to a fortune-teller. The fortune-teller says, 'I see a terrible attack on your husband. He is beaten, mutilated and murdered.' Mrs Cohen asks, 'Was I acquitted?' For this gem I thank my neighbour, Academy Award-winner Don Black, co-lyricist for Andrew Lloyd Webber's *Aspects of Love*. The revival of this great show is currently a box office smasheroo at the Menier Chocolate Factory.

Historic food in a basement too far

Sometimes I think: I'm being too kind. I must kill, kill, kill. Restaurant slaughter is always good for a laugh. So I worked myself up into a frenzy of bloodlust. A friend of mine told me he hated **Pierre Koffmann's Restaurant** at the Berkeley hotel, Belgravia. I thought, I'll get the knife out.

Things started well. I phoned the Berkeley. 'Is Pierre Koffmann's restaurant open for Saturday lunch?' I asked. A lady replied, 'I don't know.' 'Perhaps you could find out,' I said rather icily. It was. The Koffmann receptionist was polite. 'Do you have any special requirements, such as dietary requests?' she asked. 'Just a large table, please,' I responded.

Three cars were parked in front of the Berkeley. I placed my Bentley behind them. A doorman said, 'It can't stay here. We'll move it round the side.' 'Why can't it stay here?' I demanded. 'Those other cars are in the front.' 'I'm going to move them,' said the doorman. Bet he isn't, I thought. Before major hostilities commenced, a senior doorman appeared wearing a bowler hat. 'I'd like my car to stay here,' I said. 'Don't worry, Mr Winner, I'll deal with it,' said the bowler-hatted one, name of Taffy. After lunch two of the three cars that I was assured would be moved were still there. A £1m-plus Bugatti Veyron and a £535,000 chromed-up Mercedes McLaren SLR. My 1975 Bentley added dignity.

In the hotel I asked a concierge, 'Where's Pierre Koffmann's?' 'You have to go outside and walk to the street entrance,' said a woman. 'Nonsense, you go through the hotel,' I responded. So the lady led me through the bar to Pierre's pad. Why tell me I had to go outside?

The restaurant is drab. Corridor-like. Lacking in atmosphere. Comfy tables. I was led to a nice one by restaurant manager Eric Garnier. I liked him when he was at Racine. The starter canapés of stuffed cheese were ghastly. Heavy, no taste. Water was the awful Tufa. Now removed from the Wolseley and Richard Caring's The Ivy, Caprice and Scott's. The bread was only adequate. Great for the scalpel, I thought. Things are going well. Then Pierre ruined it.

My first course, fresh crab with celeriac and apple, was superb. Geraldine's foie gras with French bean salad lacked much foie gras. I asked if she wanted more, she said, 'No.' Then I saw Eric going to get her some more. She said no to me and yes to him. That's beautiful women for you. She loved it. Pierre could be seen through the glass wall working away in the kitchen. Rare for the chef to be in for lunch on Saturdays. My main course, cod with chorizo, white beans, tomatoes and a bowl of carrots and peas, was marvellous. Perfect chips, made on the premises, came in a cup of fake newsprint *Le Monde*. I asked Eric how long it would take if I ordered pistachio soufflé. He said 12 minutes. Normally they ask you to order soufflé at six in the morning. That's if you're coming for dinner. It was the best soufflé – texture right, taste fantastic, ice-cream to go in it, incredible.

A splendid meal. Simple, to the point, no plate decoration, masterful blend of tastes, not overpowering, not overworked. Service very on the ball. Pierre Koffmann had three Michelin stars, took six years off, then returned. Next Michey-star time they should give him eight.

Later I took Michael and Shakira Caine. They loved it. I had the best sweetbreads I've ever eaten. The horrid cheese puffs were off, my freebie starter was a delicious savoury pastry tart. 'The room needs mirrors,' observed Michael. Just what I'd said on my first visit. Mirror the end and one side wall. Liven the place up. Take away the boring photos of food and have a mural of flowers or something jolly. It's a basement. Make it cheerful.

So it hasn't been a murder, has it? I must leave on a low note. Let me think. The bill took too long to come. Eric, nice chap, gave me a number which he said was direct to the restaurant and it was to some woman in Bethnal Green. He took forever to return calls to his mobile, so what was the point of giving me the number? Summation: food 99.9 per cent, atmosphere minus 68. Room minus 1,006. Pierre Koffmann: the greatest cook. A cook, in case you didn't know, is much better than a chef.

Winner's Dinners Awards

2010 – 2011

Winner's Dinners Awards 2010–2011

BEST UK RESTAURANT: SCOTT'S

BEST UK CHEF: PIERRE KOFFMANN

BEST UK HOTEL CHEF: JOHN WILLIAMS OF THE RITZ, PICCADILLY

BEST UK RESTAURANT CHAIN: CÔTE

BEST UK COUNTRY HOTEL: SHARROW BAY

BEST UK HOTEL MANAGER: JOAN REEN OF YNYSHIR HALL

BEST HOTEL IN THE WORLD: LA COLOMBE D'OR, SAINT-PAUL DE VENCE

BEST RESTAURANT IN THE WORLD: HOSTELLERIE JÉRÔME, LA TURBIE, SOUTH OF FRANCE

BEST HOTEL MANAGER IN THE WORLD: HANS MEIER OF THE SETAI, SOUTH BEACH, MIAMI

BEST RESTAURANT MANAGER IN THE WORLD: GILDO BOCCHINI OF THE PALACE HOTEL, GSTAAD, SWITZERLAND

LIFETIME ACHIEVEMENT AWARD: CHRISTOPHER CORBIN AND JEREMY KING

BEST SERVICE EVER: HARRY'S BAR, VENICE

BEST SURPRISE MEAL: PLANET HOLLYWOOD, LONDON

WORST MEAL OF THE YEAR: SCALINI

RESTAURANTS IN AND NEAR LONDON I GO TO A LOT:

Murano – marvellous Italian food prepared by Angela Hartnett, Gordon Ramsay's far-and-away best protégée. The **River Café** – the best and most consistent food in London. Italian, supervised and sometimes cooked by Lady Ruth Rogers. Also the best London restaurant staff by a long way. **The Ivy**, **Le Caprice** and the **Ivy Club** – still excellent standard, simple, comfort food in glamorous surroundings. **Indian Zing** in Hammersmith – the best Indian restaurant I've ever been to. **The Wolseley** – the buzziest place in town. Celebrity-strewn, big menu, all of it excellent. The **Ritz** hotel tea room and restaurant – both places unique in London if not the world. Preserved Edwardian grandeur, immaculate service, superb food. The **Goring** – a family-run hotel in Belgravia, traditional in the best sense of the word. Every room and aspect a pleasure except for a grotesque David Linley chandelier in the main dining room, quite out of place with the restrained décor everywhere else. **Belvedere** in Holland Park. A terrific room with major Damien Hirst and Andy Warhol art lent by the owner Jimmy Lahoud. Food is pleasant and at times memorable. The **French Horn** at Sonning – the most lovely Thames-side setting, old-fashioned food of great quality, ducks roasting on the open fire as you enter. The **Royal Oak** at Paley Green, owned by Sir Michael Parkinson – English pub food at its best and most superior. A well-deserved Michelin star. **Bibendum** in Fulham Road – some of the best, simple, fantastic food in the capital. Great room in the old Michelin Building.

MICHAEL WINNER ON HIS AWARDS

This year's awards again reflect my personal view of places I've been to. Scott's restaurant in Mount Street is the most immense credit to Richard Caring, the owner and originator of it. Although the Scott's name was used on restaurants on the same premises for years, Caring completely gutted the place and spent two years restoring it and changing it and making it completely different. Namely a fantastic restaurant. It was poor before, now it's a model in seating, ambience and food. It is not over-fussed. The staff are extremely efficient and friendly. It has a very wide menu. Very comfortable seats. It's everything a restaurant should be. Absolutely deserves the title **Best UK Restaurant** even though the chef is not known to anybody. I think chefs should be cooks and shut up. They're the most boring people in the world.

* * *

Best UK Chef is Pierre Koffmann, a chef brought up and working in England. His new restaurant in the Berkeley hotel, London, serves extraordinarily simple, effective, well-balanced food. Although Koffmann was a three-Michelin-star chef before he retired six years ago, his cooking has none of the overworked complexity of so many three-star chefs. There is no plate decoration. Just proper portions, brilliantly cooked, plainly but well presented. In an age of culinary excess, Koffmann reduces cooking to its essentials. He takes dishes I have eaten in other places and does them better. What more could anyone ask?

* * *

The **Best UK Hotel Chef** I've given to John Williams of the

Ritz. He does not appear on many of the lists of great chefs. That is because newspaper critics have got their heads so far up their own arses they only see daylight when they open their mouths. He produces the most marvellous simple food. English to the core. He himself comes from Newcastle.

To go to the Ritz hotel is an occasion. It's the only hotel in London that has not ruined itself by attempting to recreate and redecorate and update. The updating in the other grand hotels means that they removed classical and fantastic decoration by absolute genius experts and replaced it with a quick fix designed by morons. Only the Ritz retains its original grandeur.

John Williams, who used to be at Claridge's (before Gordon Ramsay took over the restaurant and decreased its quality by a few million light miles), is absolutely the right person for the Ritz. He knows what he's doing and he does it superbly. On top of that he's extremely charming.

* * *

The **Best UK Restaurant Chain** award goes to a fairly new chain called Côte. It's owned by Richard Caring, who was in the rag trade, entered the restaurant business, and is now one of the biggest and most successful hotel and restaurant operators in the world. Those who smirked are now ridden with jealousy. At times when other restaurants were closing, running out of money and decreasing standards, Richard has kept everything tip-top. The Côte chain offers unbelievable value. As you can see from my article about it in this book. The food is marvellous. My staff now go there regularly.

* * *

The **Best UK Country Hotel** is Sharrow Bay. It used to be owned by two gay gents, Brian Sack and Francis Coulson. When I first asked to go there Brian said, 'We daren't have you. You're not welcome.' Later on, his partner Francis died and I tried again. This time Brian let me in. It was absolutely marvellous. Brian played the piano in the evening and sang. It was a very personal place.

Brian told me that when he died he was going to leave the hotel to his manager/managing director, Nigel Lightburn, who would carry on as one of the family. He called Nigel 'my illegitimate son.' He would run the place the way Brian and Francis would have wished. In fact Nigel sold the hotel within seconds to the Von Essen Hotel Group and settled down in the luxurious house that Brian had left him on Lake Ullswater. So much for loyalty to the dead. Brian's possessions were sold. I was rather touched that, having first refused me entry, six photos of me and Brian were in the auction.

When I went back again I was interested to see if the hotel was of the same standard under new ownership, if it was anything like before under the very personal ownership of Brian and Francis. I think it was every bit as good. The manager, Andrew King, had kept all the decoration and everything very similar. The food was fantastic! The lake view was historic. It was always a bit of a show-business hang out. Ian McKellen was eating in one corner of the room with a young man, so I didn't disturb him, even though I first met him when I interviewed him for a part in 1963. The whole thing was a delight. It well deserves my award as Best UK Country Hotel.

* * *

The **Best UK Hotel Manager** of the year is Joan Reen, who runs the delightful small hotel Ynyshir Hall in Wales. She is there from 8am until late at night. She is cheerful, totally dedicated and makes it a very personal experience. It's like being in a small country house where she is the host. She does that marvellously.

She has only one serious problem. The views from the windows of the hotel are staggeringly beautiful. They look out over the Welsh countryside and the lovely gardens of the hotel. Joan is completely bonkers when it comes to curtains. She loves curtains. So she fills the windows with curtains where you can only see the view through a tiny space. Every day Geraldine used to get up on a chair and loop the curtains up over the poles so we could see out of the window. In spite of this, or perhaps because of it, because a nutty hotel manager is always a good thing, she well deserves the title of Best UK Hotel Manager.

The **Best Hotel in the World** is La Colombe d'Or in Saint-Paul de Vence in the South of France. It is the most unique hotel that I visit. Set on the edge of a beautiful, preserved medieval village, it was frequented by all of the major Impressionist artists who lived in the area. As they couldn't afford to pay for the food, instead they gave paintings. As a result, the dining room displays important oil paintings by Picasso, Braque, Manet, Matisse and many others. There are also sculpture and mosaics by Impressionists of equal fame.

The hotel is a kind of farmhouse run by the same family for decades, currently by Daniele Roux and her husband, François. They are on the spot and on the ball. Daniele, with one glance, can destroy any human being in sight of whom she disapproves. Prices are amazingly cheap. It has the most beautiful swimming pool I've ever seen, a unique atmosphere and is one of the few unchanged parts of the South of France. I first went there in 1946. It's just as magical now as it was then.

* * *

Best Restaurant in the World is Hostellerie Jérôme, La Turbie, South of France. This extraordinary restaurant is set in the hills in a small village. You go up a cobbled street and find it hidden away. It's run by the chef Bruno Cirino and his wife, Marion, who looks after the front of house. It has two Michelin stars but that does not in any way demonstrate the extraordinary quality of cooking, which is great without being over-fussed. The room is a delight, with old murals from the 18th century. Tables are not too close together. There's a small terrace with further seating. If you want to get there, you go along the coast road toward Monte Carlo, turn left in Cap d'Ail and carry on upwards until you find La Turbie and Hostellerie Jérôme. It's well worth it.

* * *

The **Best Hotel Manager in the World** I've awarded this year to Hans Meier of the Setai hotel in Miami. I went to Miami for New Year 2010 to be with my friend Sir Michael Caine after having had Christmas dinner with him in his home in Surrey. The first week the weather was wonderful. The second week it was not cold, it was somewhat more freezing than the Arctic. It was the coldest weather they'd had in Miami since 1940.

Hans is a fantastic hotel manager because he's everywhere. He greets every guest with great charm. He was there every time I left the hotel to go somewhere and every time I came back. He behaved exactly the same to other guests. You could tell the hotel was well managed because everything ran smoothly. The food, the service, the lot. Everything comes from the top. As they say, a fish rots from the head down. If the boss is useless then the whole thing's useless. In Hans', case, he's superb and the whole hotel is superb. If you go to South Beach, Miami, go there.

* * *

The **Best Restaurant Manager in the World** I give to the wonderfully charming Gildo Bocchini of the Palace hotel, Gstaad. The Palace remains a grand hotel in the old tradition, with the most beautiful views over the mountains. Even in winter you can sit on the terrace with deep snow a few feet away.

Gildo has known everybody and everything. He's not overpowering. He's extremely organised and it's always a pleasure to enter the restaurant and see his smiling face. He is the epitome of the old-time elegant restaurant manager with his evening dress and stylish behaviour. The hotel itself I greatly like.

Although I did have a major falling out with them. They annoyed me greatly by booking me into the wrong room, so I didn't go on that occasion. A few other things happened I didn't like. I named the manager Ernst Scherz as the worst hotel manager in the world in my awards and slagged him off for years. After three years I had a phone call from the Palace saying they'd like to come and see me because a lot of the things I was complaining about they'd dealt with. They came most graciously to make amends and offer their friendship. So I went back.

Everything I'd complained about was improved. I've been going back regularly ever since. It is an absolutely marvellous hotel. In winter or in summer, when the mountain flowers are out, it is a place I strongly recommend you to visit.

* * *

The **Lifetime Achievement** award goes to Chris Corbin and Jeremy King. They are the most gentlemanly people in the restaurant business. A business not known for housing gentleman. In fact, it offers more spivs and wideboy smart-arses than any other industry I can think of.

King and Corbin are beautifully dressed, immensely hard-working and have the most extraordinary achievements. They took a run-down place that used to be very popular called Le Caprice and turned it back into a very buzzy and viable restaurant. Then they did the same with The Ivy. Then they created J Sheekey.

Their type of comfort food, served by very pleasant and efficient people, is a total contrast to the rubbish, over-decorated, clever nonsense that's served elsewhere. They have not tried to keep up with fads and fashions. They just serve the sort of things people like.

When they sold The Ivy Group they created the Wolseley. It is the most successful restaurant in England. Certainly the restaurant I go to more than anywhere else. It has taken over as the main show-business/celebrity restaurant. I don't mean by that silly celebrities. I see nearly every time I go my very old friend Lucian Freud, together with endless actors and actresses. If you're coming up to town (or you're in town), you could not do better than spend a lunchtime or evening at the Wolseley. Or indeed breakfast, tea, elevenses, late-night supper, anything.

* * *

The **Best Service Ever** I give to Harry's Bar in Venice. The downstairs bar is very crowded. The service is so quick it isn't true. The waiters glide through the tables like a ballet. Their rhythm, their speed and their efficiency are just beyond belief. I've never seen anything like it in any restaurant in the world. They're all smiling, they're all charming, they're Italian in the very best sense of the word. Of course, this comes from the top, which is Arrigo Cipriani, unquestionably one of the greatest restaurateurs. He's there, immaculately dressed, going round greeting guests, who range from the most famous writers (Ernest Hemingway was a regular) to movie stars to tourists to Venetian people. When Harry gives you a breakdown of who is who in the bar it is just extraordinary. A great, great place.

* * *

The **Best Surprise Meal** I had in the last year was, of all places, at Planet Hollywood. I'd eaten there before and it was awful. It has moved from Coventry Street to the Haymarket. The premises are much simpler than they used to be. It looks like a reasonably posh canteen. I was just amazed by the quality of the food. Everything tastes interesting except the spare ribs, which I thought were horrific. There's a whole lot of dishes that you can't get anywhere else, all exquisitely done. For what is basically a mass-catering operation it really is extraordinary. I went with the owner of Planet Hollywood, Robert Earl, who started as a waiter and then had a tiny restaurant somewhere in South Kensington. He and his wife did everything, from wiping the tables, sweeping the floor to greeting the customers. This professionalism shows. Planet Hollywood is a triumph. You may not think of going there. But I advise you to try it. I believe you'll be, as I was, extremely surprised and happy when you leave.

* * *

The **Worst Meal of the Year** was at Scalini. A restaurant I've enjoyed for a number of years. It's always been vastly overcrowded, far too noisy. Health and safety should come and deal with the noise as a health hazard. But somehow or other it overcame that. Now it has become a caricature of itself.

The noise level has risen. The tables are even closer together than they were before. The food has gone down the drain. I had very tired squares of Parmesan which had either been cut from a real Parmesan so long ago that only pensioners would remember when that Parmesan first arrived on the premises, or were bought in, or God knows what. I had a spaghetti bolognese which is one of the most awful things I've ever been served in my life. It was all a kind of brown. The brown had spread into everything and tasted of nothing. The so-called meat sauce was just horrific. The spaghetti was awful. An Italian restaurant should be able to do spaghetti bolognese if nothing else.

The restaurant manager spends a lot of time being jolly. Jolly is not enough. You have to run a restaurant with a rod of iron. The most awful group of people sat next to me who were not meant to be sitting there but the manager, when they looked a bit threatening, left them there. That is typical of the way the place is now run. What is once good is now miserable. Stay away.

Hotels and Restaurants Index

Hotel de Paris (112). Place du Casino, 98000 Monte Carlo, Monaco, France. 00377 98 06 30 00
Hotel Iden (173). CH-3780 Gstaad, Switzerland. 0041 33 748 49 50
Il Gabbiano (171). 335 S Biscayne Blvd # Cu100, Miami, FL 33131-2360, USA. 001 305 373 0063

Indian Zing (192, 248). 236 King Street, London W6 0RF. 020 8748 5959
Ivy, The (152, 248). 1-5 West Street, London WC2H 9NQ. 020 7557 6393
Ivy Club, The (180). 1-5 West Street, London WC2H 9NQ. 020 7557 6095

Jerry's Deli (171). 1450 Collins Avenue, South Beach Miami, Fl 33139, USA. 001 305 532 8030

Kamenice (228). Gunduliceva Poljana 8, 20000 Dubrovnik, Croatia. 00385 20 323 682□
Kensington Palace (240). Palace Avenue, Kensington, London W8 4. 08444 827 777
Kitchen W8 (129, 140, 176). 11-13 Abingdon Road, London W8 6AH. 020 7937 0120
Koffmann's (242, 247). The Berkeley Hotel, Wilton Place, Knightsbridge, London SW1X 7RL. 020 7235 1010
Konavoski Komin (227). Jasenice, Velji Do 4, Cavtat, Croatia. 00385 20 479 607

La Colombe d'Or (100, 122, 191 247). 1 place general de gaulle, 06570 St Paul de Vence, France. 0033 4 93 32 80 02
La Figa (118). The Mosaic Building, 45 Narrow Street, London E14 8DN. 020 7790 0077
La Mamounia, Hotel (202, 203). Avenue Bab Jdid, 40 040 Marrakech, Morocco. 00212 524 388 600
La Petite Maison (200, 208). 53-54 Brook's Mews, London W1K 4EG. 020 7495 4774
La Reserve de Beaulieu (96). 5, boulevard du Marechal Leclerc, 06310 Beaulieu-sur-Mer, France. 0033 4 93 01 00 01
La Tortuga (104). Via XXIV Maggio, 5, 25084 Gargnano BS, Italy. 0039 0365 71251

Le Caprice (179, 194, 248). Arlington House, 25 Arlington Street, St. James's, London SW1A 1RJ. 020 7629 2239
Lido di Adriano Gramatica (104). Via Colletta, 61, 25084 Gargnano BS, Italy. 0039 0365 791 042
Locanda San Vigilio (210, 219). Via San Vigilio, 1, 37016 Garda, Italy. 0039 0457 256 688
Louis XV-Alain Ducasse (113). Hotel de Paris, Place du Casino, 98000 Monte Carlo, Monaco, France. 00377 98 06 30 00
Luton Hoo Hotel (213). The Mansion House, Luton LU1 3TQ. 01582 734 437

Mango's Café Bar (233). 642 Oldham Road, Failsworth M35 9DU. 01616 849 958
Mariott Grosvenor Square (122). Grosvenor Square, Westminster, London W1K 6JP. 020 7493 1232
McDonald's, Wood Green (168). 97-101 High Road, Wood Green, London N22 6BB. 020 8888 1120
More (196). 00 385 98 942 6427
Mosimann's (174). 11B West Halkin Street, London, UK SW1X 8JL. 020 7235 9625
Mr Chow (200). 151 Knightsbridge, London SW1X 7PA. 020 7589 7347
Mr Chow at The W Hotel (171). 2201 Collins Avenue, Miami Beach, FL 33139, USA. 001 305 938 3000
Murano (157, 248). 20 Queen Street, London W1J 5PR. 020 7592 1222

Nautika (188, 228). Brsalje 3, 20000 Dubrovnik, Croatia. 00385 20 44 25 26

Old Boat Store (167). The Cleave, Kingsand, Torpoint Cornwall PL10 1NF. 01752 822 568

Palace Hotel (172, 235, 247). Palacestrasse, 3780 Gstaad, Switzerland. 0041 33 748 50 00
Petersham Nurseries Café (146). Church Lane, Off Petersham Road, Petersham, Richmond, Surrey TW10 7AG. 020 8605 3627
Petrus (198). 1 Kinnerton Street, Knightsbridge, London SW1X 8EA. 020 7592 1609
Planet Hollywood (117, 247). 57 Haymarket, London SW1Y4QX. 020 7437 7639
Poppy's Tea Room & Restaurant (155). 8 Milk Street, Shrewsbury, Shropshire SY1 1SZ. 01743 272 709
Porticciolo (217). Cipriani Hotel, Giudecca, 10, 30133 Venice, Italy. 0039 041 520 7744

Quo Vadis (157). 26-29 Dean Street, London W1D 3LL. 020 7437 9585

Rhubarb – Caterers (105). "rhubarb" food design Ltd, 5-25 Burr Road, London SW18 4SQ. 020 8812 3200
Ritz, The (117, 122, 133, 247, 248). 150 Piccadilly, London W1J 9BR. 020 7493 8181
River Café (121, 166, 179, 194, 248). Thames Wharf Studios, Rainville Road, London W6 9HA. 020 7386 4200
Royal Oak (121, 148, 248). Paley Street, Maidenhead, Berkshire SL6 3JN. 01628 620 541

WASN'T ALL THAT BRILLIANT?
DREAM ON MIKEY BOY
HE'S A BLOODY NIGHTMARE.
ZZZZ
MW 2010